CULTURAL HAUNTING

CULTURAL HAUNTING

❖ GHOSTS AND ETHNICITY IN ❖
RECENT AMERICAN LITERATURE

KATHLEEN BROGAN

University Press of Virginia • *Charlottesville & London*

For my parents,

Rita and Edward,

and for

Jonathan and Oliver

Contents

Acknowledgments   ix

1   Haunted Tales of Heirs and Ethnographers   1

2   Ghost Dancing: Cultural Translation in
Louise Erdrich's *Tracks*   30

3   Getting Back One's Dead for Burial: Traumatic History
and Ritual Reburial in Toni Morrison's *Beloved*   61

4   From Exiles to Americans: "Recombinant" Ethnicity in
Cristina García's *Dreaming in Cuban*   93

5   Ethnic Memory, Ethnic Mourning   129

Notes   173

Bibliography   205

Index   221

ACKNOWLEDGMENTS

I AM GRATEFUL TO Wellesley College for generously granting me a leave year in which to begin this project and for further supporting my work through an award for scholarly research. Susan Schweik, Barbara Bowen, and Vera Kutzinski, who years ago kindly agreed to examine an embryonic description of this project, offered early support. I am indebted to Louise Z. Smith, editor of *College English*, for publishing an early version of chapter 1 and to Gillian Gane, assistant editor, for her helpful suggestions. For their discerning comments on portions of this book, I thank Margery Sabin, Timothy Peltason, Michael Cooper, Vernon Shetley, and Werner Sollors. I am especially indebted to William E. Cain for his judicious and impressively swift responses to drafts. Thomas Ferraro read the manuscript for the University Press of Virginia, providing magnanimous and learned commentary. I owe a particular debt of gratitude to Lawrence Rosenwald, who helped me find my inspiration at many crucial moments; for his tact, encouragement, and thoughtful suggestions, I am most thankful.

Deborah Clarke and Susan Meyer went beyond the call of friendship in reading the entire manuscript, offering precise, invaluable advice at every step of the way. I have depended on their constancy and companionship during the long and often lonely work of writing. Conversations over the years with Ron Scapp and Marina Leslie have been a source of pleasure. For her unflagging belief in this project and in me, I warmly thank Lois Slovik. My appreciation also goes to Barbara Harman, who proffered sage advice about combining scholarship and motherhood. Thanks, too, to Lorraine Garnett Ward for her eleventh-hour encouragement and wise counsel. Cathie Brettschneider, my editor at the University Press of Virginia, has been a pleasure to work with. Deborah A. Oliver, Virginia's managing editor, patiently answered many a bibliographic query, and Jane M. Curran provided expert editorial assistance. I salute Alina Kantor and Inna Kantor, my student research assistants, for their energetic and always cheerful help in reading proof and preparing the bibliography.

I wish to thank my dear parents, Rita and Edward Brogan; my sisters, Janice and Maureen; and my brothers, Ed, Tom, and Andy, for their faith and loving support. I am grateful also to Phyllis and Bernard Spring for their inexhaustible kindness. My son, Oliver, who was born when this book was half written and who came fully into language as it was completed, has reminded me afresh of the powers and delights of storytelling. My profoundest debt is to my husband, Jonathan Spring, who proved a most rigorous, astute, and sympathetic reader. Our conversations gave me a vision for this book that sustained me through the writing of it. I am deeply grateful for the daily gift of his patience and wit, his unstinting generosity, and his enduring love.

AN EARLIER VERSION of chapter 1 appeared in *College English* under the title "American Stories of Cultural Haunting." Copyright 1995 by the National Council of Teachers of English. Reprinted with permission.

A version of chapter 2 was published in *Prospects* under the title "Haunted by History: Louise Erdrich's *Tracks*." Copyright 1996 by Cambridge University Press. Reprinted with the permission of Cambridge University Press.

CULTURAL HAUNTING

ghosts themselves—were all generously present. Yet these conventional elements play a vastly different literary role than they do in traditional Gothic novels. The Gothic generally explores personal, psychical encounters with the taboo. At the most basic level, its ghosts function as plot device—providing crucial information, setting in motion the machinery of revenge or atonement—and, of course, as source of the pleasurable thrill we derive from the uncanny. On a more sophisticated level, the ghosts serve to illuminate the more shadowy or repressed aspects of characters. Like the ghosts in Shakespeare's plays, they externalize a character's state of mind or inadequately repressed feelings ("This is the very painting of your fear," Lady Macbeth tells her distraught husband when Banquo's ghost appears to him). The ghosts in recent African-American literature, while sharing these familiar literary functions, also serve another: they signal an attempt to recover and make social use of a poorly documented, partially erased cultural history. The haunted narratives of Wilson, Morrison, Marshall, and Naylor undoubtedly offer us powerful dramas of the individual psyche, yet these dramas are woven inextricably into the recuperation of a people's history. Horace Walpole's *The Castle of Otranto* (1764), the first Gothic novel, gave Manfred's psychomachia an exclusively familial context, but in contemporary African-American ghost stories the individual's or family's haunting clearly reflects the crises of a larger social group. The figure of the ghost itself emerges from the cultural history of that group: one of the key elements of African religious thought to survive in syncretic forms of new-world religious practice and in slave folklore is the belief in ancestor spirits.[1] While contemporary African-American writers often invoke the Gothic tradition, they tend to filter its conventions through African folklore and spirit beliefs. It was tempting to think that I had come upon a rich thematic vein of contemporary African-American fiction, that the appearance of ancestral ghosts, though from Walpole a popular feature of the Gothic, registered in fact a literary Africanism.

Thinking about the ghosts in Marshall, Morrison, Naylor, or Wilson solely within the context of an African-American tradition, however, obscures a very important point: how much their haunted narratives share with other contemporaneous American ghost stories. Around the same time that Wilson's family called upon ancestral ghosts to exorcise its historical demons, similar ghosts were slipping into the writing of American writers of very different ethnic identities. Maxine Hong

Kingston mined the ghost metaphor in the mid-1970s in *The Woman Warrior*; it appears in Native American literature as well, most recently in novels by Louise Erdrich (*Tracks*, 1988; *The Bingo Palace*, 1994) and Leslie Marmon Silko (*Almanac of the Dead*, 1991). William Kennedy's *Ironweed* (1983) is haunted by the ghosts of Irish Albany, New York. In "The Management of Grief" (1989), Bharati Mukherjee invokes ghosts to dramatize the divided loyalties and ultimate transformation of immigrants to North America. The ghost of the folkloric La Llorona (like Kennedy's and Morrison's protagonists, an infanticidal parent) weeps through the pages of much contemporary Chicano literature, including Rudolfo Anaya's *Bless Me, Ultima* (1972), Sandra Cisneros's *Woman Hollering Creek* (1991), and Alma Luz Villanueva's *Weeping Woman* (1994). Richard Rodriguez opens his memoir *Days of Obligation* (1992) with an allusion to La Llorona; "crying from [his] mouth," Rodriguez himself becomes the weeping infanticidal ghost, who has killed off not his children but his own Spanish-speaking "Mexican" childhood.[2] In *World's End* (1987), T. Coraghessan Boyle moves his narrative back and forth between seventeenth-century New York, populated by Native Americans, Dutch, and English, and a twentieth century haunted by the ghosts of these earlier inhabitants. Oscar Hijuelos describes belief in ghosts as a "Cuban susceptibility" in his 1983 *Our House in the Last World*; the novel's English-speaking Cuban American, Hector, haunted by the loss of his Cubanness, envisions Cuba itself as a "mysterious and cruel phantasm," a ghost at once luring and terrible.[3] In Nora Okja Keller's *Comfort Woman* (1997), a young Korean-American woman redefines her ethnicity by opening herself to the ghosts of her mother's Korean past. Amy Tan's *The Hundred Secret Senses* (1995) casts Chinese as "the language of . . . ghosts"; Tan's cynical Chinese-American protagonist recovers some sense of her spurned Chinese heritage when she acquires the ghost-vision of her more Chinese half-sister.[4] We encounter ghosts of old Ukraine in Askold Melnyczuk's 1994 *What Is Told*, spirits of the Sioux past in Susan Power's 1994 *The Grass Dancer*, Cuban ghosts in Cristina García's 1992 *Dreaming in Cuban* and her 1997 *The Agüero Sisters*, and a ghostly cantor in Ira Levin's 1988 play *Cantorial*.[5] In a fascinating transethnic borrowing, an Italian-American immigrant, appearing like "the ghost of a woman," recovers an abandoned *Italianità* in Carole Maso's 1986 *Ghost Dance* by performing a cross between the *tarantella* and the Native American Ghost Dance.[6] Plainly, the contempo-

rary American ghost story is not solely an African-American phenomenon; it is, in fact, a pan-ethnic phenomenon, registering a widespread
concern with questions of ethnic identity and cultural transmission.

To examine each ethnic grouping separately—to study, for example,
the influence and literary transformation of African religion in Naylor,
of Chinese ancestor worship in Kingston—valuably illuminates the specific histories and local understandings these texts engage, yet to do so
obscures the fact that these contemporary American works have much
in common.[7] Ghosts in contemporary American ethnic literature function similarly: to re-create ethnic identity through an imaginative recuperation of the past and to press this new version of the past into
the service of the present. In doing so, these works have much to tell
us about our own historical moment and the range of imaginative responses it provokes. Ghost stories reflect the increased emphasis on ethnic and racial differentiation in all social groups following the ideological upheavals set in motion by the black civil rights movement. They
also register the tectonic epistemological shift we have witnessed since
the 1970s in the social sciences. A reevaluation of historical method-
ology, indeed, of what can be identified as history ("fact") versus story
("fiction"), has profoundly changed our understanding of how the past
is translated and how ethnicity is constructed. The ghosts haunting contemporary American literature lead us to the heart of our nation's discourse about multiculturalism and ethnic identity. When summoned for
close examination, they reveal much about the dynamics of social and
literary revisionism in response to cross-cultural encounters.

I would like to identify here a specific kind of ghost story—a story of
what I would call "cultural haunting"—that, while it has nineteenth-
and early twentieth-century antecedents, has emerged in large numbers
only in the last quarter of this century. For precursors in earlier American literature, we could look to Hawthorne and Faulkner, whose borrowings from Gothic romance serve their interests in memory and inheritance. In their ambivalence toward ancestors and their interest in
storytelling, these authors offer important models for contemporary
writers who turn to the supernatural to examine the troubled transmission of immigrant, slave, or native cultures.[8] We find another early example of cultural haunting in Abraham Cahan's 1896 *Yekl*, in which the
Americanized Jake's fears about abandoning his Judaism take the form
of his father's ghost, who comes in the night to seize him by the throat.
The figure of this ghostly father "attired in burial linen" (77) rises

in Jake's mind as he suffers (always temporary) twinges of regret for his spurned Russian Jewish culture (see *Yekl*, 33, 77–79). The ghost appears only because Jake has begun to sunder his connection to the old-world culture. That the ghost is always frightening to Jake is nevertheless a measure of his still close proximity to the culture he desperately wants to escape. Greater distance would more likely produce a more ambivalent mixture of fear and nostalgia.[9]

The story of cultural haunting needs to be distinguished from the more familiar ghost story, that genre of short fiction that blossomed during the nineteenth century, leaving us with thrilling fireside tales of haunted houses, graveyard revenants, and Christmases past. A homespun Victorian derivative of the more fabulously draped, exotic Gothic novel, the ghost story evolved early in this century into the subtle psychological studies of Henry James and Edith Wharton and the surrealist nightmares of H. P. Lovecraft. These modern ghost stories recast supernaturalism as the hallucinatory projections of the self. In doing so, they show a family resemblance to Macbeth's spectres but are marked by a Freudian-era understanding of psychology. The idea of the internally haunted self ("Ourself behind ourself, concealed—," more frightening, Dickinson knew, than "External Ghost") becomes central: in James's "The Jolly Corner," Spencer Brydon stalks the spectre of his rapacious alter ego; in Wharton's "The Eyes," Culwin is haunted by a figuration of his own evil nature; in Miller's *Death of a Salesman*, Willie Loman encounters ghosts of his own misguided ambitions. Though one can step back to generalize from the individual example—reading Wharton's female ghosts as expressions of women's cultural invisibility, or Loman's haunting as the bankruptcy of the American dream of masculine success—the focus of each work is first and foremost the tortured mind of an individual. This is not to say, of course, that writers like James, Wharton, and Miller have no ethnicity, or that their ghost stories, despite their individualist ethos, do not in some sense represent their authors' cultural worlds.[10] The story of cultural haunting, however, brings to the foreground the communal nature of its ghosts. When the ghost in Morrison's *Beloved* speaks of her life in the grave in terms appropriate to the slave ships, she clearly becomes more than an externalization of one character's longing and guilt; her return represents the return of all dead enslaved Africans. Stories of cultural haunting differ from other twentieth-century ghost stories in exploring the hidden passageways not only of the individual psyche but also of a people's historical consciousness. Through the agency of ghosts, group histories that have in some way been threatened, erased, or fragmented are recuperated and revised.

In investigating history through supernatural means, the story of cultural haunting needs also to be distinguished from historical novels that "bring the dead to life" without reference to any literal interaction between the living and the dead (Don DeLillo's *Libra*, for example) or from fiction in which characters can be said to be "haunted" by the past in purely metaphorical terms (as in Ralph Ellison's *Invisible Man*, William Styron's *Sophie's Choice*, or Philip Roth's *The Ghost Writer*). The turn to the supernatural in the process of recovering history emphasizes the difficulty of gaining access to a lost or denied past, as well as the degree to which any such historical reconstruction is essentially an imaginative act. Centrally concerned with the issues of communal memory, cultural transmission, and group inheritance, stories of cultural haunting share the plot device and master metaphor of the ghost as go-between, an enigmatic transitional figure moving between past and present, death and life, one culture and another. An extraordinarily hybrid category of literature drawing upon a wide range of cultural traditions, the story of cultural haunting crosses the generic boundaries of the novel, the historical novel, the novelistic memoir, short fiction, drama, and, to a lesser extent, the lyric. Reading contemporary haunted narratives together— tracking the ways in which themes of possession, exorcism, historical repetition, and the reconstruction of memory reverberate within and across the texts—identifies the American story of cultural haunting as a significant and as yet unrecognized contemporary genre.[11]

The links between these thematic obsessions establish the masterplot of the cultural ghost story, a paradigmatic movement from possession to exorcism—or more accurately, from bad to good forms of haunting. In most cases possession is established by traumatic experience, such as the loss of land or homes, deaths of family members, or acts of racial persecution. Studies of persons suffering from posttraumatic disorders have revealed characteristic "pathologies of memory" that have relevance for the shared historical traumas of some ethnic groups. Traumatized individuals suffer from an unlikely combination of amnesia and abnormally precise (and usually automatic) recall: while the traumatized may cut off from consciousness "large realms of experience" and aspects of personality, these "failures of recall can paradoxically coexist with the opposite: intruding memories and unbidden repetitive images of the traumatic events."[12] When the individual's distress derives from the larger trauma of a group, pathologies of memory take on a cultural and political significance, reflecting a society's inability to integrate with the present both traumatic experience and a pre-catastrophic lost past.

In Morrison's *Beloved*, for example, Sethe's mother-love and guilt lead to her possession by the ghost of the daughter she murdered to save from a life of slavery. The ghost must ultimately be exorcised by a reenactment of the murder scene, which occurs toward the end of the novel. Sethe's understanding of memory suggests the intrusive repetition of the past evident in traumatic disorders:

> I was talking about time. It's so hard for me to believe in it. Some things go. Pass on. Some things just stay. I used to think it was my rememory. You know. Some things you forget. Other things you never do. But it's not. Places, places are still there. If a house burns down, it's gone, but the place—the picture of it—stays, and not just in my rememory, but out there, in the world. What I remember is a picture floating around out there outside my head. I mean, even if I don't think it, even if I die, the picture of what I did, or knew, or saw is still out there. Right in the place where it happened.[13]

So intensely does Sethe suffer the intrusion of unbidden memories that she envisions memory as an external reality that can take possession of her (or even of others); her coinage "rememory" captures this sense of memory as the re-presenting or repetition of the past. The return of Sethe's murdered daughter as a full-bodied and dangerous ghost who brings back the past is clearly forecast here. The past that resists integration into the present because it is incomprehensible or too horrific takes shape as a ghost that can possess.

The novel's exorcism reenacts the scene of the murder with a crucial difference: Sethe points her ice pick at the white man Bodwin—an act of confusion that nevertheless releases her by directing her anger outward. The weapon is a symbolic pointing of the finger, naming white guilt for the evil consequences of slavery. Significantly, the ghost is not completely exorcised but is transformed into a safer presence, one about which Morrison can tell a tale, even though for Sethe remembering still "seemed unwise."[14] Morrison's narrative thus completes what Sethe cannot, the full integration of the ghostly past. Pierre Janet, who early in this century studied traumatic memory disorders, observed that narrative memory reshapes and gives meaning to past experience; he distinguished this form of memory from traumatic memory, which fails to adapt the past to the present, dooming the traumatized subject to mechanical, nonverbal reenactments.[15] Sethe's incorporation of the past in the form of a spirit possession resembles traumatic memory. In giving narrative organization to Sethe's experience (the experience of the historical Margaret Garner and, by extension, all victims of slavery), Morrison defines historical consciousness as a good form of haunting, in which the denied ghosts of the American past are finally integrated into America's national identity.

The movement from possession to exorcism plotted by Morrison's novel is repeated in other stories of cultural haunting. In exorcising the ghost of the slave-owner Sutter, Berniece Charles in Wilson's *The Piano Lesson* trades one form of haunting for another. Her invitation to family ghosts long held at bay releases her from a paralyzing and angry mourning over her husband's death. Marshall's Avey Johnson in *Praisesong for the Widow* is also a haunted survivor. Her husband's ghost—a forbidding internal voice of assimilation, race hatred, and self-denial in the name of upward mobility—is defeated (and therefore can finally be properly mourned) as a result of Avey's gradual opening to other spectral voices. When, on a trip to the Caribbean, she witnesses the performance of a traditional African-derived circular dance called a "ring shout," she has a sudden double vision: "Kin, visible, metamorphosed and invisible, repeatedly circled the cleared space together." The revelation is complete when the living dancers and their ghostly African counterparts reverse roles. Avey comes to understand that "It was the essence of something rather than the thing itself she was witnessing. . . . All that was left were a few names of what they called nations which they could no longer even pronounce properly, the fragments of a dozen or so songs, the shadowy forms of long-ago dances and rum kegs for drums." The "nation" dances Avey views are "shadowy forms" or ghosts of old tribal ritual dances. In enacting ritual movements, in however revised and truncated a form, descendants thus become ghosts of their own ancestors. The transformed protagonist will return home to "haunt" an assimilated black New York, having been filled with the spirit of a lost African culture.[16]

In the literature of cultural haunting, such haunting potentially leads to a valuable awareness of how the group's past continues to inhabit and inform the living. The exorcism of all forms of ghostliness could result in a historical amnesia that endangers the integrity of the group. Toward the beginning of *The Woman Warrior*, Kingston confesses that she is haunted by her suicidal aunt and fears a possession that duplicates her aunt's terrible fate. The task she undertakes in her memoir is the transformation of haunting as deathly possession into a haunting that enlarges self with the *selective* integration of family history and Chinese legend. Kingston knows that the very ghostliness of her aunt, her erasure from acknowledged family history, gives herself the imaginative room for revision. As Pierre Janet noticed, the movement from traumatic to narrative memory allows for the possibility of revision. While traumatic memory is rigidly inflexible, marked by pure repetition, narrative memory—essentially a social act—can be "adapted to present circumstances."[17] Stories of cultural haunting record the struggle to establish some form of historical continuity that allows for a necessary distance from the past—breathing room, as it were. They can be read as cautionary tales about the proper function of memory. Possession—the dangerous incorporation of the dead—signals a failure of memory to organize history, to render it usable. Flight from history can just as easily lead to possession as a nostalgic return to the past: denied history reasserts itself, much like the return of the repressed.

Possession in haunted American fiction marks a continuity with the past over which one has little control: history lodges within, swollen bodies (a recurring image in this literature) give birth not to the future but to a nightmarish repetition of the past. Though it is sometimes figured as a malignant pregnancy, possession is also conveyed through metaphors of consumption. Cannibal and vampire ghosts abound, feeding upon the living. The Korean-American Beccah in Nora Okja Keller's *Comfort Woman*, for example, suffers nightmarish visions of "the Korean ghosts and demons that fed off our lives"; consumed by these cannibal ghosts, she herself begins to thin into ghostliness, her once substantial American body growing dangerously "translucent" as she is absorbed into her haunted mother's fierce engagement with the ghosts of her own traumatic past in Korea.[18] When Kingston in *The Woman Warrior* describes her mother's oppressive presence with language that echoes Brave Orchid's earlier account of a "Sitting Ghost," she imagines that her mother "pries open my head," an image recalling the legendary monkey brain feasts in China that Brave Orchid describes with relish. Feeling that she is being asked to bear "responsibility for time, responsibility for intervening oceans," the young Kingston envisions her "barely real" mother as a cannibal ghost.[19] In Louise Erdrich's *Tracks*, the Algonkian cannibal ghost called *windigo* possesses characters in deep mourning for lost family members. Characters in this literature run the danger of being swallowed up by the very past they attempt to recover (or to deny). The ghost Beloved feeds off of Sethe, growing fat as the haunted mother thins toward ghostliness: "Beloved ate up her life, took it, swelled up with it, grew taller on it."[20] Consuming a past that may not nourish, the eater can be turned into the eaten—or, in a vampiric transformation, the living can themselves become ghostly. Memory is thus translated into something closer to *embodiment.* In psychoanalytic terms, the ghost as cannibal or vampire suggests a dangerous introjection of the dead, or mourning gone awry. The possessed one is locked into repetition, doomed to reenact the past without relevance to present realities.

Everywhere in this literature, possession is associated with the conditions of invisibility and voicelessness. In *Tracks,* Nanapush and Fleur's windigo spirit possession, a form of suicidal mourning, renders them speechless: "We felt the spirits of the dead so near that at length we just stopped talking." The names of dead family members, Nanapush remembers later,

> grew within us, swelled to the brink of our lips, forced our eyes open in the middle of the night. We were filled with the water of the drowned, cold and black, airless water that lapped against the seal of our tongues. . . . We had gone half windigo. I learned later that this was common, that there were many of our people who died in this manner, of the invisible sickness. There were those who could not swallow another bite of food because the names of their dead anchored their tongues. There were those who let their blood stop, who took the road west after all.[21]

Here memory is a form of embodiment: Erdrich's characters incorporate the dead they can not relinquish, threatening to join their ghostly kin in death (taking the "road west" to the afterworld). Ghostliness is equated with silence. The exorcism of the icy spirits of the dead (the completion of mourning) is consequently described as a thawing of frozen words: "My voice rasped at first when I tried to speak, but then . . . I was off and talking. . . . I began to creak and roll. I gathered speed. I talked both languages in streams that ran alongside each other, over every rock, around every obstacle. The sound of my own voice convinced me I was alive."[22] The saving movement from reenactment to enabling memory is represented as a movement from traumatic silence into language. Through acts of narrative revision—which are very often presented as acts of translation, linguistic or cultural—the cycle of doom is broken and the past digested. Translation functions like an exorcism because it reframes cultural inheritance, rendering the past in the terms of the present. Translators must allow themselves to be haunted by their "source" culture in order to render it into their "target" culture: contemporary America. In translating history into ghost stories, authors of haunted narratives transform both source and target cultures, reshaping the past to answer the needs of the present and, implicitly, the future. This double-edged revisionism—which reinvents old traditions and creates new cultural fusions—constitutes a literary form of what social scientists have called "reciprocal acculturation."[23] The ghost that makes present the past while conveying its indefiniteness (and thereby possible malleability) thus provides the vehicle for both a dangerous possession by and an imaginative liberation from the past.

IN ARGUING THAT the ghosts I track are linked to issues of acculturation and cultural transmission in a polyethnic society, and particularly in asserting that the bloodline family ghosts of different ethnic groups belong in fact to the same cross-cultural genre, I take a position congruent with the directions laid out by the scholarship of Werner Sollors, who has argued forcefully for a recognition of the syncretic and often quite modern nature of ethnic "traditions." Along with others who join him in his anti-essentialist position, he points to the groundbreaking work of social scientist Fredrik Barth, who posited in 1969 that ethnicity is not a thing but a process. Groups maintain their identity not by holding on to what Barth calls "cultural stuff" (specific food, dress, customs, symbols, language, and so on) but by establishing boundaries that mark off "us" from the heathens, the goyim, "them." Tradition is thus less a matter of content than of *form*. Sollors quotes Barth: "when one traces the history of an ethnic group through time, one is *not* simultaneously, in the same sense, tracing the history of 'a culture': the elements of the present culture of that ethnic group have not sprung from the particular set that constituted the group's culture at a previous time, whereas the group has a continual organizational existence with boundaries (criteria of membership) that despite modifications have marked off a continuing unit."[24] Barth's rejection of an autonomous and "authentic" cultural inheritance passed down through the generations helps to explain why the current emphasis in this country on ethnic difference emerges precisely when assimilation (whether forced or voluntary) is widely though not completely accomplished. Widespread assimilation threatens an ethnic group's self-delimiting boundaries, setting in motion a "return" to what in fact are newly reimagined cultural sources.[25]

For me, one of the considerable attractions of this recent approach to ethnicity is that its anti-essentialist view works against the nostalgic tendency to dissolve history (particularly unpalatable history) in the effort to achieve a sentimentally conceived identity. The lesson for the critic of ethnic writing is clear: that one must resist indulging in a naive romanticizing of roots (hunting for the "authentic" ethnic sources of every aspect of a literary work), choosing instead to look for cultural cross-pollinations, convergences, and inventions. A comparative, cross-cultural approach has the advantage of opening up the study of reciprocal acculturation, whether cultural or literary. Moreover, the emphasis on syncretism and shifting identic boundaries valuably counters the false and restrictive conception of identity as a static, bounded entity. Although the reification of identity has in the past twenty-five years come under attack by philosophers and social scientists, the older and still widely popular view of ethnic identity as a changeless substance shared by fairly homogenous social groups has proven extraordinarily difficult to supplant—especially when the alternatives seem so unstabilizing. In times of increased inter-ethnic conflict, the idea of ethnicity as a natural, timeless essence tends to revive with recharged power.

As we shall see, the ghosts in stories of cultural haunting are agents of both cultural memory *and* cultural renewal: the shape-shifting ghost who transmits erased or threatened group memory represents the creative, ongoing process of ethnic redefinition. In this literature, ghostly "kinship" replaces biological descent as the basis for ethnic affiliations. The implication is that ethnic identity is largely a matter of voluntary rather than prescribed association, an understanding of ethnicity that, while fiercely debated, has increasingly begun to take hold just as stories of cultural haunting are appearing in large numbers. As Toni Morrison observed in 1987, "Now people choose their identities. Now people choose to be Black. They used to be *born* Black. That's not true anymore."[26] To be sure, the emphasis on ethnic self-ascription continues to raise hackles—and some difficult questions. How possible is it, for example, for a dark-skinned individual to *choose* not to be black in racist

America? What of those who, perhaps never themselves having suffered discrimination, disaffiliate themselves from the dominant culture
to claim affiliation with minority groups?[27] Is ethnicity in America, as
sociologist Herbert Gans has argued, becoming merely "symbolic" and
"cost-free"?[28] Can ethnic identities be assumed and discarded like cos-
tumes (hiding, by implication, some inner "true" self or an essential
identic emptiness)? Most importantly for the writers discussed here, do
members of an ethnic group who actively redefine received tradition,
particularly through the selective incorporation of alien cultural elements, damage that tradition, inadvertently bringing on the community's demise?

The debate about "invented" traditions and "achieved" ethnicity
tends to turn on the vexing issue of "authenticity." Yet surely, as historian David A. Hollinger reminds us, "superficiality does not follow from
volition any more than authenticity follows from submission to tradition
and authority."[29] Racial authenticity, moreover, has a troubling colonial
history, tied as it has been to the defining and containing of difference
through blood-quantum laws. The authors of cultural ghost stories
counter the idea that ghostly "kinship" is somehow less authentic than
affiliations defined strictly by blood by exposing the constructed nature
of all traditions, which thrive by being repeatedly reinterpreted. They
validate their own ethnic redefinitions and cultural syntheses by observing that the group's self-defining narratives have always been invented
or revised to answer to present conditions. Yet while the figure of the
ghost ultimately affirms the principle of cultural revisionism, ghostliness is almost never treated without ambivalence. Haunting sometimes
registers the price of rebellion against tradition or the loss of cultural
roots. Neither the act of affiliating with groups nor the reinvention of
traditions is represented in these haunted tales as "cost-free." In the
masterplot of cultural haunting, the movement from bad to potentially
good forms of haunting reflects the desire both to articulate fears and
ambivalences about ethnic redefinition and to claim such redefinition as
finally rejuvenating to tradition.

The tradition-as-invention camp, as exemplified by Sollors, has also
come under attack for eliding ethnic differences in the name of what is
seen as a too narrowly conceived "common" American culture. Anthropologist and borderlands theorist Renato Rosaldo, for example, has argued passionately that academic assertions of "cultural constructedness"

err by smoothly dismissing the very real consequences of white rule in America. He contends that in the recent scholarship on "invented" traditions, "human beings and their products lose their specific gravity, their weight and their density, and begin to float." These "purely cerebral" studies of ethnicity and otherness ignore the effects of racism and "forget the dead and maimed." Rosaldo is particularly concerned with Sollors's subsumption of all ethnic texts to a Puritan model of dissent, rendering "outsiders" of any stripe essentially mainstream, a potentially totalizing aspect of Sollors's argument that has been targeted by others.[30] These critics are suspicious of a rhetoric of transcendence, in which the merely local is subsumed into the pseudo-universalism of white, Protestant culture. They also warn of conflating ethnicity and race, of wrongfully assuming the same choices are available to immigrants, particularly those who left their native lands voluntarily, as to colonized or enslaved peoples. And they ask the compelling (and, to me at least, not easily dismissable) question: how do we explain the tenacious persistence, often in the face of formidable disintegratory forces, of the culturally marked custom, the story, the verbal expression, the gesture?

I find these concerns valid, yet I see nothing here to jeopardize the position that ethnicity is a cultural construct, a variable entity reshaped by an always imperfect consensus over time. One can resist ethnic essentialism and yet remain uneasy about the implication that ethnic culture is essentially contentless. The face-off between form and content (boundary marking versus "cultural stuff" or differentiation versus essential difference) presents at bottom a false opposition: both are central aspects of ethnic identity. Differences in cultural content exist, and they matter. These differences cannot be separated from the particular histories from which they arise and to which they continue to make reference; to understand ethnic differences *only* as boundary markers is to elide the importance of the specific histories they encode. Moreover, an exclusive focus on oppositional self-definition fails to account for the ever-growing populations of people who claim membership in several ethnic groups and who may conceive their ethnicity differently in different situations.[31] Simone de Beauvoir was certainly right when she observed that "no group ever sets itself up as the One without at once setting up the Other [or, we might add, others] over against itself,"[32] yet definition purely by opposition does not fully account for the power and persistence of ethnic cultures. The commitment to a shifting and always redefined set of shared elements perceived within the group as in some way fundamental—particularly myths and memories that encode versions of history perceived as "ours"—also centrally constitutes the sense of belonging. We define ethnic identities by establishing a contrasting "otherness," and, especially in the case of visible difference, we are defined perforce by the perceptions of others.[33] But we also construct our ethnic selves through a complicated negotiation with the past in which we claim and revise the group's organizing narratives.

To understand exactly how ethnic difference in the literature of cultural haunting matters is to attend to the particular histories to which these differences attach, and the local meanings these histories engender. Attitudes toward the dead in Chippewa and Chinese cultures, for example, produce differences in the metaphorical burden borne by ghosts in Louise Erdrich's and Maxine Hong Kingston's works. There are also, of course, significant differences—particularly in the degree of nostalgia toward the past—in how writers within an ethnic group treat shared group symbols and narratives. Visible and invisible ethnic differences may inflect haunting differently. As Ralph Ellison knew, "'high visibility' actually rendered one *un*-visible," a ghostliness created by the racism that, in W. E. B. Du Bois's words, relegates black Americans to the Banquo-like role of "the swarthy spectre [who] sits in its accustomed seat at the Nation's feast."[34] By contrast, in William Kennedy's *Ironweed*, the ghosts who spur the on-the-streets protagonist toward a confrontation with his past certainly register the non-existence of the homeless in the eyes of the socially respectable, but they do not similarly reflect the protagonist's "*un*-visibility" as an Irishman in the eyes of contemporary Albany's non-Irish.

Ghostliness, as we shall see, takes on varied meanings in haunted tales that address American histories of slavery, internal colonization, or (to varying degrees) voluntary immigration. The mobility of the ghost who moves between life and death in Mukherjee's "The Management of Grief," for example, figuratively represents the geographical and cultural shifting of immigrants who look back to the old country as they negotiate the new: "Like my husband's spirit, I flutter between worlds," says the protagonist, who must decide between her new life in Canada or a return to her native India.[35] These are choices that she is free to make; her repeated contact with ghosts during a period of mourning dramatizes the turns in this painful but voluntary process of self-redefinition. In much African-American literature, the ghost's movement between worlds, generally rendered in far more traumatic terms and connected to plots of highly dangerous, life-threatening possession, reasserts ancestral connection in the face of catastrophic loss. In Marshall, Naylor, and Morrison, for example, the mediate nature of ghosts (always associated with water imagery) cannot be separated from the disaster of the Middle Passage. In the work of Chicano authors Villanueva, Anaya, and Cisneros, the ghosts who straddle boundaries can be read as hybrid inhabitants of the border. For a Native American writer like Erdrich, ghosts generally have less to do with the symbolic mobility so central to immigrant literature than with the vital but threatened relation between present and past tribal life.[36] The ghosts conjured by authors who write in a different language than their parents or grandparents speak tend to be cast as ambivalent figures of translation, literally bearing culture across linguistic and (sometimes) geographic divides. If the historical and cultural differences that emerge in these many rich and complex haunted tales are ignored, the parallels I would draw devolve into meaninglessness or, worse, would contribute rhetorically to the very ghosting or erasure of ethnic otherness that these haunted texts explore and combat. I believe that, despite these dangers, the parallels are worth identifying.

My aim here is double: both to situate the haunted stories I examine within their specific, local contexts and to show how these stories variously participate in the transethnic genre I am calling "the story of cultural haunting." To be haunted in this literature is to know, viscerally, how specific cultural memories that seem to have disappeared in fact refuse to be buried and still shape the present, in desirable and in troubling ways. Renato Rosaldo's complaint that in the recent scholarship on ethnicity human beings "begin to float" while "the dead and maimed" are forgotten could, if applied to stories of cultural haunting, be turned around: in these haunted texts, "floating" otherwordly beings are themselves the vehicles by which the "dead and maimed" are remembered, and confrontations with ghosts are a way for peoples to ground themselves anew. The ghosts in American haunted tales function similarly because they are conjured in response to shared concerns about assimilation and cultural identity. Stories of cultural haunting have everything to do with the cultural transformation engendered by immigration, as well as by those involuntary and violent movements of peoples that have rendered inextricable our senses of national identity and national guilt. They are centrally related to the questions of how cultural knowledge is transmitted and how identities are enacted in polyethnic America.

THIS BOOK ARGUES that, despite the various manifestations of ghostliness in recent haunted literature, stories of cultural haunting are drawn together not only by their conjuring of ghosts to perform cultural work but also by their tendency to organize plots as a movement from negative to positive forms of haunting and by certain thematic concerns to which they obsessively return. I sketch out here in broad outline three related aspects of American haunted narratives that are more finely limned in the chapters that follow: the emphasis on storytelling and the narrative construction of experience; the performance of ethnicity through rituals of cultural "mourning"; and, finally, the peculiar position of ethnic writers as both "heirs" and "ethnographers."

Like history, ghost stories attempt to bring the dead back to life. In contemporary haunted literature, ghost stories are offered as an alternative—or challenge—to "official," dominant history. This blurring of the historical and fictional is continuous with the interest in narrative currently emerging in metahistorical discussions. History and fiction, as Michel de Certeau has argued, are closer than we have realized, not because history lacks reference to reality, but because history relies on rhetorical and narrative strategies central to fiction in order to shape a coherent representation of reality. (Historiography, in de Certeau's view, must occlude its resemblance to fiction in order to acquire the authority of scientific truth.) We are increasingly coming to see history, in historian Lynn Hunt's words, not as a "repository of facts," but as the telling of stories. Hunt notes that history "is better defined as an ongoing tension between stories that have been told and stories that might be told."[37] Certainly we see in literature by authors from minority groups, and particularly in the writing of descendants of enslaved or colonized peoples, a heightened awareness of the disjunction between mainstream history and the group's own accounts of its past. This awareness leads to an emphasis on multiple viewpoints, the fictionality of any reconstruction of the past, and the creation of alternative histories through the telling of unheard or suppressed stories.

The creation of narrative is central to the process of reshaping the past. Storytelling has a vital function in ethnic ghost literature; in most of the works discussed here, not only do ghosts appear, but ghost stories are told: Kingston's mother relates her battles with ghosts in China; two brothers in *The Piano Lesson* chill their nephew with stories about the Ghosts of the Yellow Dog; in *Tracks*, old Nanapush tells Lulu about her family ghosts. Ghost stories like these retrieve a lost past—the China a daughter never saw, a father murdered before a son knew him well, grandparents dead of tuberculosis long before a granddaughter's birth—in ways that give new meaning to the present, which is now seen as shadowed by a past it revises and continues. The focus on storytelling shifts emphasis away from biological to adoptive models of cultural transmission (in Werner Sollors's terms, from descent to consent). Lineage is established through rivers of words; the oral transmission of group history and lore itself creates the group, rather than being merely its byproduct. Families do not simply tell stories; stories create families. Descent is reinterpreted as verbal or, in the metaphorical language of the genre, as ghostly. The transmission of stories—and most emphatically of ghost stories—creates ethnicity. Historical meaning and ethnic identity are established through the process of haunting.

The stories in haunted literature, however, tend to be tacit, multiple, conflicting, or unfinished; meaning and identity are not static, established securely and transparently. Characters struggle to piece these fragments into a coherent narrative. In Naylor's *Mama Day*, a faded and water-damaged bill of sale for an enslaved ancestor provides only tantalizing fragments of sentences, ambiguous clues about a past the descendants desperately need to understand. Beccah in Keller's *Comfort Woman*, finding her chief source of family history to be unreliable, grows "cautious of [her] mother's stories, never knowing what to count on or what to discount."[38] Kingston's mother also gives her daughter confusingly contradictory stories about her past in China, leaving the daughter to piece together a narrative that—in its nonchronological, collage form—captures even as it attempts to transcend the fragmentation of inheritance. Complicating the process are the ethnic group's own prohibitions about language, its fears that certain kinds of speech might dissolve group bonds. ("You must not tell anyone," Kingston's mother commands [3].) Partially submerged narratives powerfully, though invisibly, organize ("haunt") social groups. While these narratives are never fully articulated, hints, metaphors, pieces of the stories abound. Uncovering an occult narrative can be compared to a ghost sighting: awareness of the haunting leads to the possibility of freedom through revision, which functions in this literature like an exorcism.

The connection between revision and exorcism reminds us that the most dreadful aspect of haunting is its involuntary nature; we cannot always choose our ghosts. The attractive possibility of adopting beneficent ancestral spirits might imply that ethnicity is freely and consciously constructed, but in fact these choices are often experienced as mysterious mandates. Haunting metaphors forcefully convey the reality that cultural transmission operates partly on a subrational level. Anthropologist Michael Fischer, in an essay on ethnic autobiography, argues that ethnicity is "often transmitted less through cognitive language or learning (to which sociology has almost entirely restricted itself) than through processes analogous to the dreaming and transference of psychoanalytic encounters."[39] Richard Rodriguez has expressed this sense of ethnicity as, in his words, "a public metaphor . . . for a knowledge that bewilders us": "the past survives in my life, though in mysterious ways, deeper than choosing."[40] Ethnic identity is, indeed, as Fischer notes, "potent even when not consciously taught"—perhaps most dangerously potent precisely when it is transferred in unconscious ways. Much of what Fischer calls "ethnic anxiety" is generated by a character's inability to bring to consciousness (to put into language) the murky forces that help shape identity.[41] This view of ethnicity as a bewildering, mysterious heritage finds support in recent psychological research on the embodiment of pathology in individuals through the unconscious absorption of family narratives,[42] and in Nicolas Abraham and Maria Torok's revision of Freud, *The Shell and the Kernel,* which posits the unspoken transmission of the parent's unconscious to the child. In stories of cultural haunting, the ghost's vaporousness, its link to a twilight world of dreams and mystery, reflects the elements of ethnic identity experienced as just below rational grasp.

Frightening ghosts, however, can sometimes be put to rest, not in the sense of being forever banished, but in the sense of being transformed into memories that usefully guide, rather than overwhelm, the present. From a psychological viewpoint, the attempt to recuperate some elements of the past, to refit it for present needs, can be analogized to the process of mourning through which the living revise their relationships with the dead. Freud, in "Thoughts for the Times on War and Death," attributes the invention of ghosts to the experience of mourning for a loved one. He imagines primitive man first confronting the reality of his own mortality when witnessing the death of someone beloved: "Man could no longer keep death at a distance, for he had tasted it in his pain about the dead; but he was nevertheless unwilling to acknowledge it, for he could not conceive of himself as dead. So he devised a compromise: he conceded the fact of his own death as well, but denied it the significance of annihilation. . . . It was beside the dead body of someone he loved that he invented spirits."[43] As an embodiment of the continuity between the living and the dead, the ghost evades the finality of death. It represents a compromise, or an essentially antithetical act: a simultaneous acknowledgment of and denial of death. Ghost stories bear the message: we exist, we continue, our dead are not dead.

Yet continuity with the past can be a source both of comfort and anxiety, at times even of terror. The complexities and ambivalences of the culturally haunted ghost story cannot be overemphasized: the figure of the ghost carries both positive and negative valences, often shifting from one to the other in a single work. An angry ghost in *The Woman Warrior* who threatens to "pull down a substitute" can also be a helpful "forerunner."[44] Dangerous ghosts in *Tracks* can, in the right circumstances, be protective spirits. The connection between ambivalence and ghosts was of course explored by Freud. In *Totem and Taboo* he claims that the historical development of ghost belief reflects the conflicted emotions that, inherent in all close relationships, are particularly powerful in those with our dead:

> It is quite possible that the whole concept of demons was derived from the important relation of the living to the dead. The ambivalence inherent in that relation was expressed in the subsequent course of human development by the fact that, from the same root, it gave rise to two completely opposed psychical structures: on the one hand fear of demons and ghosts and on the other hand veneration of ancestors. The fact that demons are always regarded as the spirits of those who have died *recently* shows better than anything the influence of mourning on the origin of the belief in demons. Mourning has a quite specific psychical task to perform: its function is to detach the survivors' memories and hopes from the dead. When this has been achieved, the pain grows less and with it the remorse and self-reproaches and consequently the fear of the demon as well. And the same spirits who to begin with were feared as demons may now expect to meet with friendlier treatment; they are revered as ancestors and appeals are made to them for help.[45]

The shift from fear to veneration that Freud plots here could be aligned with the familiar three-stage model of immigrant generational succession, in which an assimilationist second generation rears children nostalgic for the lost culture of the emigrant grandparents. One generation's parental rejection succeeds another: proximity produces fear of ethnic difference, while greater distance (and the powerful desire to revise parental choices) yields reverence for ancestors. For Kingston, a second-generation writer, the ghosts of China maintain a demonic charge, associated as they are with a world of nightmares and the unconscious (as a girl she dreams in Chinese). The protagonist of Marshall's *Praisesong for the Widow*, on the other hand, makes the transition from assimilating into white culture to yearning for ancestral African connection. It may seem decidedly odd to apply a metaphor derived from immigrant experience to contemporary African-American imaginings of a preslavery heritage (many generations in the past), yet Marshall's character exhibits a "third-generation" style of triangulation, past the parents to a great-aunt, whose ghost becomes a conduit to a lost African world. Parents are also curiously absent from Naylor's *Mama Day* and Erdrich's *Tracks;* in both novels, a figure one more generation removed provides the crucial link to the past. The effects of relative proximity to loss described by Freud help as well to explain the ironic ending of Morrison's *Beloved*, with its injunction not to tell a story that has just been told: the nineteenth-century protagonist's need to forget meets the author's (and reader's) desire to memorialize. Like Sethe's forgetting of the past, Morrison's historical recovery gives expression to a survivalist instinct.

We must, however, ultimately acknowledge the limitations of Freud's scheme, which divides the components of ambivalence into two separate periods of mourning, and of the related "three-generations" model, with its simplistic framing of immigrant generational experience.[46] In Kingston, for example, the war of anger and nostalgia expressed in her conflicting desires for liberation and continuity draws a complicated, highly ambivalent portrait of ethnic redefinition. In African-American literature, a greater temporal distance from the African past—severely heightened by brutal forms of cultural erasure—tends to result in a more nostalgic treatment of ancestors. Yet even here, we find the veneration of ancestral spirits is often shadowed by the more frightening implications of being haunted.

The movement from frightening to at least potentially beneficent ghosts in this literature traces the progress from early to final stages of mourning. Freud's model of mourning, however, ultimately proves an inadequate heuristic to the work of what in this book I call "cultural mourning." My argument about cultural mourning, developed in full in the final chapter but touched upon to some degree in every reading I offer, rests upon the assumption that communities reaffirm and sometimes redefine fundamental cultural values through rituals of mourning. In his seminal scholarship on funereal rites, anthropologist Robert Hertz observes that communities are established and social identities defined by public acts of mourning. I argue here that, just as funereal rites work to organize societies, literary memorializing can be seen as the performance of a group identity. Commemoration is a central feature of every story of cultural haunting; through the enactment of commemorative rituals, ethnicities are performed. By speaking of ethnicity as a performance, I am both rejecting the concept of ethnic identity as a static and bounded entity and further refining the more recent understanding of ethnic identity as a "process." Close attention to the emergence of redefined ethnicities in stories of cultural haunting illuminates the importance of ritual in the ongoing construction or, more precisely, *enactment* of cultural identity.[47]

For my purposes, a more promising model of mourning than Freud's can be found in what anthropologists call rituals of "secondary burial," in which the dead are provisionally buried and, after a period of extended mourning, are then exhumed to be reburied properly and finally. During the intermediary period between provisional and final burials, the deceased is considered neither fully dead nor alive and appears as an often malicious, always troubling, ghost that invades the affairs of the living. Most stories of cultural haunting are set during this intermediary period of haunting and move toward a final burial that, to varying degrees of success, puts the dead to rest. While final burial reasserts the boundary between the living and the dead, the ritual transforms the dead from menacing ghosts to (at least potentially) beneficent ancestral spirits and renders them safely accessible rather than inaccessible. Stories of cultural haunting follow the model of secondary burial in demonstrating that the work of mourning requires the integration of, rather than the banishing of, the dead. Through the incorporation of the always revised past, new ethnicities emerge.

To link ethnogenesis so firmly to mourning is to acknowledge that the haunted tales examined here all bear witness to some sense of a breach with the past, even as they attest to strong continuities with that past. Cultural transmission—whether conscious or unconscious—is often complicated by the existence of substantial gaps in cultural histories. One might easily assume—an assumption supported by the fact that much of ethnic writing takes the form of personal testimony—that ethnic writers have few problems in returning to their cultural pasts: because one is Chinese American, one has more immediate, direct access to the Chinese-American experience and, by a rather large leap, to its Chinese cultural past. Oddly, though, the old-world and early immigrant past is often nearly as lost to "insiders" as it is to "outsiders" of the culture. Oceans and generations intervene, languages are lost as others are acquired; "China"—or "Africa" or "Cuba"—can seem like a myth, or a mirage—perceptible and whole only when viewed from a great distance. Ethnicity in this literature is, as sociologist Stuart Hall describes it, "an act of cultural recovery," a recovery that centrally takes the form of an exploration, via the agency of ghosts, of a group history not held securely in personal memory.[48] Most writers of culturally haunted texts—those who could be defined as ethnic "insiders"—are descendants and inheritors but stand at varying degrees of distance from the pre-Columbian or pre-American cultures from which they have sprung. They find themselves in the unusual position of being both heirs and ethnographers.

The use of the term *ethnographer* to describe that distanced position might seem inappropriate, given the colonial context of the discipline's birth. I have in mind Clifford Geertz's description of anthropology as a relation between There and Here, Then and Now. The most familiar version of this model, of course, is that of the first-world anthropologist who studies a technologically more primitive, preliterate society, producing ultimately a written document that translates "there" in terms of "here." Geertz acknowledges in a footnote that when the ethnographer belongs to the group studied—as is now more and more often the case—"special problems" arise, "including variant conceptions of what 'Being There' involves." One could argue that the movement into writing, and for that matter into Western disciplinary paradigms, tends to reestablish the "then vs. now" division. Geertz shortly returns to this point: "The textual connection of the Being Here and Being There sides of anthropology, the imaginative construction of a common ground between the Written At and the Written About (who are nowadays, as mentioned, not infrequently the same people in a different frame of mind) is the *fons et origo* of whatever power anthropology has to convince anyone of anything."[49]

The "same people in a different frame of mind": Geertz refers to "Yoruban, Sinhalese, and Tewa anthropologists" who analyze their own cultures, but the phrase has resonance for most producers of American ethnic writing. Ethnic literature is marked by a double vision; the ghostly face of a lost past—"there/then"—can be perceived in the lineaments of "here/now"—or, to wrest another Geertz phrase out of context, we sense in this literature a spectral "There shadow of a Here reality."[50] When Here and There, Then and Now draw so close as to be nearly collapsed, ghostly metaphors tend not to appear. Anzia Yezierska, for example, who must write her way out of a crushingly proximate East European Jewish culture, does not conjure ghosts. Her writing is a liberation—much as it is for Edith Wharton, who in *The House of Mirth* (1905) shrewdly anatomizes old New York family "aristocracy," a society she found at the time all too present, though it was already in the first shadow of its passing.[51] Significantly, it is in her realist fiction, not her ghost stories, that Wharton takes as her chief subject her cultural inheritance. "There it was before me," Wharton later wrote, "in all its flatness and futility, asking to be dealt with as the theme most available to my hand, since I had been steeped in it from infancy."[52] Ghosts tend to materialize when the old social bonds have loosened, when the "same people" find themselves very much "in a different frame of mind," distanced by changes in language, geography, education, social codes, and simply by the passage of time. For authors who take as their subject the dynamic of cultural loss and recovery, the ghost offers an apt metaphor for the ongoing process of ethnic reinvention.

WHY, IT MIGHT be asked, if the position of heir-ethnographer can be assumed by anyone who straddles subcultures, are so many stories of cultural haunting written by women? Men have certainly contributed strong examples of the genre; I have already mentioned the haunted tales of August Wilson, T. Coraghessan Boyle, Rudolfo Anaya, William Kennedy, and Oscar Hijuelos. But women have turned to the genre of cultural haunting in larger numbers. The three texts to which I devote chapters of this book, *Beloved, Tracks,* and *Dreaming in Cuban,* were authored by women, as are the majority of the works discussed in the concluding chapter. Why are so many women drawn to the story of cultural haunting? Or, to phrase the question more pointedly, why might a heightened interest in how ethnicity intersects with gender find especially full articulation in the telling of ghost stories?

The answer to this question is multiple and is developed somewhat differently by each writer, yet certain associations between the female and the ghostly tend to reappear. As an absence made present, the ghost can give expression to the ways in which women are rendered invisible in the public sphere. Kingston, for example, rehearsing her childhood fantasy of becoming the powerful but dutiful female warrior Fa Mu Lan, briefly mentions the woman warriors with whom she dares not associate herself, lest she lose her social status. These "witch amazons," women once abandoned by their families, sold into concubinage, and then abandoned yet again, have transformed themselves into fierce avenging viragoes who kill men and boys. Officially unacknowledged (even Kingston–as–Fa Mu Lan refuses to "vouch for their reality"), the witch amazons are "like ghosts," frightening outlaw versions of their former social invisibility.[53] The witch amazons are ghostly both because they are socially unrecognized and because they have acquired an illegitimate strength. The uncanny power of the ghost reflects the disruptive force of strong women in societies that restrict the expression of female power. In Erdrich's *Tracks*, the character most intimately associated with the world of spirits is Fleur, an unnerving woman who "dressed like a man" and whose wolflike grin unsettles by mixing female beauty with ferocity.[54] Akiko in Keller's *Comfort Woman* unseats the authority of her American missionary husband by allowing herself to be possessed by female Korean ghosts. Through ghostly possession, Akiko reclaims both her Korean identity and a specifically female power.

Beyond its double-sided figuration as powerlessness and power, the ghost also provides a metaphor for how women's more restrictively defined roles as bearers of culture might be reconceived. Because female bodies are often the site of a struggle for control over lineage, the shift from metaphors of blood descent to ghostly inheritances reframes cultural transmission in ways that women especially are likely to see as liberating. Far more often than in ghost stories by men, haunting in women's texts tends to attach to reproductive issues: the ghosts often arise from traumatic memories of rape, abortion, or miscarriage; possessed bodies are described as pregnant, or ghosts themselves may appear as pregnant; the conjuring of ghosts is sometimes represented as a form of child labor. In Keller's *Comfort Woman*, for example, Akiko learns brutally how women can be reduced to mere bodies at the disposal of others. The trauma of her repeated rapes and forced abortion in the Japanese "recreation camps" haunts her in the form of a possessing ghost, but it is paradoxically through possession (by the ghost of a murdered comfort woman) that Akiko comes to reclaim her own body. The opening chapter of Kingston's *The Woman Warrior* offers a particularly clear example of how the bondage of women's bodies to patriarchal cultural codes may be evaded through the conjuring of a spectral female body. Brave Orchid tells the cautionary tale of the "no-name" aunt to teach her daughter, just as she is entering biological womanhood, the proper cultural role of women. The lesson is that women's bodies, because of their reproductive power, must remain under tight social control. When assuming their proper, socially ascribed role as wives and mothers, women appear to Kingston less human than purely natural: the "heavy, deep-rooted women were to maintain the past against the flood."[55] Kingston attempts to release herself from the burdensome model of the "heavy" woman by transforming her "no-name" aunt into a vaporous ghost. She simultaneously casts ghostliness as a metaphor for her own imaginative reinvention of a rich but, for women, limiting tradition. The fluid, shape-shifting spectral body offers an alternative to the anchored, all too physically defined bodies of women trapped in the role of guardians of a changeless, patriarchal culture. That Kingston fears the conjured ghost might turn vengeful, dragging her bold descendant into a shared ghostliness of exile from their people, reveals how difficult and how fraught with anxiety cultural revisionism can be. In many haunted tales by women, the dangers of conjuring ghosts speak of the risks involved in reconceiving women's traditional roles.

CHAPTERS 2, 3, AND 4 of this book examine three novels that variously illustrate the workings of cultural haunting: Louise Erdrich's *Tracks*, Toni Morrison's *Beloved*, and Cristina García's *Dreaming in Cuban*. In choosing these narratives for full-chapter treatment, I have been guided by my sense of their individual richness and complexity, as well as by my understanding of how they together illuminate the cluster of themes and strategies that define the genre of cultural haunting. The three novels arise from and meditate on markedly different histories: while *Dreaming in Cuban* focuses on the self-reinventions of the immigrant, *Beloved* explores the ongoing legacy of American slavery, and

Tracks weighs the possibilities of cultural continuity in the face of internal colonization. One of my larger aims in these chapters is to demonstrate how readings deeply engaged with specific histories and attentive to local meanings can support an argument about literary transethnicity. My readings are informed by relevant scholarship in other disciplines, yet they make their case through close attention to the literary texture of each work.

For Erdrich, cultural continuity entails the development of a kind of "ghost vision," an ability to see how the present is shadowed by an invisible but palpable past. In *Tracks*, the ghost becomes a figure for the narrative reconfiguration of a threatened tribal culture. Chapter 2 examines the novel's connection between haunting and cultural translation, an act through which tradition is remembered and revised and thereby survives. The chapter focuses on two key scenes of cultural translation: Erdrich's handling of the Algonkian cannibal spirit called the windigo and her allusions to the nineteenth-century cross-tribal religious revivalist movement, the Ghost Dance. By staging a windigo possession and, at the climax of her novel, performing Ghost Dance ritual, Erdrich models varieties of cultural "incorporation," translating elements of Chippewa and pantribal cultures into the nonindigenous form of the novel. These scenes of cultural translation are presided over by the figure of the ghost: the living enter into a period of heightened association with the dead to emerge with a newly redefined relationship with the living past. The ghost ultimately stands as a figure for Erdrich's own cultural translation in producing *Tracks*.

In Morrison's *Beloved*, the subject of chapter 3, haunting signals the return of a past that can neither be properly remembered nor entirely forgotten. Morrison's novel explores the connection between historical consciousness and traumatic memory, the problem of how to represent what is experienced as "unspeakable." I read *Beloved* as a literary "secondary burial," in which the victims of the slave trade, whom Morrison calls the "unceremoniously buried," are exhumed to be reburied properly in the novel's narrative tomb. This chapter considers the implications of conceiving of literature as a form of burial, particularly when that literature responds to traumatic histories. The novel's troubled conclusion portrays trauma as an open grave, an ultimately irresolvable haunting. Yet Morrison's literary investigation into the role of memory (and of forgetting) in the shaping of group identity also suggests how haunting may be transformed into an enabling historical consciousness.

García's *Dreaming in Cuban*, treated in chapter 4, traces the fortunes of the del Pino family, riven by the exile to the United States of family members staunchly opposed to Castro's revolution. Dramatizing the tensions between communists and capitalists, older and younger exiles in America, and fervent and lukewarm revolutionaries on the island, the novel takes as its central project the definition by younger exiles of a new Cuban-American identity. The novel's ghost functions to bring the estranged Cuban and American sides of the family together, but ghostliness has a larger metaphorical significance in the novel: the ghost who bears culture across a divide stands as an emblem of cultural translation, for García the process through which new ethnicities are defined. While the novel turns on the divisive border between Cuba and the United States, Cuba ultimately provides the model for the Cuban-American's "translated" identity. I demonstrate how García validates the new ethnic syntheses of her young Cuban-American protagonist by seizing upon the often unacknowledged hybridity of Cuban culture, particularly in the form of the Afro-Cuban religion, Santería. As the ethnic go-between traveling between death and life, the United States and Cuba, the ghost represents the force of ethnogenesis itself, constructing new identities out of the interplay of memory and the imagination.

The fifth and final chapter has two purposes: in surveying a wide selection of haunted tales, it makes a case for the pervasiveness of cultural haunting in contemporary American literature. As it does so, it also mounts an argument for the centrality of mourning ritual in the haunted tales of heir-ethnographers. The connection between ethnogenesis and mourning marks all stories of cultural haunting. While acknowledging the dependency of ethnic identity on communal memory, I note how stories of cultural haunting repeatedly testify to memory's instability and capriciousness. Cultural continuity is not assumed but is achieved in the course of each haunting. Memory in this literature takes the form of mourning, a way of remembering dominated by a sense of a break with the past. I argue that in stories of cultural haunting, ethnicity is construed, not just in terms of memory, but more specifically as a function of a mourning that finds expression in rituals of commemoration. Chapter 5 closes with three more extended readings of haunted texts, in which the living negotiate new identities by mourning the past. My treatment of Marshall's *Praisesong for the Widow*, Keller's *Comfort*

Woman, and Cynthia Ozick's *The Shawl* (1980 and 1983) aims to demonstrate the pivotal role of mourning ritual in the revision of ethnic identities. Through commemorative rites, ethnicity is performatively reconceived.

The unifying theme in stories of cultural haunting is the need to identify and revise the cultural past. Ghosts figure in the folklore of virtually every culture. They are also extraordinarily useful literary metaphors in the larger process of ethnic invention and revision. The ghost gives body to memory, while reminding us that remembering is not a simple or even safe act. Like the partially obliterated records that appear in contemporary haunted literature—the family papers mildewed and faded, stories left without endings or explanations, crucial words that resist translation—the ghost's elusiveness conveys a past not easily accessible. At the end of his study of ethnic definition, *Through a Glass Darkly*, William Boelhower observes that an image of ancestral Italian ghosts in a poem by Italo-American-Canadian poet Pier Giorgio Di Cicco illustrates the "absent presence" of the poet's "originating cultural *traditio*." Boelhower, whose thesis about ethnic identity closely parallels that of Werner Sollors, argues that all ethnic reconstruction is predicated on the inevitable absence of cultural origins.[56] The curious dual force of the ghost who makes present what is absent powerfully shapes the American story of cultural haunting. As both presence and absence, the ghost stands as an emblem of historical loss as well as a vehicle of historical recovery. It offers writers who take as their subject the survival and transformation of ethnic cultures, who recognize disconnection even as they assert continuity, a particularly rich metaphor for the complexities of cultural transmission. In confronting an obscure history and a tenuous present, writers across the spectrum of American peoples increasingly conjure ghosts to solve a single problem: how to reframe the narrative organization of ethnic experience. Ghosts are not the exclusive province of any single ethnic group; they figure prominently wherever people must reconceive a fragmented, partially obliterated history, looking to a newly imagined past to redefine themselves for the future.

Ghost Dancing

Cultural Translation in Louise Erdrich's *Tracks*

PART GERMAN-AMERICAN and part Chippewa, Louise Erdrich has described the quest of the "mixed-blood" as a search for parentage, an attempt to understand self by exploring genealogy.[1] In the opening paragraphs of *Tracks*, a novel set on a North Dakota Chippewa reservation in the early twentieth century, Erdrich reveals that the investigation of background necessarily entails an entrance into the world of ghosts. When the narrator Nanapush addresses the young woman listening to his unfolding account of her familial and tribal past as a "child of the invisible, the ones who disappeared" (1), he simultaneously connects an awareness of the ghostly presence of the dead with the discovery of identity and the creation of history. The narrator's conjuring of "invisible" ancestors and "ghosts" (2) who inhabit tribal woods introduces haunting as Erdrich's central metaphor for the way the past shapes and is shaped by the present.

Erdrich's ghosts function on three main levels. The first finds clear articulation in Richard Rodriguez's acute observations about American identity: "America is an idea to which natives are inimical. The Indian represented permanence and continuity to Americans who were determined to call this country new. Indians must be ghosts."[2] As Rodriguez contends, American national presence can be seen as predicated upon a native absence. The potential confusion of mixed ancestry is heightened when one feels, as Erdrich does, a member of two distinct nations, one of which founded its identity on the erasure or "ghosting" of the other. Noting that "the population of Native North Americans shrank from an estimated 15 million in the mid-15th century to just over 200,000 by 1910," Erdrich has explicitly linked her vocation as writer to her identity as the inheritor of a once nearly annihilated culture.[3] Spirits of the dead in her fiction thus bear witness to the destruction of traditional native cultures and the subsequent cultural invisibility of Native Americans. As one of Erdrich's characters observes of Chippewa land lost to timber interests: "The place will be haunted I suppose, but no one will have ears sharp enough to hear the [ghosts'] low voices, or the vision clear to see their still shadows" (204).

Ghosts, however, can also represent continuity with the past. Ancestral ghosts have, in the context of traditional Chippewa religion, powerful and positive connotations. For the Chippewa, as for many Native American cultures, the living and the dead participate in one integrated reality.[4] The return of ancestor spirits ensures a continuity between present and past. The retrieval of lost traditions in much contemporary Native American literature is signaled by the appearance of spirits. N. Scott Momaday has related how the imagining of a dead grandfather he never knew "invested the shadow of his presence" in certain objects and words; the ghost thus replaces what experience and memory alone cannot provide, a vital connection between the generations.[5] In James Welch's *Winter in the Blood*, a "reghosting" of what had formerly been perceived as an empty, dead land marks the alienated, deracinated protagonist's spiritual catharsis. Repopulating family land with "the presence of [ancestral] ghosts," Welch's character finally inherits the Blackfeet tradition that had been lost to him.[6] In Erdrich as in Welch and Momaday, the entrance of the ghost signals the entrance of tradition.

The double role of the ghost as metaphor for cultural invisibility and cultural continuity plays upon the curious "there/not there" status of the ghost. On the simplest level, the ghost can articulate a nostalgic return to the past or despair about its ineradicable loss. Yet ghostliness has a third, more complex function in Erdrich's work, one that releases the ghost from the either/or of presence and absence. The vaporous body of the ghost provides Erdrich with an apt metaphor for the malleable, partly remembered and partly imagined nature of tradition. It is the ghost as symbol of the imaginative element in the construction of ethnic identity and group history that will receive closest scrutiny here. The turn to the ghost as reconstructive agent simultaneously testifies to and attempts to transcend terrible loss. In the case of cultures subject to near annihilation by more powerful groups, the invocation of the supernatural can be seen as a survival strategy, through which loss or absence becomes, by awful necessity, generative. "Faced with extinction, we imagine reprieve," begins a review of (non–Indian) post–nuclear catastrophe novels that Erdrich wrote with Michael Dorris before his recent untimely death.[7] We might revise this formulation to apply to Erdrich's fiction about Native Americans: faced with the threat of cultural near extinction, she imagines lost cultural origins through the telling of ghost stories.

The implications of the ghost as reconstructive agent become clearer when we consider more closely Erdrich's understanding of "tradition." Erdrich's treatment of the supernatural can be seen as a reflection of her understanding of the tradition she claims as her legacy:

> I think all Native Americans living today probably look back and think, "How, out of the millions and millions of people who were here in the beginning, the very few who survived into the 1920s, and the people who are alive today with some sense of their own tradition, how did it get to be me, and why?" And I think that quest and that impossibility really drives us in a lot of ways. It's central to the work, and so as we go about telling these stories, we feel compelled. We're, in a way, survivors of that tradition; there aren't a lot of people who are going to tell these stories, or who are going to look at the world in this particular way.[8]

Erdrich clearly sees herself as continuing Native American tradition, yet her qualification that she is "in a way" a survivor of that tradition reminds us of Erdrich's simultaneous participation in and distance from what she has called "a tribal view of the world."[9] The "old-time" Chippewa (as they are sometimes referred to in Erdrich's novels) believed the element of water was invested with the presence of *manitous*, or spirits, but as her character Lipsha Morrissey observes in *Love Medicine*, "we live on dry land" now. When the ghost of his mother (cruising the roads in her ghostly Firebird) leads Lipsha toward an icy death at the end of *The Bingo Palace*, we need to consider how Erdrich redefines a purely traditional context to understand this confluence of human and spirit worlds.[10]

We might best approach Erdrich's understanding of tradition by considering the significance for her of "the land," almost universally associated in Native American cultures with tradition.[11] In an essay on a writer's sense of place, Erdrich contrasts what Alfred Kazin has described as the European-American attraction to and repulsion from an alien landscape with a pre-invasion, tribal worldview, in which place, inhabited by a people for time immemorial, is "enlivened by a sense of group and family history." The "unchanging landscape," a nearly mythic setting for numerous stories that encode a people's past, grounds tribal identity: "People and place are inseparable."[12] The land is invested with meaning, providing a spatial symbolic order that reflects cultural values. Identity—both personal and tribal—emerges in relation to a particular territory. This equation of land and tradition remains strong in contemporary Native American writing, though often as a negative inversion that attributes the fragmentation of cultural identity to the loss of aboriginal land or to a blindness to the land's cultural significance. In Welch's *Winter in the Blood*, Momaday's *House Made of Dawn*, and Leslie Marmon Silko's *Ceremony*, for example, disaffected, alienated protagonists must rediscover tradition by learning the forgotten meaning of particular places.

Erdrich's novels, like those of Welch, Silko, and Momaday, and like those of authors identified by Erdrich as favorites—the regionalists Faulkner, Cather, and Welty—are grounded in a particular territory. Erdrich grew up in a small North Dakota town near the Minnesota border, the child of teachers at a local boarding school run by the Bureau of Indian Affairs. She lived off-reservation, frequently visiting family members on the Turtle Mountain reservation, where her grandfather was a tribal leader. This is the land she returns to in her quartet of novels set in North Dakota. Her novels contain scant physical description, yet the land is felt as a force, a link to the past, a support for Chippewa identity. It is, like Welch's Montana, haunted land. In her essay on place, Erdrich speaks of how a vision of this North Dakota landscape comes to her often as she writes. She adds, somewhat oddly, that she has "never been able to describe it as well as Isak Dinesen," even though Dinesen wrote of Kenya, not the American Plains. Erdrich seizes upon a passage from *Out of Africa*, in which Dinesen describes the vastness of the African sky, its "everchanging clouds," and the curiously alive, flamelike quality of its air. The passage ends with Dinesen's supreme accommodation to Africa: "Here I am, where I ought to be."[13]

Bringing her experience of the American Plains to her reading of the European Dinesen, Erdrich loops back to what is her own by leaving it, modulating the native and familiar through the foreign. What is more remarkable than the fact that she cedes the best description of North Dakota to Dinesen, who had never seen it, is that she draws an analogy between Dinesen's colonial, expatriate presence in Africa and her own native connection to formerly Indian land. It is an extraordinary gesture, particularly when we consider the familiar Native American understanding of identity as rooted in the land—a sense of identity undermined by colonial invasion. This is, ironically, the understanding that Dinesen comes to at the end of *Out of Africa*. Reflecting on the dismay of the African "squatters" who are evicted by her sale of the farm (and who are legally unable to own property in their native land), she concludes that "It is more than their land that you take away from the people, whose Native land you take. It is their past as well, their roots and their identity."[14] Yet Erdrich sees in Dinesen not the colonial but the imaginative appropriator, and she clearly admires Dinesen's ability to establish an "at-homeness" even in the alien. By linking her own perspective with that of a nonindigenous writer living under colonial jurisdiction, Erdrich distances herself subtly both from the pre-invasion tribal view of culture she describes and from contemporary Native Americans whose reservation land is, in her words, "still informed with old understandings."[15] Returning to the Dinesen passage selected by Erdrich, we note that it is significantly the mobile, "everchanging" quality of the landscape that is emphasized, rather than, say, its solidity or permanence. The unfixing of the land as the *terra firma* of tradition allows for a more fluid sense of cultural identity. Erdrich intimates that one's home—"where I ought to be"—and the cultural identity that place fosters are chosen rather than simply inherited—and may even be, as her later references to the reality of Gabriel García Márquez's Macondo and William Faulkner's Yoknapatawpha County hint, partly invented.[16]

"Incorporation" is the word Erdrich frequently uses to describe the process of cultural revision and invention. She has often spoken of her grandfather, a tribal leader, storyteller, and something of a family legend, as a man adept at incorporating alien elements into a traditional framework. Incorporation takes the new into the old, changing both, creating an entity different from either that is nevertheless experienced as continuous with the past. In an interview, Erdrich recalls how her grandfather translated the geography of the reservation into verbal legend. Pointing to the low hills, he would identify features of the land for his young granddaughter, each receiving the name of an animal its shape resembled. Orienting her to the place that later becomes the location of her fiction, he "even incorporated the highways into the shapes because some of them got their tails cut off." This detail, which Erdrich laughingly recalls, seems significant to her, a small emblem of what she calls the "resilience" of the Turtle Mountain Chippewa. Erdrich identifies the ability to "incorporate" new, anomalous elements into a traditional framework as "one of the strengths of Indian culture": "you pick and choose and keep and discard." [17] In the case of her grandfather's reservation stories, parts of the animal are indeed cut off, but the agency of division—the invasive highways laid down by whites—is nevertheless incorporated into the animal's story. Her grandfather's verbal revisions supply Erdrich with a model for the way tradition is continually reshaped and thus survives. What threatens to "cut off" elements of tribal tradition is accepted, and becomes survivable, through a kind of imaginative accommodation. The severed tails, representing the violation of tribal culture as embodied in the land, are in a sense recovered through the grandfather's "tales": through the integrative power of narrative, the land continues to be tribally storied, an essential part of tradition. The storytelling scene Erdrich recalls, in which a grandfather revises and transmits tribal tradition to a granddaughter, provides a model for a key narrative transaction of *Tracks* (in Nanapush's chapters addressed to his adoptive granddaughter Lulu), a resemblance suggesting that the reconfiguration of cultural resources through narrative is a central preoccupation of the novel. [18]

The value Erdrich places on incorporation and her understanding of "home" as a mental habitation indicate that she views tradition not—as it is often understood—as a static, originary inheritance but as a flexible, mutable entity, ceaselessly evolving through a dynamic process of selection and revision. She sees the shaping of ethnic identity as a process of investigation and revision: "You look back and say, 'Who am I from?' You must question. You must make certain choices. You're able to." [19] Erdrich's emphasis on the necessity of questioning and the possibility of choice defines tradition not as a changeless essence but as imaginative construction, built from but not limited to the familiar materials of a people's cultural treasury. Though she draws on a traditional Chippewa vocabulary of ghosts, "medicine," and *manitous*, her grammar is postmodern. She maintains a distinctively constructivist vision, in which absence itself is made generative; the ghost stands as emblem of the active shaping of history. Her fictional ghosts, unlike spirits of Chippewa religion, register—even as they attempt to bridge—a distance from traditional culture. The bridging of this distance should be seen as an act of cultural translation, requiring the sort of "resilience" that Erdrich sees manifest in her grandfather's stories of incorporation.

Translation—linguistic and cultural—has emerged as a central and fiercely debated issue in Native American scholarship. As Arnold Krupat has noted, the question is not only how properly to translate from one language to another but also how to translate from one medium (orality) to another (textuality). Despite his belief that "there is no way to translate and present Indian oral performance in any completely satisfactory way," translation, both linguistic and cultural, remains for Krupat an ideal worthy of our most strenuous efforts. The aim "is not to overthrow the Tower of Babel but, as it were, to install a simultaneous translation system in it; not to homogenize human or literary differences but to make them at least mutually intelligible." Citing Krupat, David Murray in *Forked Tongues* similarly calls for "a view of translation and communication" that steers between total untranslatability and linguistic transparency, or between the reification of difference and the construction of false universals. Yet Murray points out that in the context of colonial domination, mutual translation, a two-way process of cultural interchange, may be the dominant culture's myth, while the reality remains that "the cultural translation is all one-way, and the penalty to the subordinate group for not adapting to the demands of the dominant group is to cease to exist." Against the "translative violence" that Murray describes here, Krupat positions the "anti-imperial translation" of much contemporary Native American literature. For the majority of Native American writers—who may have some familiarity with indigenous languages, but who generally write in English—this translation generally takes the form of incorporating (and inevitably revising) elements of their oral traditions into Euro-American literary forms, producing an English, in Krupat's words, "powerfully affected" by "indigenous perspectives" for a mixed (Native American and nonnative) readership.[20]

Other critics view the translation that Krupat champions in less sanguine terms. For Robert Silberman, the book in Native American literature is "a necessary evil," while for Karl Kroeber, the novel is "an Anglo-American literary structure that must prohibit any authentically Indian imaginative form."[21] The "authentically Indian" is, of course, a highly problematic notion, viewed with suspicion by many Native American writers. Critic Jana Sequoya points out that "the 'authentic' Indian is a figment of the imagination—a symbolic identity invested with meanings of temporal inequality vis-à-vis the colonizing real(m)." Yet Sequoya, like Kroeber, worries about "the replacement of traditional Native American structures of identity with those of Euro-America." Voicing concern about the potential damage to tribal societies by the commodification of an exoticized tribal culture as local color for the dominant culture, Sequoya argues that the Native American writer who translates aspects of Native American culture in terms of the dominant culture "inevitably betrays some of the social rules of the former, just as does translation between languages."[22]

In *Tracks*, Erdrich exposes some (though certainly not all) of the dangers of bicultural mediation (largely through her second narrator, Pauline) and amply illustrates the terrible cost of enforced, one-way translation. The novel's first narrator, Nanapush, fears the murder of tribal life by a culture that uses the written word as a form of domination, conjuring the image of "bureaucrats sink[ing] their barbed pens into the lives of Indians" (225). Erdrich, however, views writing and the oral tradition as "not incompatible." Acknowledging the crucial importance of the oral tradition to her work, she adds, "At the same time I believe in and deeply cherish books and believe the library is a magical and sacred storehouse. . . . The town library was my teacher every bit as much as sitting in the kitchen or out under the trees swapping stories or listening to older relatives."[23] She accords to the library qualities ("magical," "sacred") usually associated with the oral tradition. By insisting on the possibility of choice in the redefinition of tradition, and by affirming continuities between older and newer manifestations of Chippewa culture, Erdrich speaks for the regenerative potential of translation, whether linguistic or cultural. This chapter examines two key sites of cultural translation: Erdrich's treatment of the windigo, an Algonkian cannibal spirit, and her allusions to the Ghost Dance, a nineteenth-century cross-tribal revivalist movement. Through the staging of a windigo possession and exorcism, and through the implicit performance of Ghost Dance ritual, Erdrich models varieties of cultural "incorporation," translating elements of Chippewa and pantribal cultures into the nonindigenous form of the novel. These scenes of cultural translation are presided over by the figure of the ghost: the living enter into a heightened association with spirits of the dead and emerge from this ghostly encounter with a newly redefined relationship to the living past.

CULTURAL SURVIVAL FOR Erdrich hinges upon the establishment of historical perspective, the commitment to seeing the present as shadowed by the palpable but invisible past. Erdrich's view parallels Michel de Certeau's assertion that history is born of a conversation about the dead. The ghost is not simply an emblem of the returned past but, like de Certeau's dead, stands as "the objective figure of an exchange among the living" in which group members negotiate an identity through reference to the absent past.[24] The recovery of the past is not an end in itself but a vehicle through which group identity, in response to present conditions, is newly reconfigured—not merely reasserted or repeated. As William Boelhower has observed in his discussion of ethnic fiction, "the goal is interpretation of the past and not the past itself. . . . Far from being a mere archeological exercise in the quest for origins and natural bonding, serious ethnic semiosis claims the right to redefine the boundaries of ethnic interaction and the place of ethnicity in American culture."[25] Cultural ghost stories, which feature the haunting of a people by the ghosts of its own past, represent one way a group actively revises its relationship to the past. Not surprisingly, these stories tend to emerge in the aftermath of times of swift and often traumatic change, when old social bonds have been unhinged and new group identities must be formulated.

Erdrich's *Tracks* indirectly reflects on current anxieties about cultural survival and ethnic reinvention by returning to a particularly dire time for the Chippewa, when traditional tribal life was severely threatened. Set in the early twentieth century, *Tracks* is chronologically the first of a quartet of novels that follows the intertwined fortunes of several families living on and near a North Dakota Chippewa reservation. The novel opens in 1912, reaching back to a time when many Chippewa still spoke the old language, still knew the old religion. Yet it is a past rapidly disappearing. By 1912, the incorporation of elements of nonnative cultures was already far advanced. Catholic missionaries were a long established presence among the Chippewa; Jesuits, following on the heels of French fur traders, had made contact with the Chippewa as early as 1641.[26] By the early twentieth century, religious practice tended toward an amal-

gamation of Christian and native elements. Intermarriage had considerably changed the constitution of the tribe; according to government
census data, in 1910 only about a third of the Chippewa were full-
bloods.[27] By that time the tribe had already been restricted to reservation land, a confinement that severely reduced available game and led to
yearly winter famines. Government land-allotment and fee-patent policies that turned communally used tribal land into individually owned,
salable property allowed starving Indians to sell off large chunks of
reservation land to nonnative farmers, lumber companies, and land
speculators. Those who refused to sell often were unable to pay the annual holding fees on land mortgaged to buy provisions and lost the land
to foreclosure. On the Turtle Mountain reservation, 90 percent of Chippewa landowners sold or mortgaged their allotments by 1915, many returning destitute to the reservation to live off already burdened relatives.[28] The policy of educating children in off-reservation government
or church-run boarding schools generally served its intended purpose of
weakening the links between the young and the ways of their elders.
Erdrich's novel opens with references to a recent epidemic of tuberculosis, one of many diseases spread by contact with nonnatives. The
"greatest single menace to the Indian race" as it was termed in 1908 by
the commissioner of the U.S. Bureau of Indian Affairs, tuberculosis was
in fact the most deadly of the diseases threatening Native American
populations, with mortality rates far higher than among Euro-American
communities.[29] Erdrich's character Nanapush, at fifty the oldest member of a tribe thinned by starvation and illness, knows he has witnessed
the end of an era: "In the years I'd passed, I saw more change than in a
hundred upon a hundred before. My girl, I saw the passing of times you
will never know" (2).

Survival, physical and spiritual, is the central project of the novel's
characters. The narration is shared by two survivors, Nanapush, the
tribal elder, and Pauline Puyat, a Catholic convert, each the last living member of their respective families. In alternating chapters, they
offer different perspectives on the life of Fleur Pillager, the powerful
and mysterious character at the heart of the novel. Like Nanapush and
Pauline, Fleur is a survivor. With the exception of her half-mad cou-
sin Moses, Fleur is the last of the Pillager clan, reputed for their medicine, or shamanic knowledge. The story begins with Nanapush's rescue of young Fleur, when she lay half dead from tubercular plague in

her family's cabin, surrounded by the corpses of her relatives. Pauline takes up the story in the off-reservation town of Argus, where Fleur has sought work, and relates the gang rape of Fleur and the eerie ensuing death of her violators. Fleur returns to the reservation but remains something of an outsider. She exudes a potent female sexuality yet dresses and hunts like a man. More disturbing to the community, she is associated with the spirit world: we are told that when she arrives on the reservation, "Things hidden were free to walk" (34–35). Nanapush's and Pauline's alternating narratives reconstruct the rest of Fleur's story: her scandalous choice to live alone in her family's remote cabin, her involvement in shamanic medicine, her romance with Eli Kashpaw, and the birth of her daughter, Lulu. Fleur struggles to save her family from the long winter famines that strike the reservation, and fights unsuccessfully to save her land from falling to loggers. In the process, Nanapush is increasingly drawn into Fleur's life as adopted father and, later, as grandfather to Lulu. As the novel progresses, Pauline, torn by her powerful attraction to and envy of Fleur, becomes more and more bent on destroying her.

The story of Fleur is inseparable from the larger story of the near devastation of Chippewa culture. Fleur's very outsiderhood on the reservation testifies to the degree to which traditional life has been dismantled. Fleur's power is associated with the *manitous*, spirits still believed in but demonized by the Christian perspective increasingly gaining ground. Her struggle to save her allotment land from purchase by loggers, her inability to meet the government's annual tax on allotments, and the corruption of self-serving Chippewa who collude with the Indian Affairs agent to seize potentially lucrative allotments illustrate the mechanisms by which reservation land was carved up and the sense of an integral community eroded. After Fleur loses her land and can no longer care for her daughter, Lulu is sent to a government boarding school, designed to ensure that children will assimilate to Euro-American culture and will no longer be able to speak their native language or understand native gods. We know from the novel's opening chapter that Lulu has returned from school bitter and alienated from the past, refusing to recognize her mother. The combination of illness, starvation, loss of land and religion, and the estrangement of the young progressively undermines the social coherence of the Chippewa who had managed to survive in diminished numbers to 1912. As Nanapush observes, "Our tribe unraveled like a coarse rope" (2).

Nanapush's and Pauline's framing of Fleur's story reveals the deeper plot of possession and attempted exorcism that defines the genre of the cultural ghost story. The paradigmatic movement from possession to exorcism that unfolds in stories of cultural haunting is closely related to the process of mourning. Anthropologist Arnold van Gennep has proposed that death, like all rites of passage, has a tripartite structure involving separation (dying), transition (funereal rites), and the incorporation of the deceased into the world of the dead (burial or arrival at the end of the journey to the land of the dead). Mourners become counterparts to the deceased in this process; they must endure separation from loved ones through death and enter into the transition of mourning, eventually to reintegrate into society.[30] During the transitional period of mourning, the living and the dead share a liminal existence that Victor Turner, in his own study of liminality in ritual, has analogized to ghostliness.[31] This liminal period is potentially dangerous because longing for the dead in a state of heightened identification can lead to longing for one's own death. The living join the deceased in being incorporated into the world of death or, in an equally self-destructive inversion, in incorporating the dead into themselves. The ghost of the past lodges within, not as memory, but in the form of a possession.

We first discover this deadly incorporation of the past in the opening chapter of the novel, when Nanapush speaks of his rescue of Fleur Pillager and their subsequent absorption into unutterable grief for families lost in the 1912 tubercular plague. Knowing themselves to be the last living member of their respective families, the two survivors enter into a nearly suicidal period of mourning. For the duration of a winter month, they never leave Nanapush's cabin, losing interest in both food and talk. Nanapush remembers the near speechlessness of grief, the fear that if the names of the dead were spoken aloud, "they would hear us and never rest, come back out of pity for the loneliness we felt. They would sit in the snow outside the door, waiting until from longing we joined them" (5). The transposition of the survivors' emotion to the dead who may "come back out of pity" suggests an identification of the mourners with the dead, an equation hinted at earlier when Nanapush found the corpses of the Pillager family and was "stilled by their quiet forms" (3). What begins as the honoring of the customary Chippewa prohibition against naming the recent dead develops, through this identification, into a pathological mourning marked by complete silencing:

> We felt the spirits of the dead so near that at length we just stopped talking.
>   This made it worse.
>   Their names grew within us, swelled to the brink of our lips, forced our eyes open in the middle of the night. We were filled with the water of the drowned, cold and black, airless water that lapped against the seal of our tongues or leaked slowly from the corners of our eyes. Within us, like ice shards, their names bobbed and shifted. Then the slivers of ice began to collect and cover us. We became so heavy, weighted down with the lead gray frost, that we could not move. Our hands lay on the table like cloudy blocks. The blood within us grew thick. We needed no food. . . . We had gone half windigo. (6)

The "windigo" to which Nanapush here refers is a Chippewa spirit shared by other tribes of the Algonkian language family, generally represented as an enormous cannibal made of ice and endowed with a voracious appetite for human flesh. Hunters who never return from the woods are said to have been devoured by the windigo. But the windigo can also possess a human being, vampirically turning the person into a cannibal like itself. People possessed by the windigo suffer a horrible distortion of perception: they begin to see those around them, particularly family members, as edible game. Thus when Nanapush says that he and Fleur have "gone half windigo," he means not only that they have gone half mad but that their madness specifically results from having cannibalistically consumed their (dead) families. They reject food, battening instead on the ghosts of the dead.[32] Their tongues, rather than functioning as organs for speech or eating, become a "seal" in the attempt to hold in the dead, in the desperate attempt not to lose them. The description of their hands as "cloudy blocks" recalls the appearance of ice blocks the Chippewa cut from the frozen lake in winter: "weighted down with lead gray frost," Nanapush and Fleur are being metamorphosed into creatures of ice, like the windigo. The term "cloudy blocks" also conveys the paradox that their heavy despair is accompanied by a growing insubstantiality, as if they themselves are becoming "cloudy" or vaporous. This suggestion is confirmed when Nanapush adds that "I learned later that this was common, that there were many of our people who died in this manner, of the invisible sickness" (6). The sickness is aptly called "invisible" because, having eaten ghosts, they themselves are being transformed into ghosts. Nanapush and Fleur risk becoming trapped in a pathological extension of van Gennep's transition period of mourning, so closely identifying with the dead that they may leave the living to follow the deceased into the realm of death.

It is not only the psychological but also the dominant social tenor of van Gennep's "rites of passage" that I wish to underline here. The parallel Erdrich establishes between mourning and windigo possession underlines the degree to which Nanapush and Fleur's private grief for family members can also be seen as a response to a larger cultural devastation. With its imagery of ice and references to overwhelming hunger, the windigo myth probably alludes to winter starvation—always a threat to Native Americans, but turning into a year-round calamity once the spread of the fur trade and enforced settlement severely reduced available game.[33] Malevolent spirits like the windigo, however, operate within the traditional Chippewa belief system as necessary balances. Windigo stories function like cautionary tales for the Chippewa: the voracious windigo illustrates the dangers of selfish, greedy excess, a particularly dangerous violation of the tribe's behavioral norms during times when essential resources like food are limited. Erdrich accordingly develops the windigo as emotional excess in *Love Medicine*, where the cannibal spirit is associated with consuming passion.[34] In *Tracks*, however, she revises this traditional function of the windigo to emphasize the connection between two dangerous forms of consumption: the eating away of tribal culture by an invasive new culture and the consumption of one's own dead as a traumatized response to this assault on the tribe's traditional values and social coherence. Traumatic responses typically mirror the outrage that provokes them: trauma "tells" its history of damage by reenacting a version of that history.[35] Nanapush and Fleur's "eating" of ghosts, while an obvious attempt to hold on to their tribal history, nevertheless echoes to a certain degree the "consumption" of tribal life by assimilation, disease, and starvation. There is, in fact, historical support for Erdrich's revised reading of the windigo: that the windigo quickly progressed during decades of colonial expansion from one of many Algonkian spirits to one of the most powerful strongly suggests a link between the legendary "windigo madness" and what is often called "acculturation trauma." Mourning as ghostly possession, a nearly suicidal process of incorporating the dead, has not only psychological but broader social implications in *Tracks*. The incorporative dynamics of personal grieving become emblematic of a culture's potentially self-destructive response to rapid, traumatic change.

The connection between windigo possession and acculturation trauma is first hinted at just before the mourning scene, when Nanapush and Pukwan, a largely assimilated member of the tribal police, venture out into the woods surrounding Lake Matchimanito to see if any of the Pillager family survived the plague and to deal with the dead bodies. The woods near the lake are very old and said to be haunted by ghosts. The combination of the eerie atmosphere and the anticipated dreadful encounter with the dead has its effect: when Nanapush and Pukwan arrive at the deathly silent Pillager cabin, Pukwan is suddenly paralyzed with terror. We are told that he "did not want to enter, fearing the unburied Pillager spirits might seize him by the throat and turn him windigo" (3). The particular visual image Pukwan's fear creates in the novel's first reference to the windigo forecasts the later "invisible sickness" of Fleur and Nanapush. To seize by the throat is to cut off both breath and consumption, to silence and to starve. Though no windigo monster shows up, Pukwan's fear is prophetic. After his disrespectful and callous treatment of both the dead Pillager bodies (which by tribal tradition should be buried and not burned as the whites insist) and the one barely surviving Pillager, the girl Fleur, he returns home, "crawled into bed, and took no food from that moment until his last breath passed" (4). The windigo cannibal (probably in the form of tuberculosis) defeats him after all. We are clearly meant to see in Pukwan's death a kind of grim justice: through his embrace of colonial policies, his eagerness to "carry out the [U.S. government] Agency's instructions to the letter" (3), his unfeeling disregard for Chippewa tradition, the policeman has symbolically devoured his own tribal culture.

Whether taking the form of assimilation, as in Pukwan's case, or of a consuming grief, as in the case of Nanapush and Fleur, windigo possession in *Tracks* clearly reflects the near undermining of Chippewa culture. The novel's odd association of possession with tuberculosis supports this connection. Nanapush's description of grief as an "invisible sickness" bears remarkable resemblance to the symptoms of tubercular infection. Tuberculosis is a pulmonary disease, contracted through the respiratory tract and leading to the ruin of the lung (hence the loss of voice Nanapush describes). The progression of the tuberculosis often leads to a massive accumulation of fluid in pleural cavities, causing breath-lessness. The internal drowning ("We were filled with . . . water") Nanapush and Fleur undergo recalls the liquefaction of the lungs typi-cal of advanced tuberculosis. Referred to in the novel by its popular nineteenth-century name ("The consumption, it was called by young Father Damien" [2]), tuberculosis can be read as a highly appropriate metaphor for deadly forms of cultural consumption. That the disease is named by the whites seems significant; Erdrich may have had in mind the other popular nineteenth-century name for tuberculosis: the "great white plague." The "consumption" and its symptoms carry a figura-tive burden in Erdrich's novel: the name points to the eating away of Chippewa culture through disease, loss of land, and assimilation. The name also refers to a form of self-cannibalizing evident on the reserva-tion, a despair and traumatic self-destructiveness that follow devastating change. Nanapush refers to this self-consumption when he argues that the tribe's troubles come not from "dissatisfied spirits" of the dead but "from living, from liquor and the dollar bill. We stumbled toward the government bait, never looking down, never noticing how the land was snatched from under us at every step" (4). For Erdrich, windigo posses-sion functions as a symbol of cultural starvation linked, with terrible irony, to eating one's own.

Nanapush and Fleur's windigo possession is broken when a benevo-lent Catholic priest arrives with the good news that Moses Pillager, thought dead, has also survived. "We could hardly utter a greeting," states Nanapush, "but we were saved by one thought: a guest must eat." The return to custom and the consumption of food rather than of ghosts begins the process of recovery:

> My voice rasped at first when I tried to speak, but then, oiled by strong tea, lard and bread, I was off and talking. Even a sledge won't stop me once I start. Father Damien looked astonished, and then wary, as I began to creak and roll. I gathered speed. I talked both languages in streams that ran alongside each other, over every rock, around every obstacle. The sound of my own voice convinced me I was alive. I kept Father Damien listening all night, his green eyes round, his thin face straining to under-stand, his odd brown hair in curls and clipped knots. Occasionally, he took in air, as if to add observations of his own, but I pushed him under with my words. (7)

The feast of the dead in which Nanapush and Fleur partake leads to complete silencing: the past lodges within them as an indigestible and unspeakable ghost. The exorcism of the dead is therefore marked by a return to voice: the power to survive, as suggested by the substitution of revised "tales" for tails by Erdrich's grandfather, lies at least partly in the ability to authorize the self and the tribe through narrative. The sudden verbal release is described as a rushing flow of water, the spring avalanche that follows the melting of winter's (and the windigo's) ice. Nanapush's metaphorical drowning of Father Damien, who is "pushed . . . under" by the deluge of words, hints that when speech has been repressed, its return may be marked by an element of violence. The torrential narrative ensures Nanapush's survival by aggressively displacing any competing discourse. Yet what particularly interests me here is that the surge of speech is double: "both languages," Ojibway and English. The forces ranged for and against voice are surprisingly not defined in terms of a strict cultural opposition. Nanapush's bilingualism is no doubt a response in part to the presence of a sympathetic white audience ("his thin [also malnourished] face straining to understand"). More importantly, it establishes translation—of the past in terms of the present, of one culture in terms of another—as a life-sustaining act that transforms without (at least wholly) eradicating the past. The ghostly past is digested, rendered usable, through its translation into narrative. The successful completion of mourning releases the living from possession by the past, allowing for a simultaneous continuity with and separation from the past necessary to the creation of history. The casting of translation as the end of mourning reminds us that translations are founded on a death, an irrevocable loss: something of the "source" will never make it into the "target" language. The emergence of Nanapush's bilingualism in this scene is made possible by his taking final leave of his beloved dead, a painful naming of the past as past. The "spirits of the dead" who had once hovered "so near" are now firmly held at arm's length. Ethnic translation or revision appears to need a certain distancing from the very past with which it would assert continuity.

We learn later in the novel that, when young, Nanapush had worked as a government interpreter "until the Beauchamp Treaty signing, in which I said to Rift-In-A-Cloud, 'Don't put your thumb in the ink.' One of the officials understood and I lost my job" (100). When he listens to the pregnant Fleur's labor cries, he again demonstrates his ability to translate: "it was as if the Manitous all through the woods spoke through Fleur, loose, arguing. I recognized them. Turtle's quavering scratch, the

Eagle's high shriek, Loon's crazy bitterness, Otter, the howl of Wolf, Bear's low rasp" (59). By the end of the novel, he employs his translator's skill to master the Euro-American art of "leading others with a pen and piece of paper," using this "new way of wielding influence" (209) to save Lulu from virtual imprisonment at a federal boarding school. His ability to move between Chippewa and Euro-American cultures, Ojibway and English, visible and invisible realms, allows him to bridge generations, to translate the past for the present and future. Nanapush is a translator in other ways. His name refers us to the legendary Chippewa trickster hero, Nanabushu, who is an intermediary; supernatural, but born of a mortal mother, he is sent to the Chippewa as a healer. He also possesses powers of transformation, a physical form of translation. He is the most beloved of all Chippewa spirits, the trickster who is often tricked, whose foolishness endears, whose fallibility brings him closer to the human.[36]

Trickster folk figures in all cultures are associated with verbal ambiguity. It is no accident that cultures that have experienced long periods of political oppression elevate their trickster figures to the status of folk hero. The trickster is a translator, conveying meaning in words confusing to enemies. Susan Stewart has noted that the trickster is associated with the taboo and with the violation of cultural rules, while also being identified as, in the words of anthropologist Paul Radin, "the establisher of culture." Stewart observes that "As the embodiment of disparate domains, trickster is analogous to the process of metaphor, the incorporation of opposites into a new configuration. He represents both the breakdown and the emergence of the classifications constituting culture."[37] The process of metaphor as described by Stewart closely approximates a process of cultural incorporation or consumption that stands in positive contrast to the self-cannibalizing of windigo possession. It recalls Erdrich's description of her grandfather's ability to "incorporate" the new into the old, a form of "resilience" that makes possible cultural survival.

Tracks brings home the idea that translation is essential to cultural survival, that it is, in fact, the vital, life-giving act. Just as the trickster Nanabushu works as an intermediary between the supernatural and the mortal, so does Erdrich's Nanapush stand between the world of the living and that of ghosts. He is highly sensitive to the hovering presence of the dead, who flicker just beyond the edges of his vision (6). Despair draws him nearer to the ghost world; when he knows his last efforts to save Fleur's land from logging companies have failed, he feels the seduction of joining the invisible. This final transformation would represent the end of translation:

> Farther on as I neared Fleur's cabin, the woods were still untouched in sameness, so high, so cool. The wind in their branches was a shelter of air. I didn't know why I had ever found them frightful, why I ever wished to translate the language of their leaves. The path narrowed again and I felt my wandering relatives draw near, felt the rustle of their airy thoughts and complaints. I was lost in my arguments and wonder when a small wild girl with twigs caught in her hair ambushed me, held me by the leg and rifled my pockets for a drop of horehound. (209–10)

Reference to the "language" of the forest appears earlier in the novel, when Nanapush warns Eli of the dangerous, haunted woods near Matchimanito in terms that recall his own earlier windigo possession: "The leaves speak a cold language that overfills your brain. You want to lie down. You want to never get up. You hunger" (42). The imagery of a fearful "cold language" returns when Fleur, facing the failure of her powers, sings words never heard before by Nanapush, "chilling and cold as the dead, restless and sharp as the wind" (171). The connection Nanapush makes between his fear of the cold and restless dead and the motive to translate the language of the leaves reinforces the idea that translations work to distance the very dead they recall and revise. When he loses his desire to hold off the dead, the impulse to translate also diminishes. Nanapush now hears "the airy thoughts" of the dead but no longer wishes to translate back to the language of the living, until the appearance of the child Lulu pulls him back from absorption into the ghost world—she will of course later become the recipient of his story, his translation of the past. His act of translation (of the Chippewa language, of the old tribal ways, of the ghosts of the dead) for the English-schooled, modern young woman aims to assure the survival of the Chippewa. Lulu's estrangement from Fleur and her anticipated marriage into the Morrissey family, known for sacrificing tribal unity for their own financial advantage in dealings with whites, give urgency to Nanapush's project. Through his storytelling, Nanapush attempts to recall Lulu to tradition by establishing a connection between her and the world of the dead. His narrative, moving from a posttraumatic possession by the dead to a more positive form of haunting that proves necessary to the creation of historical meaning, stands as a model of attachment to the dead that opposes the more dangerous possession it describes. Nanapush says he once suffered "like a woman," "gave birth in loss," delivering all his plague-ridden children into death. "It was contrary, backward," he reflects, "but now I had a chance to put things into a proper order." Nanapush has the novel's ninth and final chapter, suggesting the completion of a (verbal) pregnancy. In a scene in which he nurses a badly frostbitten Lulu through the night to save her from amputation or death, Nanapush in a sense delivers Lulu into life, with the umbilical cord being "the string [of words] between us."[38] Pressing her icy feet against the warmth of his body, Nanapush "talked on and on" to dull the painful burning of her frozen feet, until the girl "entered the swell and ebb and did not sink but [was] sustained" (167). The imagery of the frozen body and of swelling water in this scene echoes the earlier exorcism of the windigo, but unlike the cold, black, deathly water that swelled the bodies of the possessed mourners, Nanapush's flowing river of talk, like his earlier spring avalanche of words when released from mourning, sustains rather than drowns. Mediated by Nanapush's language—that is, both summoned and held at a safe distance—the dead present no danger to Lulu. Through his narrative, he invites her to internalize the ghostly past in "a proper order," in the form of organized memory. The novel suggests that Nanapush's ghostly vision is related to the art of narration, the active shaping of the past. "Only looking back is there a pattern," he tells Lulu, "never visible while it is still happening. Only after, when an old man sits dreaming and talking in his chair, the design springs clear" (33–34). To reconnect Lulu, the "child of the invisible," to her family and tribal history, Nanapush must school her in the art of seeing invisible, ghostly patterns.

Nanapush's position as the novel's model translator raises the obvious question of why the narration should be shared with Pauline Puyat. Each attempts to exorcise the ghosts of the past, Pauline through denial, Nanapush through an incorporation of the past into the present. Though their attempts to exorcise the invisible past that possesses them take different forms, they both represent acts of cultural translation. As the sole survivors of their families, both narrators begin a process of mourning that involves a translation of the invisible spirit world of the Chippewa in other terms. In translating for the alienated Lulu, Nanapush turns to and revises traditional tribal culture, while for Pauline the spirit world of Catholicism, with its devils and saints, provides the code by which she interprets the tragedies of the Indians. Erdrich uses the parallels and oppositions between the two narrators to underline her argument about the necessity (and potential dangers) of cultural translation.

Nanapush's account of Fleur and the Chippewa serves to define and support group identity, establishing a continuity with the dead that guides the living. It is precisely this social function that Pauline's narrative lacks. Strikingly, Pauline's sections of the novel, unlike Nanapush's, fail to address a specific auditor. Some commentators have understood Pauline's chapters to be similarly addressed to Lulu, but the text offers no evidence for such a reading. Her narrative always refers to Lulu in the third person, containing none of the affectionate, teasing, exhortatory direct addresses that punctuate Nanapush's narrative and that function to establish a familial relationship between speaker and auditor. Pauline has no interest in founding a continuity with the past: "I tried to stop myself from remembering" (15), she acknowledges. Her phrasing here implies the impossibility of amnesia, yet Pauline battles fiercely against a haunting memory she can never fully relinquish. Pauline understands history as a burden to be shed, rather than an asset to be shared.

Pauline's attempts to reject history flow from a desired self-erasure. A mixed-blood, Pauline denies her Chippewa heritage: "I wanted to be like my mother, who showed her half-white. I wanted to be like my grandfather, pure Canadian. That was because even as a child I saw that to hang back was to perish" (14). Driven by an intense self-hatred and a concept of progress predicated on the eradication of the past, Pauline refuses to speak Ojibway, enters a Catholic convent, begins to talk of "The Indians" as "them" (138), and, in her growing madness, entertains the fantasy that "despite my deceptive features, I was not one speck of Indian but wholly white" (137). Taking up the work of tribal undertaker, she secretly relishes the swift diminishment of the Chippewa by influenza and tuberculosis, seeing herself as ferrying the limp, diseased bodies to the gates of heaven, where Christ, "dressed in glowing white," congratulates her on her catch (140).

Pauline's perception of her body as loathsome in its plainness and above all Indianness finds theological justification in the Christian rejection of the sinful body in favor of the invisible spirit. In her effort to shed her Indian identity and its recent humiliating history, she attempts a self-dissolution, which she sees as a kind of payment for her vocation as saint and soul gatherer: "I must give myself away in return, I must dissolve. I did so eagerly. I had nothing to leave behind" (141). Pauline's descriptions of her dissolution strangely echo Nanapush and Fleur's windigo possession. She begins by mortifying her body with physical torments and with a fasting that recalls Nanapush and Fleur's winter starvation, when their blood "grew thick" with frost: "All winter, my blood never thawed. My stomach never filled. My hands were chafed raw. And yet I grew strong" (136). The freezing effect of windigo possession is also recalled in a wildly comic scene in which Pauline, in response to Nanapush's merciless teasing (about her practice of relieving her bladder only twice a day as a form of "martyrdom"), clings to her holy resolve by "strain[ing] to make myself into a block of ice" (150). As a participant in the Catholic sacrament of communion, Pauline incorporates or "eats" the body of Christ, seeing herself as now "abid[ing] in His mystical body" (138), just as Nanapush and Fleur consume their dead only to be in turn consumed or possessed.[39] When Pauline confesses that she "swelled" (138) on her devotion to Christ, we are reminded of how the ghosts of the dead "swelled" (6) within Nanapush and Fleur.

The novel's association of ghostly possession with consumption finds expression in Pauline's vision of her life in Christ's "mystical body." Her aspirations to martyrdom and particularly her pride in her spiritual humility strongly suggest that Erdrich modeled Pauline in part on the life of St. Thérèse of Lisieux, who died in 1897 of consumption. Thérèse, who followed an older sister named Pauline to a Carmelite convent, developed what she came to call "The Little Way," a spiritual path to God that emphasized the believer's "littleness" before the Lord. When Erdrich's Pauline boasts, "I am small," one of the nuns is reminded of "The Little Flower" (138), a nickname Thérèse embraced for herself. A scene in which Pauline spits out hot broth fed to her while being nursed in the convent during an illness, throwing her caretaker into a white anger, echoes a moment in Thérèse's life when she offends a fellow nun by refusing broth offered during an illness.[40] Thérèse's intense fascination with suffering led to her renunciation of bodily pleasures, particularly eating, a sacrifice Pauline imitates in her obsessive fasting ("I drank only hot water, took the thinnest cut of bread" [152]). Pauline's self-starvation mirrors her "consumption" by the white ways she desperately embraces in the effort to expunge her Indian identity. Speaking of the dangers of translation, George Steiner reminds us of those translators who "lose belief in their own identity under the voracious impact of premature or indigestible assimilation."[41] Pauline is such a translator: desiring to consume white culture, she herself is consumed.

Pauline and Nanapush clearly offer alternative responses to the devastation of Chippewa culture by encroaching whites. The similarities between Pauline's immersion in Catholic mysticism and Nanapush's possession by the ghosts of the past suggest, however, that Pauline functions not only as an alternative but as a parody of the model of cultural revision Nanapush provides. Like Nanapush, Pauline can be understood as a cultural translator.[42] At the very height of her madness, when she begins to perceive Christ as "weak . . . a tame newcomer in this country that has its own devils" (192), she concocts a new, strengthened version of Christianity by suffusing the new religion with elements of the old.[43] She decides to fight for her pallid God by transforming herself into a "dangerous lion" possessed of "the cunning of serpents" (196, 195). Pauline's version of a *miles Christi* recalls descriptions of the lake *manitou* Misshepeshu appearing much earlier in the novel; "armored" (195) in her new identity, Pauline resembles the brass-scaled Chippewa spirit who can take "the body of a lion" or a "worm" (11). In her frenzied state, Pauline sees "double, or not at all" (202), mistakes her former lover for an Indian anti-Christ, and brutally murders him. That the man is killed by strangulation with a rosary chain both mirrors Pauline's own consumption by white culture and recalls the windigo who seizes victims "by the throat" (3). Pauline says she "devoured" (202) her victim, a metaphor that further invokes the windigo, who transforms victims into cannibals who feed off their own people. Pauline is thus consumed and consumes in a cycle of destruction propelled by her demonization of all things Indian. Her double vision during the murder, like Nanapush's bilingualism, signals her ability to translate between cultures, creating a strange new brew of Catholic and shamanic religions. Yet Pauline's "translation" fails as an exorcism because the incorporation of old symbols into a Christian framework is predicated on a need to destroy the past. In *Tracks*, what an eater cannot digest eventually consumes him. Nanapush feeds on the ghosts of the dead but learns to digest or integrate them; Pauline cannot digest the past, refuses to allow it to be integrated into her body, and is thus herself consumed.

CULTURAL SURVIVAL IN *Tracks* depends upon the ability to translate, to move fluidly between past and present, old and new cultures. The novel defines successful translation as a form of consumption in which ghosts of the past are internalized, digested, and integrated with the present. Nanapush's linguistic and cultural translation offers a model of how tradition is remembered and revised, and thereby survives. The narrative he constructs (and the cultural identity it supports) is no longer possessed but remains haunted by the past it incorporates. His tale, like those of Erdrich's grandfather, attempts to reconnect what has been severed: the younger generation from the old traditions, the living from the dead. Haunting provides a metaphor for historical consciousness, for the way the dead past, pressed into the service of the present, inhabits and informs the living. The ghost thus becomes a figure for the imaginative reconfiguring of the past. It also becomes the figure for Erdrich's own act of translation in producing *Tracks*. Re-creating a history that has been, to recall Rodriguez's terms, ghosted or erased by the selective amnesia of America's nation building, Erdrich's fictional narrative makes the invisible visible by incorporating elements of Chippewa and pan-tribal cultures into the nonindigenous form of the novel.

One such element is the Ghost Dance, a late nineteenth-century religious revivalist movement that lost much of its momentum in the catastrophe at Wounded Knee.[44] The loss of Fleur's trees to lumber interests toward the end of *Tracks* recalls the historic timber scandal on the (Chippewa) White Earth Reservation, in which some tribal members colluded against others to profit from the federally assisted razing of forest land.[45] In the description of Fleur's revenge, Erdrich layers on to this restaging of Chippewa history allusions to the cross-tribal Ghost Dance religion, with which the Chippewa were familiar, but which they themselves did not practice, at least in any large numbers. Through her allusions to the religion's songs, Erdrich appropriates the Ghost Dance as a pantribal cultural phenomenon of symbolic significance to all Native Americans.[46] Central to the Ghost Dance, a millennial doctrine that spread rapidly among North American Plains tribes, was the belief in the "return of the ghosts" of dead Indians, the end of colonial dominance, and the restitution of land to the tribes.[47] Natural cataclysms would cause a covering over of the earth's present surface, restoring a plentiful natural world and bringing dead ancestors to life. Adherents believed that by dancing the circular Ghost Dance, they would hasten the apocalypse; they also held that they could preview the paradisal world to come by meeting dead loved ones in a dance-induced trance. Although the Ghost Dance is never directly referred to in *Tracks*, echoes of Ghost Dance ritual surface in a climactic scene late in the novel. The Ghost Dance can be viewed as a ritualistic mourning that, like the haunted vision of Nanapush, attempts to recuperate the invisible through an act of translation. The Ghost Dance not only provides Erdrich with historical material for literary treatment but also exemplifies Erdrich's own vision of successful cultural translation.

A syncretism of Christian messianic and native religious elements, the Ghost Dance originated at a dire time for Native Americans, representing a desperate imaginative response to the endangering of native cultures. Nineteenth-century ethnologist James Mooney, who published a monograph on the Ghost Dance in 1896 after years of information gathering and direct observations of the dances, argued that the Ghost Dance was a response to an acculturation crisis: dwindling populations due to epidemics and starvation, alcoholism, loss of land, the erosion of tribal traditions, and assimilation to white culture.[48] Erdrich takes much the same position when, at the beginning of a review of contemporary post–nuclear catastrophe novels, she speaks of the Ghost Dance:

> Faced with extinction, we imagine reprieve. The 19th-century Paiute prophet Wovoka postulated that through the revitalization of ancient beliefs and through the newly begun practice of the Ghost Dance, military defeat, slaughtered buffalo herds and cultural genocide could be exchanged for a utopia guided by traditional values of cooperation and moderation. The devastating history of European invasion and dominance were, these Indians desperately theorized, but a test of their faith, a punishment for assimilation, a catalyst through which the past might become the future. For both the individual and the tribe, hope of continuity was antidote to annihilation, and there was a dream life accessible beyond the apparent destruction of the familiar world.[49]

The "dream life" projected by the Ghost Dance provides both an antidote to and a reflection of Indian devastation. Ghost Dance songs, an integral part of the dance, tend to emphasize the joyous reunion of the dead and living, or the immense power that the returning dead will bring the living:

> You shall see your kindred—*E'yayo'!*
> You shall see your kindred—*E'yayo'!* [50]
>
> We shall live again,
> We shall live again. [51]

Other songs, however, focus on present loss, portraying the singers themselves as ghosts, living a life become shadowy and insubstantial:

> Down west, down west,
> Is where we ghosts dance.
> Down west, down west,
> Is where weeping ghosts dance,
> Is where we ghosts dance. [52]

This dual sense of ghostliness as representing power and abjection clearly permeates *Tracks.* The Ghost Dance songs are most strongly revived, however, in Nanapush's account of Fleur's revenge against the loggers who have come to take her foreclosed land—a crucial event in the narrative because it explains to Lulu why her mother has to send her away to boarding school, a painful separation that Lulu's bitterness toward her mother now prolongs. When the loggers approach the stand of oaks surrounding her cabin, Fleur has already surreptitiously sawed through each tree at its base, leaving the trees standing erect by mere "splinters of bark" (223). She then draws on her shamanic powers to call forth a powerful wind to topple the trees, bringing them crashing down on the men and their wagons. Nanapush, witness to the event, first begins to sense trouble when, upon entering Fleur's woods, he hears "the hum of a thousand conversations" of dead relatives and perceives that the "shadows of the trees were crowded" with the relatives' ghostly forms. In Ghost Dance mythology, this humming sound was thought to accompany the covering of the present-day world by a newly restored earth:

> The earth has come,
> The earth has come,
> It is rising—*Eye'ye'!*
> It is rising—*Eye'ye'!*
> It is humming—*Ahe'e'ye'!*
> It is humming—*Ahe'e'ye'!* [53]

The nearness and concentration of the dead that Nanapush notices in Fleur's woods just before her revenge suggest the approach of the spirit nation heralded by Ghost Dance songs. After an ominous, deathly stillness, in which Nanapush comes upon Fleur and the loggers locked in a silent standoff, a wind begins to rise: "It was then I felt the wind building on the earth. . . . I knew the shifting of breeze, the turn of weather, was at hand. I heard the low murmur of the voices of the gamblers in the woods" (222). "The gamblers" refer to the ghosts of the dead seen earlier in the novel in a dream vision. Their presence here links the rising wind with the return of spirits and recalls the many Ghost Dance songs about visiting the dead at play in the afterlife.[54] The winds in traditional Chippewa religion are spiritual personages who intervene in human life for good or ill; the rising wind that Nanapush notices signals the entrance of spirits and attests to Fleur's shamanic power in being able to summon them.[55] The intensifying wind is also a very common element of the Ghost Dance vision; numerous songs refer to the whirlwind that heralds the coming of the new earth. This Cheyenne Ghost Dance song, for example, links the wind with desired reunion between the living and dead:

> I am coming in sight—*Ehe'ee'ye*!
> I am coming in sight—*Ehe'ee'ye*!
> I bring the whirlwind with me—*E'yahe'eye*!
> I bring the whirlwind with me—*E'yahe'eye*!
> That you may see each other—
> That you may see each other.[56]

The natural cataclysm that will destroy white rule has also been represented as an earthquake, as in this Cheyenne Ghost Dance song:

> When you meet your friends again—*Ähe'e'ye*!
> When you meet your friends again—*Ähe'e'ye*!
> The earth will tremble—*E'ähe'e'ye*!
> The earth will tremble—*E'ähe'e'ye*!
> The summer cloud (?)
> It will give it to us,
> It will give it to us.[57]

Again we can hear an echo in Nanapush's account. As the wind on a summer afternoon builds around the unnerved loggers,

The earth jumped and the shudder plucked nerves in the bodies of
the men who milled about, whining softly to each other like nervous
cattle. . . .

One man laughed and leaned against a box elder. Down it fell, crushed
a wagon. The wind shrieked and broke, tore into the brush, swept full
force upon us. . . . With one thunderstroke the trees surrounding Fleur's
cabin cracked off and fell away from us in a circle, pinning beneath their
branches the roaring men, the horses. The limbs snapped steel saws and
rammed through wagon boxes. . . . Then the wind settled, curled back
into the clouds, moved on, and we were left standing together in a landscape level to the lake and to the road. (223)

The "thunderstroke" of the falling trees perhaps recalls the powerful
Chippewa "Thunderers," *manitous* who in storms speak in the voice
of the thunder; if so, their message is ambiguous.[58] The final dispirit-
ing vision of the land "level to the lake" reminds us that Fleur's revenge
changes little, at least immediately, about the forest's fate. The whites
are humiliated, not stopped; no paradisal Indian world suddenly springs
from the wind's wreckage. Fleur's desperate magic is no more effi-
cacious, in a purely pragmatic and immediate sense, than the Ghost
Dance's ritual in stopping the encroachment of whites. The Ghost
Dance movement met disaster in December of 1890, when U.S. soldiers,
made nervous by Ghost Dance participants congregating in large numbers under the guidance of Sitting Bull, massacred hundreds of Sioux at
Wounded Knee.[59]

Yet the meaning of the Ghost Dance for Native Americans reaches
beyond its immediate failure to rescind white dominion. Returning to
Erdrich's discussion of post–nuclear war novels, we note that while she
excoriates the "facile hopefulness" and "cozy survivalist endings" of
most of these works, she nevertheless values the act of imagining reprieve in the face of near extinction. Equally distasteful are those novels
that sink into "utter nihilism." The two novels she distinguishes for
praise, Kurt Vonnegut's *Galapagos* and Ursula K. Le Guin's *Always Coming Home*, differ in presenting a postapocalyptic world both "more drastic" and "more benign." Le Guin's novel, which undertakes a revision of
"traditional values," is compared to the Ghost Dance in its "hope of
continuity" between past and future.[60] The Ghost Dance represents a
triumph of the spirit, an assertion of continuity, a defiance of cultural
annihilation that transcends the pathos of Wounded Knee. Similarly,

Fleur walks off the reservation at the end of the novel in a triumph stolen from defeat, pulling a wagon constructed of her oaks, on which are fixed the grave markers of her family. She becomes the bearer of a tradition (now itinerant, displaced from reservation land) that, despite defeat, will carry on. In the cleared forest around Matchimanito, "weak seedlings" (224) are now visible; although highly vulnerable and of uncertain future, the reservation's new growth hints at the possibility of tribal continuity despite devastating changes. Fleur's forced absence at the end of *Tracks*, however, underscores the unavoidable violence of many cultural translations, particularly in situations when "target" and "source" cultures are embroiled in a politics of dominance and subservience. She comes, at least in this novel, to represent an untranslatable residue, that which resists even the canny efforts of that experienced translator, Nanapush. This is not to say that the novel finally undermines its translational momentum, but that it recognizes the limits of translation. As Jerome Rothenberg points out, "Every translation is a divergence, and the interest of translation as such is as a record of its own divergences: a comment on its failure to be source." The best translations remind us of what resists translation.[61]

The Ghost Dance, though it espoused a return to aboriginal traditions, was ironically not a purely nativistic movement. Ghost Dance mythology borrowed Christian elements; Weston La Barre cites as examples of "contact-borrowing" the "explicit identification of the shaman-prophet with Christ," "the appearance of God to his prophets, the Mosaic commands, the prophet's death and resurrection, the apocalyptic end of the world and a new Heaven on earth."[62] In terms of our discussion of *Tracks*, the hybrid (mixed-blood?) Ghost Dance revised tradition through the incorporation of new, alien material into the old. As a cross-tribal movement, the Ghost Dance contributed to the development of a pan-Indian culture inconceivable before the advent of white rule. Moreover, as Gerald Vizenor has noted, the revival of traditional ways advocated by the Ghost Dance was often transmitted through the language of the white domination: "English, a language of paradoxes, learned under duress by tribal people at mission and federal schools, was one of the languages that carried the vision and shadows of the Ghost Dance, the religion of renewal, from tribe to tribe on the vast plains at the end of the nineteenth century."[63] A translation of tradition in a non-indigenous language, a return to the past that revises the past, an invocation of the ghosts of the dead as a vehicle for continuity, the Ghost Dance remarkably parallels Erdrich's own reconfiguration of Native American history. Vizenor, like Erdrich a mixed-blood Chippewa, has seized upon the Ghost Dance as a model for contemporary ("postindian") Native American writers: "English, that coercive language of federal boarding schools, has carried some of the best stories of endurance, the shadows of tribal survivance, and now that same language of dominance bears the creative literature of distinguished postindian authors in the cities. . . . The shadows and language of tribal poets and novelists could be the new ghost dance literature, the shadow literature of liberation that enlivens tribal survivance."[64] The irony that the Ghost Dance, an "impure," hybrid religion not widely practiced by the nineteenth-century Chippewa, can function for Vizenor and Erdrich as a symbol of the contemporary rejuvenation of tradition underlines the degree to which they understand cultural renewal as a process of reinvention. By weaving allusions to the cross-tribal Ghost Dance into her story of the Chippewa, Erdrich signals both her interest in the recuperation of tradition and her allegiance to the invented and syncretic; the ghost for Erdrich finally stands as a figure of ethnic reinvention. Haunted by a spirit-shadowed past, *Tracks* can be read as a contemporary Ghost Dance, aiming to promote Native American survival by recuperating a people's history through acts of cultural translation.

Nanapush's account of Lulu's return from boarding school in the novel's last lines captures the novel's grim but hopeful perspective. After Nanapush works tirelessly to secure her release from her prisonlike government school, the young Lulu returns to the reservation angry and scarred, her ugly "smoldering orange" dress hinting at a new potential for violence. The dress with its "shameful color like a half-doused flame" (226) uneasily recalls Nanapush's claim, in a moment of deep despair, that the diminished Chippewa now "can be scattered by a wind, diminished to ashes by one struck match" (225). Given up by Fleur and placed in the hands of educators dedicated to eradicating her Indianness, the embittered Lulu may represent the lit "match" that will incinerate what remains of the old tribal life. Waiting to receive her embrace, the tribal elders Nanapush and Margaret are described as "creaking oaks" that momentarily give way as the girl rushes into their arms. Yet against the onslaught of the young, these old trees "held on, braced . . . together in the fierce dry wind" (226). Lulu, at first associated with dangerous

Getting Back One's Dead for Burial

Traumatic History and Ritual Reburial in
Toni Morrison's *Beloved*

Frustrated by the intrinsic limitations of his profession, Ralph Pendrell, the historian-protagonist of Henry James's *The Sense of the Past*, longs for total, unmediated access to the past:

> What he wanted himself was the very smell of that simpler mixture of things that had so long served; he wanted the very tick of the old stopped clocks. He wanted the hour of the day at which this and that had happened, and the temperature and the weather and the sound, and . . . the light of afternoons that had been. He wanted the unimaginable accidents, the little notes of truth for which the common lens of history, however the scowling muse might bury her nose, was not sufficiently fine. He wanted evidence of a sort for which there had never been documents enough, or for which documents mainly, however multiplied, would never *be* enough. . . . Recovering the lost was at all events on this scale much like entering the enemy's lines to get back one's dead for burial.[1]

The reconstruction of the past in all its minute detail, Pendrell realizes, entails a recovery of "the lost moment . . . as experience"; to grasp history as lived, one must "be again consciously the creature that *had* been, to breathe as he had breathed and feel the pressure that he had felt."[2] The hint here of voluntary possession by the dead is later realized when Pendrell merges with an ancestral ghost (who, in a classic Gothic

gesture, emanates from a portrait) in order to release undocumented secrets of the past. Driven by a nostalgia for a "simpler" time, Pendrell
exchanges history for ghost story, thereby retrieving a family past rendered inaccessible partly through emigration to America, but largely
through the sheer passage of time. Pendrell's turn to the supernatural
expresses the necessarily imaginative nature of complete historical recovery—a task, he believes, therefore more suited to the artist than the
historian.

Toni Morrison's *Beloved*, a historical novel in the form of a ghost
story, registers something of the recuperative desire that drives James's
historian, though it shares nothing of his antiquarian's nostalgia. In retelling the story of Margaret Garner, a recaptured fugitive slave who
killed her child rather than see her returned to slavery, Morrison quickly
moves beyond the skeletal narrative of her original source, an 1856
newspaper clipping.[3] The novel repeatedly returns to Pendrell's idea that
"documents mainly, however multiplied, would never *be* enough"; for
Morrison it is the silences in them rather than the absence of them that
frustrates. "Detailed in documents and petitions full of *whereas* and presented to any legal body who'd read it" (180), slavery, as *Beloved*'s Stamp
Paid acknowledges, already has a sizable written record. Many of the
novel's slaves, however, resist learning to read because they feel "nothing important to them could be put down on paper" (125). A version of
the newspaper clipping about Garner surfaces in the novel, but Paul D,
the former slave to whom it is offered, rejects it; the "print meant nothing" (155) to him, primarily because he is illiterate, but also because he
believes a newspaper account (particularly when cast as a morality tale
confirming a white readership's fears) would not reveal anything he
wants or needs to know. As he views the clipping with its drawing of
Sethe, the novel's Garner figure, Paul D twice objects that "That ain't
her mouth" (154), an assertion that underlines the division between oral
and written communication. Slaves learn that they cannot trust the inky
"black scratches" (155) whites put to paper to account for blacks.[4]

For *Beloved*, Morrison seeks knowledge of American slavery that escapes documentary evidence, including, curiously, those records produced by the slaves themselves. Observing that "no slave society in the
history of the world wrote more—or more thoughtfully—about its
own enslavement," she views American slave narratives as extraordinarily rich, yet essentially incomplete, records of slave life. She has

argued that repeated references in the narratives to "proceedings too terrible to relate" indicate that the authors elided the most repulsive details of their experience at least partly in deference to popular taste and literary convention, a self-censorship rendering many aspects of slavery (particularly sexual abuse) unspeakable. Morrison is more troubled, however, by what she sees as the larger omission, in the interests of focusing scrupulously on verifiable facts, of the interior, emotional life of the enslaved.[5] Given her desire for "total access to the unwritten" past, she acknowledges that "Only the act of the imagination can help me." To "fill in the blanks that the slave narratives left," to reinvest absence with presence, Morrison like James turns to the ghost as sign of the necessarily imaginative construction of a lost, unrecorded history.[6]

The difficulty to be surmounted in Morrison's case, of course, is not simply the inevitable incompleteness of history, with its insufficiently fine lens. The undocumented past she attempts to recover as lived experience is both more horrific and taboo than the rather elegant past that calls to James's historian. Like Pendrell, she wants to retrieve the "unimaginable accidents"—the minute and now forgotten details that once fleshed the lives of those who went before us—but she also attempts to convey what requires a different inflection of the term "unimaginable." Our identification of ghostliness in Morrison's lexicon with the imaginative reconstruction of the past must be qualified to include a sense of the formidable resistance to any "remembering" of a shameful and traumatic event. The "enemy" she confronts to reclaim the dead is more insidious than James's dustbin of history; it is the deliberate obfuscation of the conqueror and the intentional forgetting of the victim that amount to what Morrison has called a "national amnesia" about American slavery.[7] Yet this amnesia, it must be recognized, is anything but simple and has never been fully successful. Haunting in *Beloved* signals the return of a past that can neither be properly remembered nor entirely forgotten. The novel records a battle between anamnesis and amnesia, the desire to account for the dead struggling against the need to obliterate them. At issue is the relation between historical consciousness and traumatic memory, the problem of how to represent what is experienced as "unspeakable." *Beloved* plots the movement from trauma to history as a story of possession and exorcism in which traumatic memory— or the eruption of a denied history—is figured as a dangerous form of haunting.

I have invoked James's *The Sense of the Past* not only because it offers an apt analogy between fictionalized history and ghostliness, but also because I believe Pendrell's description of the historian's work as a recovery of "one's dead for burial" names the governing metaphor for Morrison's project in *Beloved*. The weightier implications of Pendrell's link between memory and possession on the one hand and between history, mourning, and burial on the other become fully manifest when drawn in the context of a traumatic history. The exorcism of deadly forms of haunting in *Beloved* requires a ritual burial of the unmourned dead—or, more accurately, reburial, since the task of laying the dead to rest begins with an exhumation. Morrison herself has gestured toward this metaphor when she likens the task of writing historical fiction to a "literary archeology," a kind of grave excavation in which "you journey to a site to see what remains were left behind and to reconstruct the world that these remains imply."[8] The search for "remains" leads to a revivification of the dead, often described by Morrison as a summoning of dead predecessors, an imaginative process that gives birth to the ghost as a partly invented, embodied memory.[9] Of Margaret Garner's dead child (who becomes a composite figure drawn from historical accounts of murdered black women), she tells us that "bit by bit I had been rescuing her from the grave of time and inattention. . . . Little by little bringing her back into living life."[10] The imagery of disinterment returns repeatedly in *Beloved:* the black men who form Paul D's chain gang escape from coffinlike "boxes" (109) sunken into a muddy trench. When he is reunited with Sethe, Paul D is tempted to pry open "that tobacco tin buried in his chest where a red heart used to be. Its lid rusted shut" (72–73). Beloved's questioning of Sethe opens a "slit in her mind," from which emerge forgotten memories (61). Sethe later reflects that any "casket of jewels" from the past needs to be "decently exhumed from the grave that has hidden it all this time" (176). As Edward Bodwin approaches 124 Bluestone, his mind drifts to "a time when he buried things there," and he wonders how he can locate the buried box filled with his childhood treasures (259). The unearthing of the buried past for many of these characters is prompted, directly or indirectly, by the "miraculous resurrection" (105) of Sethe's dead daughter from a dark, underwater place, the mass oceanic grave of slaves who died during the Atlantic passage.

The dead are resurrected, however, only in order to be reburied. *Be-*

loved ends with the closing of a coffin and its return to the earth: on the casket containing Beloved's memory, the novel's final page tells us, "a latch latched and lichen attached its apple-green bloom to the metal" (275). Morrison explicitly identifies the funereal function of her narrative when, in an interview with Gloria Naylor, she speaks of the "responsibility that I feel for the woman I'm calling Sethe, and for all of these people; these unburied, or at least unceremoniously buried, people made literate in art," adding that for her "the fear of not properly, artistically, burying them, is extraordinary." [11] Dedicated to the "Sixty Million and more" Africans and African Americans killed in the slave trade, *Beloved* attempts to perform a ritual burial of the forgotten, unnamed dead. It aims to shift the meaning of haunting from an unfinished, private mourning to a more openly shared awareness of what was suffered and what endures. Early in the novel we come upon a description of a pink headstone carved with the word Sethe remembers from her daughter's funeral service, the word that gives the ghost of the dead child its name. It also gives the novel its title, indicating that Morrison's writing functions as a tombstone carving that names and memorializes the dead. This chapter considers the implications of conceiving of literature as a form of burial, asks what such an idea of literature might mean in the specific context of traumatic histories, and, finally, assesses how memory—or the denial of memory—works to shape a shared group identity. These questions are explored in the context of research on funerary ritual and on trauma, framing a reading of the novel that connects the completion of mourning with the narrative resolution of traumatic silence.

Morrison's understanding of her recovery of black history as a grave excavation that afterwards finds completion in the verbal tombs she erects for the "unceremoniously buried" parallels closely the temporal structure of what anthropologists call "secondary burial," a funereal ritual in which the dead are exhumed and reburied. The connection is, I believe, worth pursuing for the light it sheds on the novel's plot development, as well as on the larger questions of how literary history can function as a act of mourning and how acts of mourning work to constitute social identity. Where the parallel breaks down—and I believe this to be generally true of most analogies generated by interdisciplinary perspectives—proves as illuminating as where the alignment is just. The novel's conformity with the model of secondary burial, and its ultimate resistance to the strong resolution offered by funerary ritual, point to the difficulties involved in giving narrative shape to the essentially anti-narrative nature of trauma. In a pioneering 1907 study of death rituals, Robert Hertz observes that for many cultures death is not understood as a sudden severance of life but as a prolonged transitional process participated in by both the deceased and mourners (a process truncated in the modern Western "wake"). The initial moment of death leads to a "provisional burial," followed, often months later, by a second burial in which the remains of the dead are exhumed and moved to a final location. Only upon final burial does the spirit of the deceased make its definitive entry into the world of the dead. In the "intermediary period" between provisional and secondary burials, the deceased is regarded as living "marginally in the two worlds," neither fully alive nor dead, manifesting itself as a restless, often malicious ghost that returns uninvited to haunt the living. During this period, mourners can be said to join the deceased in its liminal status. The living approximate the ghostly existence of the dead, rejoining the society of the living only when the deceased has finally entered the society of the dead. Hertz stresses that survivors enact a temporary and ritually circumscribed identification with the dead in order ultimately to mark more clearly the boundary between life and death and to reassert the social fabric rent by loss.[12] At the final burial, the dead lose their dangerous, uncontrollable aspect and assume the role of beneficent ancestral spirits whom the living can call upon in times of need. The rites of final burial also mark the restoration of the social order of the living, which has been temporarily disrupted by the death of one of its members. Hertz's sociological framing of grief points to the cultural role of mourning rituals in organizing communities. Later anthropologists built on Hertz's treatment of mourning, emphasizing the ways in which death rituals, perhaps more than any other socially observed rite of passage, are used by communities to reaffirm fundamental and defining cultural values.[13]

The movement Hertz describes from the preliminary to final burials, in which a dangerous, spiteful ghost is translated into a benevolent ancestral spirit, closely corresponds to the masterplot of possession and exorcism that structures so many stories of cultural haunting. The parallel suggests that the literary recovery (or exhumation) of a lost past can function as a site of communal mourning. Just as, for Hertz, funereal rites work to organize societies, literary memorializing can be seen as the performance of group identity, whether national, ethnic, or racial: the way we remember the dead structures the society of the living. Communities are established and social identities defined by acts of mourning, in which groups move toward the integration of their (revised) past by commemorating their dead. The dead, it should be emphasized, must be incorporated in some meaningful way into the community of the living; exiled, the dead would continue to haunt the living in menacing fashion. The work of cultural mourning thus differs markedly from Freud's understanding of mourning as a reality testing, in which recognition of the loved object as definitively lost leads ultimately to the healthy severance of attachments to the dead and the redirection of libidinal energies.[14] Successful mourning, according to the Freudian model, is the killing of the dead—a "second burial" of a very different sort than Hertz envisions. While Hertz's liminal period ends in the reassertion of the boundary between the realms of the dead and the living, the dead are rendered safely accessible rather than inaccessible by their ritual reinterment. Final burial operates as an exorcism in which the dead are not killed off but are revised, transformed into ancestral spirits.[15] Stories of cultural haunting similarly imply that the work of mourning requires the integration of, rather than the complete detachment from, the dead. In *Beloved*, the haunting is not completely dispelled but is redefined through the novel's performance of funereal ritual; as Morrison herself observes, the novel moves toward a "transfiguring and disseminating [of] the haunting with which the book begins."[16] *Beloved* reaches toward an integration of a revised past through the unearthing and reanimation of the forgotten dead, although the novel's incomplete exorcism and troubled conclusion interestingly complicate Hertz's model.[17]

Two points about secondary burial are important to stress: final burial shifts power from the dead to the living, and final burial, while effecting a separation of the dead and the living, nevertheless integrates the dead (as newly accessible spirits) into the ongoing life of the community. Curiously, both of these elements emerge as central in Morrison's accounts of the creative process. In fact, she describes the composition of *Beloved* in terms that strongly suggest the stages of funerary ritual. For Morrison, writing is a form of voluntary possession, much like the intermediary period between burials. She has spoken of her "terrible reluctance" to write about slavery, a subject that she felt might "drown" her (water is, of course, the ghost's original element and the grave of those who died during the Atlantic passage).[18] The process begins with a summoning: "I have to call [the "unburied dead"] by their names and ask them to reappear." This conjuring of the dead is necessary but risky: the "danger . . . in writing" the dead into existence is that the author temporarily becomes too closely identified with them. "There is a temptation," she observes, "to draw away from living people." Yet the process leads to an extraordinary power over the dead: the spirit of Margaret Garner's child, having been rescued "*from the grave of time and inattention*" by the novel, now "*comes running when called.*" The author triumphantly asserts, "*She is here now, alive. I have seen, named and claimed her.*" Assuming the role of conjurer, Morrison gestures dramatically toward the kind of safely controlled access to the dead accomplished by secondary burial: no longer haunted by the dead in a threatening way, the living can at their discretion summon the dead (who obediently "come running" when called).[19] The author exhumes and revives the "unceremoniously buried" dead, allows them temporarily to possess her, and then in "artistically burying them"—a process of naming and claiming the dead as one's own—gains the power to conjure the dead when needed. The writing of historical fiction thus constitutes a form of mourning that ends in incorporating the dead into the community of the living. The written work, as a kind of verbal tombstone, takes on the function of public memorials: to remind a people of its collective past and of the collective identity that past grounds.

To a striking degree, the novel also follows the trajectory of secondary burial rituals. The main action of *Beloved* can be said to take place during the intermediary period between first and second funerals, when the deceased, hovering between the worlds of death and life, oppressively haunts its family survivors. Opening in 1873, eighteen years after Sethe tried to kill her children in order to spare them the agony of an enslaved life, the novel relates the increasingly menacing haunting of 124 Bluestone Road by the one child she succeeded in murdering. The ghost's uninvited intrusions into the lives of the survivors testify to the unsatisfactory and provisional nature of Beloved's first burial, recalled by Sethe in the novel's opening pages. Much like mourners during the intermediary period between first and final burials, Sethe, her mother-in-law Baby Suggs, and her daughter Denver assume a ghostlike, marginal existence in relation to their community. Ostracized by neighbors they refuse to seek out for help or pity, they live like the undead. "Suspended between the nastiness of life and the meanness of the dead" (3–4), Baby Suggs shares the ghost's liminality. Sethe, whose blood-stained dress dries "stiff, like rigor mortis" (153), has in a sense died along with Beloved; she continues to exist in a kind of ghostly afterlife for the sake of her surviving children. Yet Denver, who immediately after the murder accompanies her mother to jail, has "died" along with Sethe; Denver's memory of their jailhouse experience as a dark place crawling with rats looks forward to Beloved's later description of the grave. Moreover, in the presence of her resurrected sister, Denver grows strangely insubstantial: her "skin dissolved under [Beloved's] gaze and became soft and bright like the lisle dress that had its arm around her mother's waist. She floated near but outside her own body, feeling vague and intense at the same time" (118). When Denver's floating body takes on the look of Beloved's earlier manifestation as a white dress, we scarcely need Ella's later exclamation that "Anything white floating around in the woods . . . it's something I don't want *no* part of!" (187) to confirm Denver's transformation here into a ghost. Sethe follows Denver's example in something closer to a trading of identities: she "changed beds and exchanged clothes" (240) with Beloved, and as the ghost increasingly "imitated Sethe, talked the way she did, laughed her laugh and used her body the same way" (241), the mother, her eyes "bright but dead" (242), takes on the status of the ghost child.[20] Near the opening of the novel Sethe remembers how, standing with "her knees wide open as any grave" (5), she sold her body for the child's engraved stone. Her open-legged stance above the grave hints at a kind of reverse birth, a suggestion that is realized at the height of her haunting: Sethe reabsorbs Beloved back into herself, until she herself in a sense becomes the child she killed.

The invasive and threatening quality of the haunting, the isolation of the mourners, and their close identification with the deceased (including the symbolic exchange of clothing with the dead) are all common elements of the transitional period preceding secondary burial. The novel proceeds toward an exorcism of the ghost that, in reasserting the boundary between the living and the dead, prepares for the closing allusion to the sealing of a coffin. The novel's brief coda presents us with Beloved's second burial: she is returned to "the place where long grass opens," the grave in which she will disintegrate into "her separate parts," then be "swallow[ed] . . . all away" (274). Yet here the parallel with secondary burial becomes troubled. We might expect upon exorcism and reburial an end to the haunting, and possibly a transformation of the dead into a more benign spirit, along the lines of secondary burial. The fact that the coda's reburial is immediately preceded by the happy resolution of the novel's romantic plot (Paul D's revival of Sethe by asking her to reclaim from the dead what is "best" in herself) pushes toward a similarly positive resolution of the haunting. Yet any expectations we may have for a Hertzian transformation of menacing ghost into beneficent spirit, safely relegated to the world of the dead but accessible in controlled ways by the living, are flatly defeated. While Morrison has defined her purpose in the novel as properly reburying the "unceremoniously buried," Beloved is hastily put away, forgotten by the other characters "like a bad dream" (274). To a certain degree, the aims of final burial are achieved: by the novel's end, the most troubling aspects of the haunting are removed, and the mourners experience some form of healing and are reabsorbed into a community that reconfirms its wholeness in the face of loss. The boundary between the worlds of the dead and living has been more clearly redrawn, with power shifting from the dead to the living. Yet the novel's vampiric ghost, while in a sense defanged by exorcism and reburial, remains as a vaguely troubling, potentially dangerous presence. Rituals of secondary burial work to reaffirm damaged social bonds, but here the reburial of the dead has a more ambiguous effect. The community of the living reaffirms its solidarity against the ghost in the novel's powerful exorcism scene, yet the ghost's very exclusion gives it the power to reinsinuate itself, much like the inevitable return of the repressed. "Sometimes," we are told, "the photograph of a close friend or relative—looked at too long—shifts, and something more familiar than the dear face itself moves there. They can touch it if they like, but don't, because they know things will never be the same if they do" (275). The unacknowledged ghost retains a disruptive and—because the intimately "familiar" is experienced as unnameably strange—uncanny power that puts at risk the stability of community. The living continue to be haunted by what they refuse to remember or to name as their own.

The novel's reburial diverges from rituals of secondary burial and from Morrison's own descriptions of the novel's composition as a process that moves the author from dangerous possession to confident conjuring, in its refusal to assimilate the dead, an integration of the dead necessary to the construction of history. The novel's black community, needing to forget pain too close to bear, rescues itself by closing off a piece of its history. For Sethe and the others, the haunting of Beloved is "not a story to pass on" (274); the past is relegated—at least within the world of the novel—to silence. The novel has, of course, just "passed on" the unspeakable story, suggesting that we may also read "pass on" in the sense of "pass away": this is "not a story to [let die]."[21] The inescapable ironies of the prohibition against telling force us to distinguish what the novel itself accomplishes, as a fictional "slave narrative" that gives voice to the formerly silenced "interior life" of the enslaved, from what the tormented characters within the novel find possible. *Beloved* arguably enacts a ritual burial in reanimating the past and claiming the unnamed dead as our own legacy, yet on the level of plot it tells a story of incomplete mourning, an inability to incorporate the past.

What emerges from the curious disjunction between the novel's reclamation of the past and its characters' flight into amnesia is a heightened awareness of the powerful resistance of trauma to the consolations of ritual, or to any attempt to limit and contain suffering by establishing a continuity between the traumatic and the ordinary. Because trauma is defined primarily by its effects, rather than by the kind of experience that traumatizes (the same event may traumatize one person and not another), I use the word *trauma* to refer to a complex of reactions to something experienced as so disturbing that it threatens the very structures by which meaning is made of the world. Trauma consequently proves resistant to the integrative powers of narrative, which like ritual works to connect, contextualize, and contain. While the completion of mourning through ritual reburial provides a metaphor for the recovery and integration of a lost past through narrative, trauma names a disastrous alternative to history, one that leaves the traumatized highly vulnerable to revictimization. Trauma is, to cite Werner Hamacher on the Holocaust, a "'history' [that] cannot enter into history," or, to take a definition from Cathy Caruth, a "pathology . . . of history itself." For Caruth, the traumatized "carry an impossible history within them, or they become themselves the symptoms of a history that they cannot entirely possess."[22] Ghostly possession in *Beloved* signals the inability to "possess" one's own history—or, given the cannibalistic cast of the ghost—to be possessed or traumatized is to be eaten by a history one cannot digest. Yet while the ghost can be said to stand as an antihistorical figure of trauma, Morrison has claimed that her purpose in making the ghost real was "making history possible."[23] An examination of how traumatic memory operates in the novel reveals why Morrison must paradoxically make history by conjuring ahistoricity and must bury the dead by leaving the grave open.

In shifting the antebellum story of Margaret Garner to a Reconstruction setting, Morrison underscores the issue of how the past is recovered or reconstructed in the present. This is, for Morrison, the work of any historical fiction that imaginatively supplements recorded facts ("you journey to a site to see what remains were left behind and to *reconstruct* the world that these remains imply" [emphasis added]), but *Beloved* distinguishes itself as a highly self-reflexive example of the genre, taking as its subject the distinction between healthy and pathological forms of historical reconstruction. The danger lies in repetition: the past reinstated rather than adapted for present purposes. Traumatic memory constitutes a pathological form of historical "reconstruction" in which the present and future are sacrificed to the reliving of an indelibly fixed and hence "timeless" memory. For many of the novel's characters, postwar Reconstruction only brings more of the same; the ex-slave Ella, for example, reduces the Emancipation to a semi-colon: "Slave life; freed life—every day was a test and a trial" (256). The syntactical echo of Ella's thought, "Slave life; freed life," captures one of Morrison's central stylistic and narrative strategies. The novel's nonchronological, disrupted narrative is given coherence by a web of repeated words, phrases, and scenes—a repetition that conveys how the past can be reconstituted in, or can possess, the present, while it also, as demonstrated below, gestures toward more desirable forms of reconstruction. Verbal repetition characterizes addresses to the ghost ("Come on. Come on. You may as well just come on" [4]); marks the return of the past in memory ("suddenly there was Sweet Home rolling, rolling, rolling out before her eyes" [6]); flags the entrance to deepest possession by the past ("Nobody saw them falling," repeated as a refrain three times followed by "nobody saw them fall" [174–75]); and expresses pain that continues and intensifies over time ("loneliness wore her out. *Wore her out*" [29]). Rather disturbingly, verbal repetition also tends to accompany the characters' aggressive efforts to forget the past, suggesting a connection between willed evasion and unwilled return. Hoping to erase a shameful memory that has unmanned Paul D, Sethe "rubbed and rubbed" the "stony curves that made up his knee," a repetitive action that is compared to her morning's work of kneading bread: "Working dough. Working, working dough. Nothing better than that to start the day's serious work of beating back the past" (73). Beaten back dough, however, rises. In fact, it rises all the more assuredly because it is kneaded. The repetitive action of "beating back" the past ensures its continued life: Paul D's memories, like Sethe's, prove as viable as yeast, as durable as stone.

The novel's emphasis on repetition directly relates to the central role past traumatic experience plays in organizing the characters' present lives. Traumatic memory can be defined as the reexperiencing of an event too overwhelming to be integrated into understanding. Pierre Janet, whose work on memory and trauma early in this century strongly influenced later research on posttraumatic disorders, describes traumatic memory as the involuntary retention of an "unassimilable" past. Often taking the form of flashbacks and behavioral reenactments, the pathology of trauma is marked by the intrusive, unwanted return of an indelibly fixed, painful memory; it is also strongly connected to unfinished mourning. Sethe's disturbingly literal recall of the past, coupled with a selective forgetting of certain details (she can, for example, more readily recall the "wonderful soughing" of Sweet Home's sycamores than the lynched boys hanging from the branches [6]), resembles the pathology of memory peculiar to trauma.[24] Traumatized persons suffer from an unlikely combination of amnesia and abnormally precise (and usually involuntary) recall; while the traumatized may cut off from consciousness "large realms of experience" and aspects of personality, these "failures of recall can paradoxically coexist with the opposite: intruding memories and unbidden repetitive images of the traumatic events."[25] The extraordinary precision and inflexibly unchanging nature of traumatic recall in fact depend upon its exclusion from consciously willed memory. Traumatic memory, precisely because it remains unassimilated into existing mental constructs for making sense of experience, tends to establish a parallel reality; the realms of trauma and ordinary life are experienced as a double existence, the one governed by ordinary chronology, the other, being "in a sense, timeless," liable to spring to life at any moment.[26]

Battling a recurring and hence "timeless" memory becomes the central occupation of many of the novel's characters. Concluding that the past was "something to leave behind," Ella decides that "if it didn't stay behind, well, you might have to stomp it out" (256). Similarly, Sethe expends most of her energy in "keeping the past at bay" (42), and Paul D vows to keep his memories "in that tobacco tin buried in his chest" (72). The evaded past, however, resurfaces to haunt, the violence with which it is stomped out or beaten back serving only to charge unwanted memory with an uncanny force. The uncanny, as Freud argues, subsists primarily as "involuntary repetition" ("something repressed which *re-curs*"), its chief figure being that of the ghost or the double.[27] Sethe's description of memory early in the novel hints at this phantasmal repetition of the past:

> "I was talking about time. It's so hard for me to believe in it. Some things go. Pass on. Some things just stay. I used to think it was my rememory. You know. Some things you forget. Other things you never do. But it's not. Places, places are still there. If a house burns down, it's gone, but the place—the picture of it—stays, and not just in my rememory, but out there, in the world. What I remember is a picture floating around out there outside my head. I mean, even if I don't think it, even if I die, the picture of what I did, or knew, or saw is still out there. Right in the place where it happened." (35–36)

Sethe experiences the undesired, intrusive recall of the past so powerfully that she conceives of memory as a fully dimensional reality that can take possession of her and, even more startlingly, of others—hence she warns Denver that "if you go there . . . it will happen again." As the phrase "Places, places" suggests, "rememory" (a neologism created by the prefix for return or repetition) repeats the past as a kind of spatial echo, literally reconstructing (or re-membering) past experience in the present. This spatialization of memory has the effect of dissolving time; the rememberer does not mentally return in time to recall the past to the present but literally re-enters the past. "Rememory" is thus a form of repetition or reenactment. The physical externalization of memory "out there, in the world," no longer dependent on or controlled by the rememberer, clearly forecasts the imminent return of Sethe's dead daughter as the embodied past. The double nature of the novel's trauma (the horror of slavery compounded by the horror of infanticide within the black community) itself reflects this repetitive quality of trauma. Sethe's desperate attempt to save her children from slavery by destroying them can be seen in part as a traumatized reaction that reenacts its

One of the most marked symptoms of haunting and possession in *Beloved* is the disruption of normal chronology typical of traumatic memory. For Sethe, "ten minutes" in the past "were longer than life" (5); in her slave days at Sweet Home, "time didn't pass" (244); now, years after her escape, "time didn't stay put" (272). Sethe and Denver conclude that "nothing ever dies" (36). "Today is always here," Sethe tells Denver, "Tomorrow, never" (60). For the novel's characters, the word *future* is drained of meaning when the past no longer can be distinguished from the present. Learning that "Time never worked the way [he] thought," the slave Sixo for a period stops speaking English because he is convinced there is "no future in it" (21, 25). A Cherokee tribe Paul D meets in Georgia, dispossessed of their lands and devastated by smallpox, assume an apocalyptic time frame; drastically truncating the future, they "retire into the forest and await the end of the world" (111). Slave mothers bitterly learn that "it wasn't worth the trouble to try to learn features [of children] you would never see change into adulthood anyway" (139). To Sethe, "the future was a matter of keeping the past at bay" (42), yet she is nevertheless obsessed by the past she struggles to forget: her "brain was not interested in the future. Loaded with the past and hungry for more, it left her no room to imagine, let alone plan for, the next day" (70). At the height of her possession, Sethe is "wrapped in a timeless present" (184); she leaves the haunted realm of 124 Bluestone Road only with great reluctance and, after her clock-measured hours of work at Sawyer's restaurant, hurries back to the ghost and its "no-time waiting for her" (191). Having come "from the timeless place" (182), the ghost erases chronological time, substituting for linear movement an eternal present: "All of it is now   it is always now" (210). Sethe initially believes that the eternal present brought by the returned dead, described ominously in terms of a permanent winter (176), relieves her of the oppressive burden of the past; "I don't have to remember nothing," she rejoices, as she trudges home to the haunted 124 "in the ruts left earlier by wheels" (183). But as the image of the "ruts" hints, Sethe relinquishes both future and present to tread the past again. Only when the ghost's power is dispelled can the characters resume sequential time, which rewards them with a future—the "tomorrow" (273) Paul D asks for near the end of the novel. "No-time," in which a traumatic past intrudes upon the present, is ghost time, the stopped clock of the revenant.

Beloved exhibits symptoms of the "abortion to time" that Lawrence

Langer finds in the testimonial narratives of Holocaust survivors. "Anguished memory," according to Langer, "hovers in a space inaccessible to normal narrative. It has no place of its own." Drawn out of chronological time, traumatic memory is spatial, iconic, static. It is, as Sethe notes, a "picture" of a "place" disturbingly located "out there," displaced from both the past and present—hence Sethe experiences her mind as "homeless" (204) because her memories have "no place" in any familiar story of maternal love and protectiveness. The tension between normal chronology and the stasis of trauma exerts extraordinary pressure on narrative coherence and continuity. Langer describes Holocaust testimonies as dominated by two different "clocks": "a time clock (ticking from then to now) and a space clock (ticking from there to here)." The spatial clock, much like Sethe's pictorial "rememory," deranges the plot; the narrative consequently "meanders, coils back on itself, contains rocks and rapids, and requires strenuous effort to follow its intricate turns," an apt description of Morrison's narrative.[30] Two opposing senses of time—sequential and simultaneous, linear and traumatic—similarly organize *Beloved*, reflected in the novel's loosely chronological narrative that repeatedly loops back to the past. Remembered experiences, such as Sethe's escape from Sweet Home, are recounted in fragments scattered across several chapters. Partially told stories are abruptly laid aside; Denver learns to recognize the signs that her mother's storytelling "had reached the point beyond which [Sethe] would not go," "for now anyway" (37). Engaging in her own form of reconstruction, Denver retells the past for Beloved by "giving blood to the scraps her mother and grandmother had told her—and a heartbeat" (78). Denver's narrative fleshing out of the "scraps" of the past finds an equivalent in Beloved herself, an embodied past that always threatens to rive into its originary fragments: the ghost is herself haunted by the repeated nightmare of waking up to find her body in "pieces" (133, 212), a self-dissolution reflected in her fragmented sentences. Throughout the novel we find, in its many scenes of storytelling, a straining toward a narrative ordering of the past that is repeatedly thwarted by the unspeakable nature of the events the telling would organize. What, asks Baby Suggs, "was there to say that the roots of her tongue could manage?" (141).

Nowhere do we observe more clearly the difficulty of establishing narrative coherence than when Sethe finally attempts, more than halfway through the novel, to tell the "unspeakable" story of the murder to Paul D. Her narrative concentrates the twisting, circuitous aspects of the

novel's own narrative. She begins with a detail about her dead daughter—that she was already crawling when Sethe made it to 124—and
moves on to her concern about what to feed infants, her frustration
about raising babies without advice, her remedies for containing dangerously rambunctious children, the help she received from Sixo. Paul D is
unconcerned that he catches only "pieces" of this opening because he
knows Sethe "hadn't gotten to the main part" (161), but fragments of a
story are all Sethe can manage. Her physical movement as she speaks to
Paul D mirrors her evasion of the story's "main part": she is "spinning"
about the room, "turning like a slow but steady wheel," "Round and
round, never changing direction" (159, 161). The repetitive nature of
her circling, and her corresponding inability to move forward or strike
out in a new direction, physically dramatize her entrapment in the past.
Recognizing that "the circle she was making around the room, him, the
subject, would remain one" (163), Sethe breaks off her narrative, shifting
abruptly to static, wordless mental pictures of the murder scene. When
she finally spits out "I took and put my babies where they'd be safe," an
outrageous euphemism to her auditor but literal truth to Sethe, she
speaks a language Paul D does not share, drawing on a vocabulary
wrenched from ordinary meanings. "This here Sethe talked about love
like any other woman," he reflects, "but what she meant could cleave the
bone" (164).

Sethe's inability to construct a coherent story of her past illustrates
her subjection to the power of haunting. For Paul D, listening to Sethe
"was like having a child whisper into your ear so close you could feel
its lips form the words you couldn't make out because they were too
close" (161); his uncomfortable sensation registers the co-opting of
Sethe's voice by the ghost of her murdered child. Elsewhere linguistic
confusion is more explicitly linked to the ghost's presence. At the height
of possession, when the women of 124 shut themselves off from the
world, their "unspeakable thoughts" merge with the "undecipherable
language" (199, 198) of the dead. Stamp Paid describes the sound
emerging from the haunted house as "a conflagration of hasty voices—
loud, urgent, all speaking at once so he could not make out what they
were talking about or to whom. The speech wasn't nonsensical, exactly,
nor was it tongues. But something was wrong with the order of the
words and he couldn't describe or cipher it to save his life" (172). He
names the ghostly babble "the mumbling of the black and angry dead"
(198), but the next paragraph further identifies the "mumbling" as the

sound of a "new kind of whitefolks' jungle" (199)—the projection onto blacks, as a justification for slavery, of an entirely white-invented animality. Curiously, then, the voice of the "people of the broken necks, of fire-cooked blood" (181), is also the voice of "whitefolks" defining blacks as inhuman. The furious response of the black dead thus carries within it the echo of the outrage that provoked it, just as traumatized reactions repeat the originating event.[31] Something is wrong with "the order of the words," and as hinted by Stamp Paid's fretting that "he couldn't describe or cipher it to save his life," lives depend on knowing how to translate that verbal chaos into a comprehensible narrative. Haunted language in *Beloved* can be described as a traumatic language, distinguished by its repetitiveness, fragmentation, unhinging of vocabulary, and at times odd dislocations of syntactic logic, but chiefly by its wily resistance to conventions of narrative organization.[32]

One of *Beloved*'s strengths lies in Morrison's powerfully compelling representation of the tortured internal world of those traumatized by slavery. Although she may have no familiarity with psychological studies of trauma, the connection Morrison makes between trauma and linguistic chaos finds ample support in trauma literature, particularly in the groundbreaking work of Pierre Janet. Janet's findings on the relationship between trauma and language shed light on Morrison's treatment of traumatic memory and help to explain how the novel's exorcism fails to translate the menacing ghost into a safely accessible spirit. Janet's most valuable contribution to the study of traumatic memory is his move to distinguish this disastrous form of memory, which dooms the traumatized subject to mechanical, nonverbal reenactments of the past, from what he calls "narrative memory," which reshapes and gives meaning to past experience by adapting it to present circumstances. Janet observes that traumatic memory is rigidly inflexible: the past is seen and relived exactly as it was first experienced, without the filter of later interpretations. Janet acknowledges that traumatic memory is not, strictly speaking, memory per se but is a "repetition," a nonverbal "reproduction" of the event. True memory, for Janet, is essentially *"the action of telling a story."* A "linguistic operation," active recollection requires a fairly elaborate mental adjustment to the event remembered:

> The teller must not only know how [to tell the story], but must also know how to associate the happening with the other events of his life, how to put it in its place in that life-history which each one of us is perpetually building up and which for each of us is an essential element of his person-

ality. A situation has not been . . . fully assimilated, until we have achieved, not merely an outward reaction through our movements, but also an inward reaction through the words we address to ourselves, through the organisation of the recital of the event to others and to ourselves, and through the putting of this recital in its place as one of the chapters in our personal history.[33]

The action of telling the story imposes an organization on the events that allows them to be "assimilated," that is, subsumed into the larger narrative of one's own history.

For Janet, then, the resolution of trauma—the exorcism, we might say, of a possessing past—requires a movement into narrative. He often illustrates the difference between traumatic and narrative memories with the example of his patient Irène, a young woman traumatized by the loss of her mother to tuberculosis. The case is worth examining briefly because it so clearly demonstrates both the centrality of narrative in the dissolution of trauma and the social function of narrative adaptations. Having nursed her invalid mother night and day through her long illness, Irène herself fell gravely ill after her mother's death. She denied that her mother had died, refused to wear mourning, and, most distressingly, for months after the death would frequently fall into deliriums that lasted for hours. At the sight of an empty bed she would obsessively and unconsciously reenact her deathbed ministrations, cleaning and rearranging an invisible body. Her automatic behavior reproduced in minute and exact detail her actions on the night of her mother's death. Irène's hallucinations ended when she was finally able to narrate, rather than reenact, the story of her mother's death. Significantly, Janet notes that after recovering the narrative memory, Irène told different versions of the story to different people, depending on her relationship to them and her intentions in telling the story. He concludes that while traumatic memory is rigidly inflexible and a solitary activity, narrative memory is, at its very heart, a social act and is characterized by adaptability to present needs. The movement from trauma to recovery entails a movement from unyielding literality to the possibility of adaptation: in order to assimilate the past, memory shifts from repetition to revision. To release the future from the death grip of the past, the past must be revised.[34]

The fascinating case of Irène suggests that traumatic memory can be viewed as a form of perverse faithfulness; it remains absolutely true to its originary event. When this event is the death of a loved one, the faithfulness of trauma becomes a substitute for mourning.[35] Irène vainly attempts to keep her mother alive by returning obsessively to the harrowing moments just before and after her mother's death. Her repeated reenactments constitute a kind of somatic memory, which, being spatialized in her own body, appears to evade death by stopping the clock. She must learn how to tell rather than embody her history, yet the transition from embodiment to verbalization demands a painful relinquishing of the dead to death; hence it is ferociously resisted. Janet's research makes clear that trauma can be understood as an embodied or somatic, as opposed to linguistic and narrative, history. Trauma usurps history by encoding damage in the body, which mutely "tells" its history, often by reenacting it.

The rather surprising corporeality of Beloved—I can think of no other story of cultural haunting that features such a substantial, fully fleshed ghost interacting independently with multiple characters—illustrates this concept of unspeakable and therefore embodied histories. Like Irène's physical reenactments, the ghost's returned body substitutes for the ritual mourning that has yet to be accomplished. Janet's distinction between traumatic reenactment and narrative adaptation illuminates the central tension between words and bodies in *Beloved*. Like Irène, Sethe embodies a history she cannot tell. She does not, of course, literally reenact the past as Irène does, and unlike Irène, she is fully cognizant of the event that haunts her. Sethe's concept of "rememory," however, bears striking resemblance to Janet's account of trauma in reproducing portions of the past so exactly that she relives them. Moreover, the novel contains many scenes in which memory is presented as physicalized and silent. When Sethe acknowledges that the memory of Sweet Home returns "whether we want it to or not," for example, no specific memory from that time is articulated. Instead, her body registers the passage of a memory: "She shivered a little. A light ripple of skin on her arm, which she caressed back into sleep" (14). Sethe and Baby Suggs "agreed without saying so that [the past] was unspeakable," but "the hurt was always there—like a tender place in the corner of her mouth that the bit left" (58). For Sethe, past experience yields not a tellable history but a bodily zone of pain. The injury, a wound to the mouth caused by the silencing bit (the "tongue . . . held down by iron" [71]), makes explicit the substitution of bodily for verbal memory. The novel's symbol for this substitution is the scar, the bodily mark that silently "tells" a story of past damage. With the whip as his pen, Schoolteacher has one of his pupils inscribe upon Sethe's body her status as object and animal.[36] Like the bit's injury to the mouth, Sethe's welter of scars connects directly to a prohibition against speech; she is beaten because after her rape she "told on em" to Mrs. Garner (17). The beating is also accompanied by further symbolic injury to the mouth: while the whip opens her back, she bites off a piece of her tongue. Not only has Sethe not authored the scars that dumbly memorialize past pain, but she can neither see nor interpret them, as do both Amy Denver and Paul D. She bears physically an unspeakable history, over which she exerts neither an author's nor a reader's control.

Sethe's unspoken memories, like her scarred back skin "dead for years" (18), erupt in spectral form to haunt her. The effects of haunting are registered most dramatically on her black female body—visible sign of race and site of violent conflict over control, ownership, and reproductive authority. Sethe's internal cry as she bites down on her tongue— "Good God, I'm going to eat myself up" (202)—links traumatic silencing to self-cannibalism and prepares for the later cannibalistic turn of the ghost who gives bodily form to the unspeakable. She will be consumed by a past she cannot digest, possessed by the history that she cannot herself possess. Beloved's devouring of Sethe—we are told that she "ate up [Sethe's] life, took it, swelled up with it" (250)—is to a certain extent the punishment a guilt-ridden Sethe inflicts on herself for the murder, but the ghost's cannibalism also functions as a projection of white myths about blacks, who are viewed as both self-destructive (the murder is taken as evidence of "the cannibal life [blacks] preferred" [151]) and predatory (their "red gums ready for . . . sweet white blood" [198]). The particular form of Sethe's self-punishment surprisingly enacts a white-invented cannibalistic "blackness." Sethe in a sense relives and repeats her victimization by whites, just as in trauma a damaging history is obsessively relived by the traumatized person. Ghostly possession, in the historical context of slavery, figuratively represents the invidious claim of human possession asserted by slave owners, the damaging effects of which continue long after legal slavery is abolished. As Baby Suggs understands, "Freeing yourself was one thing; claiming ownership of that freed self was another" (95). Such self-possession requires the ownership of one's own body, as Baby Suggs realizes when she suddenly sees her hands differently ("These hands belong to me. These *my* hands" [141]), but it also requires possession of one's own history, in this novel an even more challenging feat than freeing the body.

Janet's emphasis on trauma as an "unassimilated" event finds a close parallel in Morrison's descriptions of slavery as an "undigestible and unabsorbable" history.[37] For Morrison as for Janet, trauma is a pathology of both mourning and history: the past that cannot be properly mourned lodges within the body as a mute history, over which the traumatized person has no control. Morrison's use of the ghost as metaphor for an unspeakable and therefore repeating history also resembles Janet's concept of traumatic reenactment, though she does not insist on the strict literality of the repetition. "The past," she has observed, "until you confront it, until you live through it, keeps coming back in other forms. The shapes redesign themselves in other constellations, until you get a chance to play it over again."[38] Morrison's phrasing here suggests that what distinguishes the two kinds of return—the past that "keeps coming back" and the replaying of it—is the element of conscious control: the past returns until "you" seize agency and confront that past by organizing a reenactment. The shift in subject position from "the past" to "you" inserts a crucial and saving revision into the reenactment, a shift that may be compared to Janet's definition of narrative memory as distinguished from traumatic memory by its intentionality and ability to revise. Indeed, the novel's exorcism succeeds through the insertion of difference in the recasting of the past, thereby adding the crucial element of revision that occasions the release from traumatic repetition. Yet the exorcism quite dramatically refuses the narrativization that for Janet is essential to resolving trauma. *Beloved* curiously raises and then rejects the possibility of assimilating the traumatic through specifically narrative adaptation.

The exorcism is accomplished through a reenactment of Beloved's murder with, as Mae Henderson and David Lawrence have noted, the crucial difference that Sethe's violent response to slavery is turned outward, toward a representative of the white oppressor and away from her own family.[39] During the course of the exorcism, Sethe is whisked nineteen years into the past, to the day of her daughter's death. The rememory is signaled by verbal repetition: Sethe's observation that "The sky is blue and clear. Not one touch of death in the definite green of the leaves" repeats (changing only the verb tense) Baby Suggs's earlier memory of the day (261, 138). When Sethe mistakes Bodwin for Schoolteacher, the passage echoes nearly verbatim earlier accounts of the murder scene: "He is coming into her yard and he is coming for her best thing. She hears wings. Little hummingbirds stick needle beaks right through her headcloth into her hair and beat their wings. And if she thinks anything, it is no. No no. Nonono. She flies. The ice pick is not in her hand; it is her hand" (262). The last line, however, introduces a new element—the transformation of Sethe's body, once the possession of another, into a weapon that she turns against the "owner." Her directing of the ice pick at Bodwin, however mistakenly, represents a symbolic pointing of the finger, a bodily speech that names white guilt for slavery.

More importantly, Sethe's reenactment differs from the original event in being properly "witnessed." The thirty neighborhood women who gather at 124 Bluestone Road to undertake the ritual exorcism of the ghost provide the community support denied Sethe at the time of the murder. Their presence asserts—and Ella's memory of starving her own child confirms—that Sethe's story (and Sethe's mother's story as well) is also their own. As Mae Henderson rightly observes, by intervening when they originally had refused to warn Sethe of the approaching slave catchers, the women also perform a revised reenactment, now accepting their own responsibility for the crisis.[40] As they near 124, the women step into a rememory of the day before the murder:

> the first thing they saw was not Denver sitting on the steps, but themselves. Younger, stronger, even as little girls lying in the grass asleep. Catfish was popping grease in the pan and they saw themselves scoop German potato salad onto the plate. Cobbler oozing purple syrup colored their teeth. They sat on the porch, ran down to the creek, teased the men, hoisted children on their hips or, if they were the children, straddled the ankles of old men who held their little hands while giving them a horsey ride. Baby Suggs laughed and skipped among them, urging more. (258)

The women, however, edit the past by recapturing only the fullness of their pleasure, "not . . . the envy that surfaced the next day" (258). Their revision reabsorbs Sethe into the community that had expelled her. The cries of response to their lead prayer, "Yes, yes, yes, oh yes" (258), revise through reversal the terrible negation of the killing (the "No. No. Nono. Nonono" that enters Sethe's head just before the slaying [163]), while openly affirming Sethe's inclusion in the community.

One damaging aspect of the past, however, is not revised in the reenactment—or one might say that it is revised by becoming more prominent. Sethe was betrayed by her own community through their jealous silence, their refusal to speak a word of warning or, when a destroyed Sethe is led away, a word of sympathy. The novel underlines the point: "Sethe walked past them in their silence and hers. . . . And then no words. . . . No words at all" (152). This failure of speech becomes, in the exorcism, the women's chief weapon against the ghost. After some prefatory prayer, they open the exorcism proper with a turn on John's gospel: "They stopped praying and took a step back to the beginning. In the beginning there were no words. In the beginning was the sound, and they all knew what that sound sounded like" (259). The "sound" they search for is "the key, the code . . . that broke the back of words" (261), which they had once found in Baby Suggs's Clearing ceremonies. Staged as an attack on language, the exorcism casts Beloved as a demonic (or anti-) Logos, a role supported by the fact that the exorcism occurs at "three in the afternoon on a Friday" (257), the timing of the Crucifixion. The allusion to the Crucifixion establishes the ghost as a diabolical "Word made flesh," an emblem for the traumatic embodiment of unspeakable histories. It also hints that the exorcism will fail to prevent the ghost from "rising again."[41] When the word-breaking wave of sound washes over Sethe's trembling body like a wordless baptism, she is recalled to Baby Suggs's ceremonies in the Clearing. Baby Suggs, who "talked as little as she could get away with" (141) and who does not so much preach as "let her great heart beat in [the black community's] presence" (87), provides the model for the women's antiverbal strategy: Baby finds her spiritual vocation in an affirmation of the spurned slave body and, when words fail her, turns to the body language of dancing to express "the rest of what her heart had to say" (89). Spurning words, the women's exorcism works almost entirely on a somatic level.

Most readings of the exorcism scene emphasize the clearly important affirmation of female community. In triumphantly superseding Scripture, the women recover a spirituality anterior to Christianity, the master's religion acquired through exile and enslavement.[42] Mae Henderson argues that in revising the gospel of John, the "black women's voices" give priority to "the semiotic (rather than the symbolic)," thus challenging "the dominant white and male discourse in which the text of black womanhood is constructed." Yet while we can agree that through the ritual exorcism Sethe is symbolically "'delivered' from the constraints of the master('s) discourse," it is also true that she is delivered to a suicidal depression. Henderson contends that through the exorcism,

"Sethe is released from possession by the spirit of a *now speakable past*" (emphasis added), but the novel in fact offers us no vision of Sethe's movement into narrative.[43] Henderson's feminist reading of the novel rightly stresses what is unquestionably a celebration of female communal power, but at the cost of overlooking the desperate aftermath of the exorcism, which requires the saving return of the male lead, Paul D. When Paul D returns to 124 Bluestone after the exorcism, he encounters the sounds of trauma: silence (the house is "stone quiet" [270]) and babbling. The ghost has vanished, but Sethe is found lying in Baby Suggs's deathbed, her eyes expressionless, half singing a lullaby-like tune that, in its references to wildflowers ("Jackweed raise up high. . . . Lambswool over my shoulder, buttercup and clover fly" [271]), echoes Ophelia's final mad scene and death in *Hamlet*. The implicit comparison to Ophelia, the mourner who does not survive, suggests that Sethe still retains the inappropriate daughter's role she assumed during her possession, and that she remains too closely identified with Beloved, who like Ophelia leaves by water (the ghost is last seen "down by the stream . . . a naked woman with fish for hair" [267]). The allusion to *Hamlet*, a play that links haunting with violent death and disrupted mourning, also signals the failure of the exorcism to perform the proper ritual burial of the dead. Like Ophelia undone by grief and romantic abandonment, Sethe is as close to death after the exorcism as she was during the height of her possession.[44]

The exorcism works almost entirely on the somatic rather than the symbolic level, eschewing language to heal the soul through the body, because the body is where traumatic history is housed. Elaine Scarry has argued that bodily "pain does not simply resist language but actively destroys it, bringing about an immediate reversion to a state anterior to language, to the sounds and cries a human being makes before language is learned."[45] In their exorcism, the women return to this "state anterior to language," translating the isolated cry of pain into a communal battle cry; the fact that it is based on a collective memory ("they all knew what that sound sounded like") gives the women's cry its power over the ghost. Yet as Scarry has also observed, the failure of pain to find verbal representation has grave political consequences, since experience that is by nature verbally inexpressible is all too often rendered politically invisible (12). The implication of language in the subjection of the slaves, primarily through the figure of Schoolteacher, who positions himself as

ritual bears a dual function: it affirms the connection between mourners and the deceased even as it works to reassert the boundary between the living and the dead. Mourning rituals allow us ceremonially to relinquish the dead in order, paradoxically, that they may reenter our lives differently. The novel's exorcism repudiates the ghost, successfully reestablishing the proper division between the living and the dead, but it does so without allowing for any reintegration of the dead into the society of the living. The exorcised ghost, far from being translated into an ancestral spirit to be safely invoked in times of need, is still feared and intentionally forgotten: "Remembering," the community decides, "seemed unwise" (274). Tales are briefly told about the vanished ghost, but these hastily put aside stories, like the fragmented, traumatic narratives Sethe tells during the course of the novel, ultimately fail to repossess the "undigestible" past. The integrity of the community has been defined *against* the history that threatens it—a powerful and necessary survivalist act, but not a model for the kind of historical reconstruction Morrison herself undertakes in writing the novel.[47]

The disjunction between the novel's reclamation of the past and its characters' flight into amnesia, however, itself gestures toward the strategy necessary to translate a paralyzing possession by the past into a historical consciousness that usefully informs present action. The possibility of narrative is hinted at in the novel, if never fully realized. It emerges most clearly when Sethe confirms her love for Paul D and looks forward to the sharing of their pasts: "Her story was bearable because it was his as well—to tell, to refine and tell again. The things neither knew about the other—the things neither had word-shapes for—well, it would come in time" (99). This confidence is later dashed, of course, when Sethe struggles to find the "word-shapes" for her daughter's death: an appalled Paul D retreats into silence by echoing Schoolteacher's definition of slaves ("You got two feet, Sethe, not four" [165]), one of several examples of black characters mirroring the racist aspersions of slave owners.[48] Despite this failure, romantic love continues to be associated with the power of narrative. When Paul D returns to Sethe after the exorcism, he recalls Sixo's description of his beloved "Thirty-Mile Woman": "She is a friend of my mind. She gather me, man. The pieces I am, she gather them and give them back to me in all the right order" (272–73). Understanding that loving relationships, like narrative, "gather" the "pieces" and put them in "the right order," Paul D looks at Sethe and decides that he "wants to put his story next to hers" (273). Affirming the power of narrative, like that of love, to give meaningful "order" to the fragments of the past, this scene of reunion points to an eventual, if yet unrealized, narrative resolution of trauma. The women's destruction of language succeeds in silencing the ghost's voice and in exorcising the possessed body, yet Paul D's reappearance after the word-breaking exorcism indicates the need to couple the reclaiming of the body with the repossession of history.

Paul D and Sethe's reunion scene, with its forecasting of a narrative recovery of the past in service of "some kind of tomorrow" (273), stood as the novel's original ending when Morrison gave her manuscript to her editor at Knopf.[49] Morrison's decision to append the coda, which shadows the optimism of the reunion scene and reasserts the resilience of traumatic silence, has two important implications. Baby Suggs's claim that "Not a house in the country ain't packed to its rafters with some dead Negro's grief" (5) asks us to read the haunting of 124 by Beloved as emblematic of a nation's haunting by its ugly racial history—a haunting that Morrison, in other contexts, calls "the ghost in the [national] machine" or the racial "shadow" that continues to darken American optimism.[50] The continued presence of this ghostly "shadow" in the coda figures the continuing effects of slavery in a nation that has not fully come to terms with its shameful past. Inheritors of this improperly buried past, lacking a fully acknowledged past and therefore a future, are locked into a liminal existence that Victor Turner, building on Robert Hertz's tripartite structure of death ritual, discusses as invisibility or ghostliness with social structure. Like Hertz, Turner sees social liminality as a potentially regenerative period, a difficult but temporary passage to a more desirable state. Turner's description of the liminal subject as structurally "dead" within the social system, however, uneasily resembles Orlando Patterson's recent redefinition of slavery not as bondage per se but as a permanent state of "social death." Originating as a substitute for death upon capture by enemies, slavery, Patterson argues, never loses its metaphorical association with death. The slave is incorporated into society as *the living dead*, a negativity that defines by opposition what lies within the bounds of social order.[51] Existing in a state of marginality, albeit institutionalized, the anomalous slave partakes of the liminality of the ghost. The implications of Hertz's "intermediary period," when viewed in light of Patterson's argument about the essential nature of slavery, helps to explain how ghostly haunting in Morrison's novel can be read as a metaphor not only for a Jamesian imaginative recovery of the past but more ominously as the perpetuation of the culture of slavery well after legal emancipation. The novel's unfinished mourning thus works against safely historicizing racism as primarily a slavery-era phenomenon and intimates that what has been called America's "master narrative" continues to be predicated on a selective historical amnesia.[52]

The novel's uneasy ending also raises what is at once a literary and moral issue: what language is available to speak the unspeakable, to render comprehensible the unthinkable, without diminishing the horror? In his study of Holocaust literature, James Young has argued that "violent events—perceived as aberrations or ruptures in the cultural continuum—demand their retelling, their narration, back into traditions and structures they would otherwise defy. For upon entering narrative, violent events necessarily reenter the continuum, are totalized by it, and thus seem to lose their 'violent' quality. . . . For once written, events assume the mantle of coherence that narrative necessarily imposes on them, and the trauma of their unassimilability is relieved."[53] While this relief is certainly desirable, does the "totalizing" power of narrative paradoxically undermine the attempt to derive meaning from "violent events" by too easily and quickly resolving what is unpalatable?[54] What if these events are not perceived as "aberrations or ruptures in the cultural continuum," but as the flaring out of a society's intrinsic, structural violence? Werner Hamacher sees the narrative assimilation of historical trauma as a futile attempt to escape the consequences of the past:

> We do not just write "after Auschwitz." There is no historical or experimental "after" to an absolute trauma. The historical continuum being disrupted, any attempt to restore it would be a vain act of denegation. The "history" of Auschwitz, of what made it possible, supported it, and still supports it in all its denials and displacements—this "history" cannot enter into any history of development or progress of enlightenment, knowledge, reflection, or meaning. This "history" cannot enter into history. It deranges all dates and destroys the ways to understand them.[55]

Hamacher eloquently expresses the quandary of the post-Holocaust writer, yet the very eloquence of his formulation raises for me the spectre of another danger (one to which I do not accuse Hamacher himself of succumbing)—that of glamorizing or fetishizing the traumatic condition of unspeakability. Trauma as an open grave that cannot be closed, a haunting that can never be fully resolved, a history that cannot be told, an endless mourning: *Beloved* acknowledges this to be true but at the same time refuses to accede to this defeated position. The novel's nonchronological, disrupted organization, through which the traumatic voice at times breaks with its "indecipherable language," suggests that the proper narrative for trauma must in some sense be fractured and unresolved, so that it struggles for continuity and closure, while allowing us to hear the sound of words being broken by a history that deranges reason, order, meaning. It is primarily through this opening of her narrative to trauma, while refusing to be ruled by it, that Morrison revises her slave-narrative models. Morrison's project of historical recovery is more complex than "filling in the blanks," as she has described it: the task involves not simply supplying or imagining missing information but also showing the process by which such information has been, and continues to be, suppressed. The "indecipherable" ghost voice, never fully integrated into the black community's story about itself, records the magnitude of violence against that community and reveals the limitations of narrative in the face of historical trauma: after closure there remains a residue, a ghostly trace, something of the past that resists being contained, the still unassimilable aspect of slavery. Nevertheless, the incomplete nature of the antiverbal exorcism, the association established between love and storytelling, and above all the example of the novel itself as an act of historical recuperation compel us to understand narrative as a crucial, if not always possible, means of confronting the consequences of the past. *Beloved* records the struggle toward narrative, performs the final burial, but leaves the grave open.

Although its haunting remains unresolved, *Beloved* holds open the possibility that readers may join the author in forming a community of mourners who commemorate the dead. The novel works to translate trauma's community of silence (the community of its characters) into a community grounded in—in fact, created by—open, shared remembering (the community of its ideal readers). Organized as a ritual reburial of the dead, the novel positions its readers as mourners who gather around the grave of American history. Sympathetic readers replace the faceless congregation at Beloved's first, unsatisfactory funeral, the "Dearly Beloved" who give the ghost her name. In thus taking on the name of the ghost as their own, readers also become inheritors of a claimed legacy, performing the promise of the novel's biblical epigraph: "I will call them my people, which were not my people." Addressed presumably to black readers who may have, like the novel's traumatized community, disowned portions of their own history, the epigraph perhaps more pointedly challenges nonblack, and particularly white, Americans to assume the responsibility of redefining exclusive conceptions of "my people." Most emphatically, Morrison does not invite whites to the funeral to engage in a national version of what Mary Louise Pratt calls the postcolonial mode of "anti-conquest," in which Europeans seek a sentimental identification with the colonized that barely masks the continued (even strengthened) assumption of superiority.[56] The invitation can only be read as a challenge to take responsibility for both the past and the present, an undertaking that may involve an unpalatable identification with the novel's Schoolteacher or well-meaning but condescending Bodwins. By working to shape a collective memory, literary memorializing, like ritual reburial, carries the potential to construct a new and enlarged group identity.

As Stanley Rosenman and Irving Handelsman have observed of Holocaust testimony, when the proper burial of the dead has been obstructed, the needed "laying to rest" can take the form of a narrative reconstruction of the past that creates of its readership a haunted community: "[Eli] Wiesel acknowledged that writing for him expressed the wish to carve words on his father's tomb. (No doubt, he wished too that his father, who died during the forced march from Auschwitz before the arrival of the liberating Russians, had a tombstone.) Now, the creative product, the readership, the group join the author in becoming vessels, abodes of the spirits of the dead. The dead may know that by way of their story being told, they have left traces, that they did not just disappear up a chimney."[57] Significantly, the dead are not "buried" in their verbal tombs in the sense of being hidden or put away from the present; rather, sympathetic readers join the author in becoming "abodes of the spirits of the dead." The community of survivors established by the text allow themselves to be haunted in order that a continuity between past and present be established. The potentially dreadful haunting of the unburied dead may thus be translated into the weighty but more benign haunting that we call historical consciousness.

From Exiles to Americans

"Recombinant" Ethnicity in Cristina García's *Dreaming in Cuban*

SET BETWEEN 1972 and 1980, Cristina García's *Dreaming in Cuban* (1992) opens with the children of the first massive wave of Cuban emigrants, those who left shortly after Castro's triumphant march into Havana, coming of age in American cities. It closes with the April riot at Havana's Peruvian embassy, which set off the most recent mass exodus to the United States, the Mariel migration. The novel's endpoints thus refer us to events that fractured the Cuban-American exile community, which was drawn largely from Cuba's overwhelmingly white, traditionally Christian economic elite. The arrival of the less privileged and racially mixed Marielitos, many of whom were practitioners of the syncretic Afro-Cuban religion Santería, introduced new social, racial, religious, and economic tensions. The Mariel boatlift, according to historians James and Judith Olson, "created, for the first time, a real generational and ethnic division in the Cuban-American community, a sense of 'old Cubans' versus the 'new Cubans.'" Yet, as the Olsons note elsewhere, signs of division preceded the Mariel migration; a "generational" conflict was already underway, as the children of the original exiles, most of whom had little memory of their native country, began to define a new Cuban-American identity.[1] While their parents established a group solidarity in the new country chiefly through a fervent anticommunism, Cuban Americans who came of age in the era of Watergate and Vietnam tended to define an ethnicity less centered on the Cuban revolution and exile politics. Feeling connected to Cuba, but no longer aspiring to return to the island should Castro be ousted, young Cubans in the United States began in the 1970s to make the transition from exiles to Americans.[2]

García, herself a member of this younger generation, describes the shift chiefly in terms of language: "Immigrants have to make their way into the U.S. Eventually, English becomes the first language in terms of social interaction, of education. Those of us who kind of straddle both cultures are in a unique position to tell our stories, to tell our family stories. We're still very close to the immigration, we're in the wake of that immigration, and yet we weren't as directly affected by it as our parents and grandparents were. So we are truly bilingual, truly bicultural, in a way the previous generations were not." Born in Havana and raised in New York, speaking Spanish at home and English at school, García found her Cuban-American youth to be "a schizophrenic situation without the negativity that this implies." The "negativity" of her insider-outsider status certainly emerged later: as a journalist meeting Miami's fiercely anti-Castro Cuban community for the first time in the mid-1980s, she found that her opposition to the conservative politics of the Cuban-American National Foundation and her interest in a more inclusive debate about Cuba's future made her "not a welcome daughter in the community."[3] García's experience in Miami finds reflection in her second novel, *The Agüero Sisters*, which negatively portrays anti-Castro exiled "patriots" whose violent politics are spurred by "their habit of fierce nostalgia, their trafficking in the past like exaggerating peddlers," and their vainglorious (male) fantasies of military heroism. "*El exilio*," one new arrival to Florida concludes, "is the virulent flip side of Communist intolerance" (45–46, 197). García insists that it is not only their intimacy with but also their distance from the Cuban exiles' experience that enables the new hyphenated, bilingual Americans to "tell our family stories," presumably in a way they have not been told before. The issue is not simply the shift from stories heard in Spanish to stories retold in English to a larger public audience, or the mediation of family culture for outsiders. As shown in my reading of *Dreaming in Cuban*, García's first novel, interlingual translation provides the central, highly ambivalent metaphor for an intracultural (Cuban-American) regeneration. The novel ultimately privileges the perspective of those Cuban Americans whom García champions as the first "truly bilingual, truly bicultural" generation over both their Cuban relatives and their exile parents. Yet it also implies that bicultural translation necessarily involves a death: Cuba must in some sense be killed off as "home" to survive as a ghostly memory that sponsors a new ethnic American identity. The novel's model for the Cuban American's translated identity is, ironically, Cuba itself, which is portrayed as a hybrid composed of imported, translated elements. When a young Cuban-American character describes Cuba as "a peculiar exile" (219), we are alerted to how Cubans in the United States can view their exilic condition as, paradoxically, an essentially Cuban experience. While García seizes upon the often repressed hybridity of Cuban culture to validate the new ethnic syntheses of the "truly bilingual, truly bicultural" Cuban Americans, *Dreaming in Cuban* also registers the losses attendant upon relinquishing the exile's dream of final return.

These losses find reflection in the novel's imagery of haunting. Like the exile Lourdes, who "tossed and turned all night, as if she were wrestling ghosts" (221), many of the other characters are haunted by what they have been forced to leave behind. Ghostliness also figuratively represents the loss of cultural ties. A grandmother in Cuba imagines her Cuban-born granddaughter growing up in New York as "pale, gliding through paleness, malnourished and cold without the food of scarlets and greens" (7). Although at times shot through with painful nostalgia, this pale, gliding girl finds that Cuba in turn begins to "fade" into ghostliness: "Every day Cuba fades a little more inside me, my grandmother fades a little more inside me. And there's only my imagination where our history should be" (138). In this girl's American teenage dialect, fading Cuba is, like the ambiguous ghost, "kind of dead" (137). Ghostly imagery here points to the replacement of a vital cultural embeddedness with a *merely* invented ethnicity, an identity based less on collective memory than on an individual's fabrications. Yet ghostliness will gradually come to be reenvisioned in the novel as the "matrix" of successful cultural translation, the proper medium through which new ethnic fusions emerge in a complex interplay of imagination and history. *Dreaming in Cuban* lacks the explicit and dramatic scenes of possession and exorcism that we find in Erdrich's *Tracks* or Morrison's *Beloved*, but it is organized by a similar movement from dangerous to (at least potentially) regenerative forms of haunting. In *Tracks*, the bilingual translator ensures cultural survival by mediating between the world of the living and that of ghosts, between the new generation of Chippewa and their tribal history. The translator in *Dreaming in Cuban* must also enter into a ghostly "in-between" state in which clear ethnic boundaries are blurred and ultimately redefined. Cultural translation, however, has its pitfalls: in the characters of Lourdes and Felicia, sisters divided by exile, García models two opposed but equally unsuccessful versions of translation, as well as two varieties of "possession." Each presents dangers that Pilar, Lourdes's daughter and the family's candidate for the role of Cuban-American "translator," must avoid in order to define a new ethnic identity seen as continuing, without being possessed by, a ghostly Cuban legacy. Pilar never quite accomplishes this feat, but by the novel's end she is positioned to do so.

Dreaming in Cuban traces the fortunes of the members of the del Pino family, which has been split (as García's own family was) by opposing responses to the revolution. The splitting of the family is reflected in the novel's organization, which divides into two long sections comprised of chapters that alternate between Cuba and New York, followed by a third short section in which the separated characters are briefly reunited in Cuba. The chiefly third-person narration moves from the perspective of one family member to another, returning most often to the matrilineal line of Celia, her daughter Lourdes, and granddaughter Pilar; Pilar's importance as the novel's potential Cuban-American "translator" and family historian is indicated by her first-person narration.[4] Each of the three sections includes a collection of secret, unmailed letters written by Celia from 1935, the year of her marriage, until the revolution in 1959, a collection that at the novel's close will be inherited by Pilar.

Like Morrison's *Beloved*, the novel closely follows the three-part structure of secondary burial rituals, in which a provisional funeral is followed by an intermediary period of active haunting, to be concluded upon second or final burial. At the novel's opening, Jorge del Pino has just died. Disgusted with the passionate commitment of his wife, Celia, to the revolution, Jorge years before has followed his beloved and equally anticommunist daughter Lourdes to Brooklyn. There she has established her tribute to democracy and capitalism, the "Yankee Doodle Bakery," which is a gathering spot for Cuban exiles, in the words of Lourdes's rebellious daughter, Pilar, to "talk their dinosaur [anti-

Castro] politics and drink her killer espressos" (177). Forty days after Lourdes buries Jorge "like an Egyptian king" (64), his spirit returns. The forty-day absence, together with the description of Jorge's "death and resurrection" (78) by an attending nun (he rises from his deathbed in a glowing "nimbus of holiness," puts on his hat, and passes through a window [19]), echoes a biblical "secondary burial": Christ's ascension into heaven forty days after his resurrection, during which time he appears to his disciples. Jorge similarly visits his loved ones before he departs forever. He shows up once in Cuba, emerging at daybreak to greet Celia as a colossal, luminous figure on the shore. Although he "moves his mouth carefully" (5), his wife fails to understand his words. To Lourdes he makes regular appearances over a period of seven years, to discuss the family, the bakery, American baseball, the fight to "win Cuba back" (132). As the novel's second section draws toward its close, Jorge explains that "the time he's stolen between death and oblivion is coming to an end," and Lourdes realizes with renewed grief that her father is "dying all over again" (193–94). Until this point in the novel, Jorge is so deeply entrenched in his conservative politics that as a ghost he only mirrors to Lourdes her own predilections and intolerances. As he faces his final departure, however, Jorge's ghost undergoes a change, acknowledging for the first time his responsibility for Celia's deep unhappiness and bouts of madness, a condition that wrecked Lourdes's childhood. He finally admits to abandoning his young wife to his monstrously cruel and jealous mother while he fled on long business trips, punishing Celia for her undying memory of an earlier lover: "I wanted to break her," he confesses to Lourdes, "may God forgive me. When I returned, it was done" (195). Just before he departs, he pleads with Lourdes to return to her estranged mother in Cuba to speak words of reconciliation, a final request that sets in motion the brief reunion of divided family members in the last section. Upon Jorge's final disappearance, Lourdes "imagines white azaleas and an altar set for high mass on an April Sunday. She sings in a high, pure voice, carefully pronouncing each word" (197). The allusion to Easter service marks Jorge's second funeral; resurrected from his ghostly term on earth, he departs finally for the otherworld. Although Lourdes, after so many years of hoarding bitterness against her mother, will find herself unable to fulfill the ghost's directive, she brings with her to Cuba her daughter, Pilar, through whom a limited reconciliation between the Cuban and American branches of the family is realized. The novel's ghost functions not only to illuminate the character of Lourdes but to direct the plot toward a Cuban/American rapprochement, from which Pilar will emerge with a newly redefined Cuban legacy.

As discussed in chapter 3, funereal rituals, like other social rites of passage, work to organize communities by reaffirming, or in some cases redefining, fundamental cultural values. The parallel García establishes between exile and the intermediary period of mourning suggests that the ghost's presence signals a period of heightened ethnic reevaluation in the face of severed family ties. The very mobility of the ghost, who roams between his native and adopted countries, reflects the displacement of exiled Cubans. The first del Pino to be buried outside of Cuba, Jorge rises from his grave in "a cemetery on the border of Brooklyn and Queens" (64) to become a spectral embodiment of permeable but divisive cultural borders. His language no longer understandable to Cubans (Celia "cannot read his immense lips" [5]), he becomes principally associated with his favored daughter, Lourdes, the novel's conservative, "old-guard" exile who has seized upon American capitalism as her best revenge against the revolution. While her mother labors in the hot cane fields, Lourdes makes money by selling sugary confections that she photographs to torment her Cuban relatives: "Each glistening éclair is a grenade aimed at Celia's political beliefs, each strawberry shortcake proof—in butter, cream, and eggs—of Lourdes's success in America, and a reminder of the ongoing shortages in Cuba" (117).[5] While viewing capitalist enterprise as her avenue to triumph over Celia and the regime her mother so ardently supports, Lourdes also eagerly embraces English as the language that will erase revolutionary Cuba. She "considers herself lucky. Immigration has redefined her, and she is grateful. Unlike her husband, she welcomes her adopted language, its possibilities for reinvention. Lourdes relishes winter most of all—the cold scraping sounds on sidewalks and windshields, the ritual of scarves and gloves, hats and zip-in coat linings. Its layers protect her. She wants no part of Cuba, no part of its wretched carnival floats creaking with lies, no part of Cuba at all, which Lourdes claims never possessed her" (73). The desperation of Lourdes's "reinvention" is belied by her insistent repetitions ("no part," "no part," "no part . . . at all") and by the extreme seasonal imagery she associates with her adopted home. Lourdes desires a mind-numbing, amnesiac coldness, hungers for "layers" of protection against memories of Cuba that, despite her disavowals, still possess her. The denial that Cuba ever "possessed" her covertly alludes to Lourdes's most haunting memory: her rape by the revolutionary soldiers who came to claim her wealthy husband's estate. Details of this incompletely repressed rape leak into Lourdes's images of winter. The "cold scraping" of the sidewalks returns us to the rape's conclusion, when "the soldier lifted the knife and began to scratch at Lourdes's belly with great concentration. A primeval scraping. Crimson hieroglyphics." Lourdes afterwards tries to read his carvings in the bathroom mirror but cannot: her body is inscribed with an "illegible" (72) writing that forecasts her linguistic and emotional alienation from Cuba. Lourdes will never again be fully "at home" in her own body (hence her gross fluctutations in weight)—or, for that matter, in her native tongue. When she finally returns to Cuba toward the end of the novel, she finds that the Cubans "can't understand a word I'm saying." This cannot, of course, be literally true; Lourdes means that the Cubans do not accept her capitalist ideas. Lourdes expresses the magnitude of her alienation from Cuba by using linguistic metaphors; she feels that her "mother tongue" has become a "foreign tongue," suggesting that her frustrating encounter with the Cubans mirrors her estrangement from Celia. Pilar relies on the same metaphors, observing that the Spanish Lourdes "speaks is lost to them. It's another idiom entirely" (221). Lourdes's "reinvention" suggests that ethnicities are constructed through language, that we live in languages as much as we do in countries. However, languages are subject to strange permutations: to speak in an exile's Spanish is not at all the same thing as speaking in Cuban. García will return to this idea in *The Agüero Sisters*, when a newly arrived Cuban emigrant finds the Spanish of Miami's established exiles bizarrely archaic: while her own Cuban Spanish is "quotidian," spiced by "an explosive lexicon of hardship and bitter jokes at the government's expense," the exiles' Spanish, "florid with self-pity and longing and obstinate revenge," is a "flash-frozen language, replete with outmoded words and fifties expressions" (236).[6]

For Lourdes, the memory of her rape is horrifically compounded by the miscarriage of her two-month pregnancy a week earlier, when she stood on her property "like a shield before her husband," staring down the gun barrels of the same soldiers. The "clot" that slides down her legs to form "a pool of dark blood at her feet" (70) is forever mixed in her mind with her vision during the rape of her "blood seep[ing] from her skin like rainwater from a sodden earth" (72). Lourdes's Cuba, the Cuban soil itself, has stolen her second child, a boy, we later learn, that "she would have named Jorge, after her father" (227). Lourdes's mourning for her father cannot be separated from her unspeakable grief for this other Jorge, the last child she would be able to conceive. Upon her return to Cuba, Lourdes drives out to the old villa, now a mental institution, and "studies the checkered linoleum, longs to dig for her bones like a dog, claim them from the black-hooded earth, the scraping blade" (227). In returning to the second Jorge's "grave," Lourdes returns to her own; she would claim "her [own] bones," her former Cuban self, from the covered earth. The fantasy of exhumation connects to the novel's secondary burial scheme: the digging up of the dead immediately precedes the final burial, at which a reconciliation with the dead occurs and mourning concludes. Revisiting the site of the second Jorge's death could complete the final burial Lourdes has already performed for her father. The return of the "scraping" image, however, indicates that for Lourdes there has been no healing, and there is no possible reconciliation with Cuba. The "scraping blade" can be read in apposition to the "black-hooded earth," as if the Cuban soil itself is the agent of destruction; "black-hooded" Cuba is transformed into an executioner.

At this point Lourdes suddenly "remembers a story she read once about Guam, about how brown snakes were introduced by Americans. The snakes strangled the native birds one by one. They ate the eggs from the nests until the jungle had no voice" (227). This apparently unrelated memory bears a double significance. The destruction of the native "eggs" points to the miscarriage of her two-month-old son, an identification supported by her earlier vision of his face "pale and blank as an egg" (174). But the devouring, imported snakes also express the desire of Lourdes, now an American, to avenge herself, to destroy the revolutionary Cuba that aborted her family's Cuban life.[7] The American snakes may hint at Lourdes's subliminal sense of America as destructive of her Cuban self, yet she fully identifies with this American voraciousness. Indeed, she "hungers for a violence of nature, terrible and permanent, to record the evil. Nothing less would satisfy her" (227). The double, contradictory meaning of the snake memory (the snakes as Castro's soldiers, the snakes as America) reflects Lourdes's desire to enact an appropriate revenge: because she sees revolutionary Cuba as the snakelike devourer of her unborn child, Lourdes wants to see Cuba in turn devoured by American snakes.

Insatiable hunger has been Lourdes's instinctual response to crisis in the past. She gains 118 pounds as her father declines toward his death from stomach cancer, an illness he ascribes to his bitterness over Celia's devotion to the revolution (194): Jorge's shaved and stitched stomach (21), much like Lourdes's knife-scarred belly, is taken as evidence of communist Cuba's violence. Lourdes's quickly massing body and voracious sexual appetite would deny her father's slow diminishment; in her dreams of bread multiplying prodigiously, she counters death (and Cuba's betrayal) with a yeasty affirmation of life. "What sorrow could there be" in "work[ing] with bread," she thinks as she establishes her bakery. Comforting herself with "the sustaining aromas of vanilla and almond" (18), Lourdes seeks to forget terrible memories of Cuba, inextricably associated with certain scents: the bodily smells of her rapist (71–72) and the "aroma tree" (70) near which she is thrown from her horse, a fall that precipitates her miscarriage. When Lourdes loses all 118 pounds five years after her father's death, longing "for a profound emptiness, to be clean and hollow as a flute" (169), her desire for physical "purity" (167, 172) can be read as yet another denial of Cuba or, more precisely, of what is to her an unspeakably filthy Cuban history. Lourdes, like her father, sees in cleanliness and coldness an antidote to Cuba's "tropical squalor," that sickening spawning ground for dreaded *microbios*. (Complaining that "food spoils quickly in our climate!" Jorge obsessively turns the refrigerator's dial "to near freezing," until Lourdes's teeth ache when she bites into her meat [22]). For Lourdes, however, uncleanness acquires another, more personal and devastating association with Cuba. After her rape by the soldiers, she "scoured her skin and hair with detergents meant for the walls and the tile floors" (72), yet to Lourdes her invaded body remains forever tainted. Understanding her self-starvation as a form of cleansing, Lourdes attempts once again to purge her body of the dirty revolution. When she finally breaks her fast, beginning another precipitous weight gain, she significantly does so at a family Thanksgiving Day meal. Her startling bodily fluctuations consistently register her attempt to reinvent herself as non-Cuban by "incorporating" America through its food or by purging revolutionary Cuba from her body.[8]

In her revenge fantasy of the imported snakes, Lourdes changes her tack slightly: having been unable to shed Cuba, she will devour it. It is significant that the snakes kill off birds: in her Cuban home, Lourdes had "built an aviary in the garden, stocking it with toucans and cockatoos, parrots, a macaw, and canaries that sang in high octaves" (130). When she lives in New York amidst drab wrens and dirty pigeons, she "misses the birds she had in Cuba" (131). The extermination of the native birds constitutes a kind of self-murder: she must kill off even her good memories of Cuba. What seems especially important to note is that Lourdes conceives of her revenge as the violent silencing of a native language: the loss of the island birds leaves the jungle with "no voice" (227). Although she continues to speak Spanish (Pilar refers to her impressive Spanish curses), Lourdes's ethnic "reinvention" is motivated by the desire to destroy her "mother tongue."

The price of figuratively tearing out her own tongue is hinted at earlier when Lourdes strolls past the new Arab shops of Brooklyn, representing the latest wave of immigration: "Baskets of figs and pistachios and coarse yellow grains are displayed under their awnings. Lourdes buys a round box of sticky dates and considers the centuries of fratricide converging on this street corner in Brooklyn. She ponders the transmigrations from the southern latitudes, the millions moving north. What happens to their languages? The warm burial grounds they leave behind? What of their passions lying stiff and untranslated in their breasts?" (72–73). Although she quickly dismisses this wistful line of thought to celebrate her "adopted language," with its "possibilities for reinvention," Lourdes is clearly haunted by the consequences of lost languages. The "burial grounds" of origin countries remain "warm"; the ancestral dead are not completely dead but become lodged as "stiff" corpses (the "untranslated" emotions) within the immigrants' breasts. Neither able to leave their dead firmly behind in the process of assimilation, nor to carry them into new worlds as the living presences of ethnic memory, Lourdes's imagined immigrants, like Lourdes herself, are caught in the void between languages. Significantly, the haunting memory of the still warm ancestral burial grounds is linked to a failure of translation. To translate their passions, the immigrants would need to "rebury" them in new soil, meaningfully incorporating past into present, the old country into the new. It is only when the "burial grounds" are "[left] behind," bearing no relation to the new reality in which the immigrants find themselves, that their passions lie "untranslated": the failure of cultural translation thus results in a miserable ghostly possession, in which a corpselike past takes up residence within the immigrants' bodies. Pilar tells us that her mother "tossed and turned all night, as if she were wrestling ghosts in her dreams. Sometimes she'd wake up crying, clutching her stomach and moaning from deep inside a place I couldn't understand" (221). The deep internal pain and the clutching at the stomach hint at nightmares about the miscarriage and rape, the ghosts Lourdes can neither forget nor openly confront. Pilar cannot understand the nature of her mother's ghosts, primarily because Lourdes has never spoken of them, but also because her mother's Cuban memories lie corpselike and "untranslated" within Lourdes herself. Lourdes's refusal to "translate" her past leaves her unable to realize her father's dying request; although she travels to Cuba to see her mother, new words "refuse to form in her mouth" (238). She can only replay in her mind her mother's hurtful words from the past. Her ghosts prevent her from imagining the language that reconciliation would require, the language that could recast the family along less tragic lines. She walks on Cuban soil again, but Cuba remains unapproachable, "mined" as it is "with sad memories" (24). Although technically bilingual, Lourdes represents the failure of cultural translation, a failure connected to her possession by Cuban ghosts she can never put to rest. The past she cannot herself possess, by safely reburying it in the present through "translation," in turn possesses her.

Much later in the novel, Celia returns to the issue of lost ancestral graveyards when she miserably observes to Pilar that their family has "no loyalty to our origins. . . . Families used to stay in one village reliving the same disillusions. They buried their dead side by side" (240). The confraternity of the dead attests to, and perhaps in turn ensures, the fidelity of living kin, although Celia acknowledges that this allegiance can also imprison a family in a dreary monotony of repetitions. The fear of losing the family "burial grounds" and the ethnic community they memorialize is also reflected in one of the several passages by Federico García Lorca, Celia's favorite poet, that appear in the text. Celia's daughter Felicia recalls a snippet of "Casida de las palomas oscuras" (Casida of the dark doves), which Celia used to recite as she rocked her children to sleep (109–10). In the passage Felicia remembers, untranslated for the English-speaking reader, two dark doves in the branches of a laurel tree metamorphose mysteriously into two opposed worlds, the sun and the moon. A line not recalled by Felicia, but which repeats twice in the poem as the speaker directly addresses the birds, is, "Where is my grave?" The anxiety about a final resting place, the speaker's status as wanderer, the strange metamorphoses, even the fact that the lines appear in Spanish with no English translation, link this poem both to Celia's sorrow over the dispersal of the family and to Lourdes's melancholy musings about lost languages and abandoned "burial grounds."[9]

Felicia, who remains in Cuba with her mother, might appear to share Celia's view of the proper relation of the living and the dead. When her friend Herminia Delgado loses her son in the Angolan war, Felicia takes it upon herself to arrange for the "remains to be brought home for a decent burial" (184). She is also outraged when she learns that her father's ghost has appeared in Cuba only briefly and to her mother alone ("You mean he was in the neighborhood and didn't even stop by?" [9]). Yet Felicia's understanding of the spirit world derives primarily from her immersion in the Afro-Cuban religion Santería. Her involvement with the religion begins when, as a young girl, she meets the Afro-Cuban Herminia, daughter of a *babalawo*, or high priest (whose home her parents forbid her to visit), and grows in intensity until finally she herself is initiated as a *santera*, or priest. Like her sister Lourdes, Felicia crosses cultures, although for Felicia the border to cross is internal to Cuba, being racial rather than national. Unfortunately, also like her sister, Felicia models a failure of translation.

A new-world syncretism, Santería mixes Spanish folk Catholicism and Yoruba religion, resulting in a curious "doubleness" suggestive of García's ideal of the "truly bilingual, truly bicultural." Yoruba gods and Catholic saints are "treated as replicas of one another, known as *santos* in Spanish and *orishas* in Yoruba."[10] Each *santo/orisha* therefore has two names: Santa Bárbara can also be called upon as Changó, the god of fire and war; Oshún is the same person as Cuba's patron saint, La Virgen de la Caridad del Cobre. The doubleness of Santería constitutes an ethnic survival strategy: slaves from West Africa ensured the continuity of their spiritual traditions by protectively "translating" them into the terms of the master's religion. The degree to which this translation remains central to the religion is much debated. No consensus on the centrality of the syncretism issues from Santería's believers themselves, who exhibit a "wide range of variation in ritual and degree of Catholic versus African influence."[11] In his study of the development of Santería, George Brandon observes that for "some believers today the equation of the saints and the orisha is not real but is an historical residue, a practice standing over from when the Africans used the Catholic saints to mask the worship of their own deities." From this perspective, the syncretism of Santería was purely "a strategy of subterfuge." Yet Brandon also notes that the acculturation process was partly motivated by the desire to appropriate "key symbols of the powers of the dominant society," through which "social realities" could be "manipulated by means of magical or religious rites. Viewed from below and in relation to social and magical power, to include the saints in the pantheon of the blacks was not necessarily submission to a higher power (even though it took place in the context of dominance of Catholic ideology and religious hierarchy) but was instead the acquisition of the saint's power. Thus these Africans did not convert to the saints but converted the saints to themselves; in this way the Africans came to possess the saint, in order to work their will through its means."[12] Anthropologist and Santería practitioner Joseph Murphy would have it both ways: through a process of transculturation (mutual influence and adaptation), a "new bilingual tradition emerged, at once a resistance to Catholic oppression and an accommodation to Catholic values."[13]

To understand fully Santería's attractions for Felicia, as well as its thematic function in the novel, two central aspects of the religion must be considered. The first is the gradual replacement of African (blood) ancestor worship with Santería's ritual or fictive—one might say "ghostly"—ancestry. When slavery's destruction of natal ties and interethnic marriage in Cuba made Yoruban ancestor worship difficult or impossible, the Catholic *compadrazgo* (the practice of "godparenting") and religious "fraternities" provided a new kinship model: worshippers of the *orishas*/saints become "godchildren" of the priests; all believers form one "family."[14] *Santeros* thus "have a group of ritual ancestors as well as ancestors by blood and marriage. These ritual, fictive ancestors include the people who initiated them into the priesthood and the initiators' ritual ancestors going as far back and extending as far out as the priest or priestess knows." Important ceremonies begin with devotees reciting genealogies of ancestors, both familial and ritual.[15] Emotionally abandoned in childhood by a troubled mother and a father who preferred her sister (and who, on Felicia's marriage, disowned her), Felicia is power-fully drawn to a religion that offers the consolations of ritual rather than blood kinship. Herminia, who has been "more than a sister" (189) to Felicia, and whose name reverberates with *hermana* (sister), takes her to "La Madrina," the mother priestess, who treats Felicia "like a newborn child" (187). Felicia's fascination with the divining coconut's "sweet white milk" (85) hints at a thirst for maternal nourishment. Yet her desire to replace the del Pinos with a substitute family proves super-ficial; she longs for the withheld approbation of her own flesh and blood and is finally destroyed when her family ostracizes her after her corona-tion as *santera*. Celia blames Santería for Felicia's death, but the symp-toms of Felicia's fatal illness first show themselves when she returns to her home after her coronation as *santera* to find "neither her mother nor her children were there to greet her" (188). Celia finally arrives at Felicia's home "wild-eyed, like a woman who gives birth to an unwanted child" (190), just in time to cradle her daughter into death. Although Felicia finds she cannot replace her inadequate family, Santería's fictive or ghostly ancestry later provides Pilar with an identity that firmly con-nects her to Cuba, despite her exile.

The centrality of spirit possession in Santería, in which the gods speak through the lips of devotees, also contributes enormously to the religion's attraction for Felicia. Felicia hungers for a language adequate to her experience and feelings. The symptoms of her syphilitic madness exhibit themselves largely as linguistic or translational difficulties. As her insanity intensifies, she peers at her young son, Ivanito, and wonders, "What is he saying? Each word is a code she must decipher, a foreign language, a streak of gunshot" (81). Although she cannot decipher what others say, her mind is flooded with uninvited voices and strange lan-guages (76). When Felicia nearly dies from a suicide attempt, Celia is telegraphically alerted by a polyphonic nightmare that echoes Felicia's condition: "Voices call to her in ragged words stitched together from many languages, like dissonant scraps of quilt" (95). Felicia veers from linguistic excess, in which even colors become languages ("Let's speak in green," she proposes to Ivanito [84]), to linguistic breakdown: "She opens her mouth but her thoughts erase themselves before she can speak. Something is wrong with her tongue. It forms broken trails of words, words sealed and resistant as stones" (83). Felicia's miseries rep-resent an extreme version of the linguistic confusion all the novel's characters experience; each searches, like Felicia, for an adequate language. Felicia's daughters, Luz and Milagro, for example, think they find in their father's eyes "the language we'd been searching for, a language more eloquent than the cheap bead necklaces of words [our] mother offered" (124), while her son, Ivanito, vows never to "speak his sisters' language" and secretly listens to American radio for the voice that "[talks] to a million people at once" (86, 191).[16] Felicia covets the vastly more powerful language of the gods; or rather, she longs for the *santero*'s ability to translate divine messages: "Through the mouths of the cowries the gods speak to him in clear, unambiguous voices" (147). Sinking helplessly into madness, Felicia desires a different, enabling kind of "possession," one that will provide her with both a ghostly counterfamily and divine powers of speech. But when she is finally initiated and possessed by the *orisha* Obatalá, she "could not divulge his words," even though the "*santeras* had made eight cuts on her tongue with a razor blade so that the god could speak" (187).

The sisters Felicia and Lourdes represent two opposing positions on cultural translation, but although Felicia immerses herself headlong in other languages, she is no more successful than Lourdes, who would choke off the native tongue. Their different approaches to translation reflect differing and extreme views on the value of the imagination in the pursuit of knowledge. Lourdes, who might be said to long for a unilingual world where meanings do not reverberate distressingly between languages, "abhors ambiguity" (65) and sees the world in strictly "black and white" (129) factual terms: imagination, she thinks, enters only when one has "exhausted reality" (65).[17] Felicia, who lives increasingly within her own extravagantly colorful mind, approvingly observes that "Imagination, like memory, can transform lies to truths" (88). It remains for Pilar to define a form of cultural translation that mediates between history and the imagination, a mediation that the novel will associate with ghostliness.

Pilar is, however, severely hampered by her emotional immaturity and rashly judgmental perspective, as well as by her lack of knowledge about her own family history and about Cuba generally. Having left Cuba as a young girl, she is acutely, painfully aware of how her own imaginative fabrications substitute for a real place that, though only ninety miles from Florida, may as well exist in another world altogether. As with her mother, Lourdes, Pilar's alienation from Cuba is measured by a linguistic estrangement: she writes letters to her grandmother, Celia, "in a Spanish that is no longer hers," a "hard-edged lexicon of bygone tourists" (7). She bitterly resents that her mother, who could act as transmitter of Cuban culture and family history, provides at best a faulty source. Pilar realizes that Lourdes "systematically rewrites history to suit her views of the world" with "embellishments and half-truths" that, though they make for a "good story," are "at the expense of chipping away our past." "Telling her own truth is *the* truth to her," Pilar grumbles, as yet unaware of how similar her own conception of truth as singular and exclusive is to her mother's (176–77). Pilar's obsession with "the truth" (176, 231) and her awareness of the truth's easy subordination to "a good story" leave her suspicious of all words, and especially of words in translation. She settles on abstract art as her chief means of expression and admires the Dutch expressionist painter Jacoba Van Heemskerck, who numbered rather than titled her paintings: "who needs words when colors and lines conjure up their own language?" she reflects (139). Significantly, Van Heemskerck comes to Pilar's mind as she "block[s] out" the sound of her mother's "words," suggesting that Pilar's painting registers an effort to move beyond her mother's entrapment in emotional and linguistic exile by evading verbal language altogether. "Painting is its own language," she reassures herself. "Translations just confuse it, dilute it, like words going from Spanish to English" (59). Pilar's view of painting as beyond translation is questionable but revealing: she seeks a fully embodied rather than a ghostly or mediate language.

Despite Pilar's fear that her (English-language) imagination "translates" and thus dilutes the truth of her family's Cuban history, her early and repeated connections to the bilingual religion of Santería hint at her future vocation as the family's chief heir and translator. During her first, unsuccessful attempt to return (without money or visa) to Cuba, she has a dream that evokes a religious ritual: "It's midnight and there are people around me praying on the beach. I'm wearing a white dress and turban and I can hear the ocean nearby, only I can't see it. I'm sitting on a chair, a kind of throne, with antlers fastened to the back. The people lift me up high and walk with me in a slow procession toward the sea. They're chanting in a language I don't understand. I don't feel scared, though. . . . I can see my grandmother's face" (33–34). Pilar knows little about Santería at this early point in the novel; having had some contact with the religion as a young child in Cuba through her nannies, she finally learns of the secret rites from Herminia on her trip to Cuba years later (231). Yet despite her ignorance, her dream describes a ceremony very like the *asiento*, or initiation of a new priest. Details of the dream reappear much later in the novel, when Felicia undergoes her initiation: the white gown (187), the throne (188), and the chanting in a strange language, identified as "the language of the Yoruba" (187). Pilar's seaward movement in the dream, accompanied by chanting in an unknown language, forecasts her journey to multilingual Cuba and hints at her need to shed her resistance to translation. The connection here between a foreign tongue and Santería's spirit vision also prepares readers for the novel's depiction of translation as an immersion in ghostliness.

Eight years later, Pilar's successful return visit to the island is prompted by her first visit to a New York *botánica*, where she confronts the cultural and linguistic doubleness of Santería. At this point, Pilar, now a student at Columbia University, has moved considerably away from her earlier suspicion of translation. Her readiness to investigate her Cuban heritage, an investigation that necessitates certain acts of cultural translation, is reflected in the evolving direction of her studies. Originally an art student who believes her medium transcends translation, Pilar, while continuing to paint, finally chooses to major in anthropology. Her choice of study signals her growing interest in the possibilities of cultural translation and prepares her for her role as heir-ethnographer. As she walks through the door of the *botánica*, Pilar encounters a world of doubleness created by a long history of cultural borrowings and translations. "Dried snakeskins and *ouanga* bags" hang side by side with "wooden saints" and "plastic plug-in Virgins." Special potions are named in two languages: "*amor* (love), *sígueme* (follow me), *yo puedo y tú no* (I can and you can't), *ven conmigo* (come with me), and *dominante* (dominant)" (199). Examining beaded necklaces (symbolic of the various *orishas*) that "come in two colors," Pilar instinctively selects the "red-and-white one," the colors of the *orisha*/saint Changó/Santa Bárbara. When she lifts "an ebony staff carved with the head of a woman balancing a double-edged ax," the symbol of Changó/Santa Bárbara, she identifies herself as, in the words of the *botánica santero*, "a daughter of Changó." The gesture hints at the possibility that Pilar may embrace the bilingual (in fact, multilingual) heritage of Cuba to assume what García calls the "truly bilingual, truly bicultural" identity of the Cuban American (as opposed to the only technically bilingual Cuban exile). Her entrance as "daughter" into the ritual, as opposed to biological, "family" of Santería marks her entrance into the realm of translation that she has, until this point, vehemently attempted to resist.[18] The alternative to translation appears to be silence. A gift of ritual herbs "from our father Changó" triggers the memory of a story Pilar's Cuban nanny had once told her about how Changó renders mute a fearful lizard who had failed to execute his assigned mission. The story, in conjunction with the *santero*'s instructions ("You must finish what you began" [200]), darkly implies that the cost of ignoring her mission (to rediscover Cuba) comes at the price of her voice.

By casting Pilar's return to her longed-for Cuban grandmother—a visit that proves crucial to her understanding of her ethnic identity—as an election to *santera*, Pilar's dream positions Santería as the essential key to "Cubanness," an identification that the visit to the *botánica* confirms. Moreover, Pilar's comparison of her resurgent Cuban ethnicity upon her return to the island to a "magic . . . working its way through my veins" (235) implicitly connects the essentially Cuban with Santería's magical, spirit-infused worldview: the acts of cultural translation through which Pilar's newly redefined ethnicity will emerge inevitably lead her into the realm of ghosts.

This equation of recovered Cubanness with Santería raises the question of what it might mean for a white Cuban author, with little personal knowledge of Santería, to appropriate the religion as a symbol both of Cuba's cultural hybridity and of Cuban-American biculturality. García has spoken of her family's disdain for Santería, with its "mumbo-jumbo African rites," and of her own determination to include the religion in her novel because "It's part of our cultural landscape." To do so, she needed to research the subject.[19] The irony of the situation—the writer who has always strongly identified herself as Cuban nevertheless needing to investigate her own "cultural landscape"—is peculiar to the phenomenon I describe as the "heir-ethnographer." In García's case, unlike, say, African-American writers who conjure a lost preslavery "Africa" or Chinese-American writers who imagine a "China" never known firsthand, the unknown aspect of Cuban culture is both contemporary and close at hand: one need only walk into any New York *botánica*, as Pilar does, to encounter Santería.[20] In making the Afro-Cuban Santería, which is feared or dismissed by many white, upper-class Cubans, crucial to a white Cuban American's struggle to define her ethnic identity, García conjures the spectre of racism, pointedly raising the issue of the white exiles' repression of Cuba's often violent racial history.

The recasting of often marginalized or repressed aspects of a culture as central to cultural identity is a well-known strategy of ethnic regeneration. In their work on the "folk religions" of the Pacific basin, anthropologists Jeanette Mageo and Alan Howard point out that "parts of cultures often became metonyms for cultural continuity; in the process, specific segments of reconfigured historical experience came to stand for 'tradition.'" Mageo and Howard argue that in the societies they examine, "spirits—pagan and pre-Christian, irredeemable and recalcitrant"—frequently provide emblems of this reconfigured cultural identity, an observation congruent with my own argument about the role of ghosts (often drawn from "old country" myth) as figures of ethnogenesis in American writing.[21] Brandon offers an example of the phenomenon Mageo and Howard describe when he notes that the variant of Santería to develop in Puerto Rico, Espiritismo, "which has a lower-class black image on the island of Puerto Rico and is associated with areas reputed to have a high concentration of people of African descent, is redefined by Puerto Ricans who migrate to New York. There it ceases to be represented as confined to one segment of the population or restricted to only a few areas of the island. In the new context practitioners begin to view Espiritismo as a strong symbol of a specifically Puerto Rican identity." The religion "becomes a symbol of the homeland, almost a national or ethnic symbol representing an identity that contrasts with general American norms and values."[22] The fact that some of the Cuban Marielitos practiced Santería in Cuba, but that more became devotees after they arrived in the United States, strongly suggests that Santería similarly gained strength as a guarantor of Cuban identity in response to the threat of assimilation. Brandon observes that "Santeria now almost certainly has more devotees in the United States than it had in Cuba at the time of the revolution."[23] Cuban ethnicity in America is thus reaffirmed through the mediation of Afro-Cuban spirits. Pilar's turn to Santería parallels this strategy of ethnic reinvention, in which the formerly marginal becomes central to a displaced people.

The idea that Afro-Cuban culture, long despised by Cuba's white population, in fact distills the essence of Cubanness has a tradition within Cuban literature. The movement called "Afro-Cubanism," shaped by writers such as Alejo Carpentier, Nicolás Guillén, and Ramón Guirao, and propelled by the work of social scientist Fernando Ortiz, attempted in the 1920s and 1930s to recuperate black culture as the essentially "authentic" Cuban culture. Vera Kutzinski, in her impressive study of Cuban literature, comments that Afro-Cubanism "can more profitably be seen as a historically specific instance of *cubanía*. Fernando Ortiz's term for what he understood as a spiritual condition, *cubanía*, unlike the more passive national identification expressed by the concept of *cubanidad*, signifies an active desire to be Cuban, and its various articulations in literature, the arts, and the social sciences were to provide indigenous ideological antidotes to the economic, social, and political crises induced by United States interventionism."[24] Afro-Cuban culture, the banner of the indigenous for the Afro-Cubanists, is, of course, a syncretism of nonindigenous elements; moreover, the recuperation of black culture to invigorate modernist art is not an originally Cuban phenomenon. Afro-Cubanism can be seen as an extension of the aesthetic "primitivism" of the European avant garde, evident in Picasso's painting and García Lorca's poetry. The effect of Afro-Cubanism was to grant "a degree of legitimacy" to Santería (which now could be viewed "as folklore rather than witchcraft and crime"), although as Kutzinski shrewdly observes, the movement "defused potential ethnic threats to national unification by turning them into original (and originary) contributions to Cuban culture."[25]

The inclusion in *Dreaming in Cuban* of passages from three of Lorca's poems, as well as a description (in the form of Celia's girlhood memory) of the last lecture Lorca delivered during his 1930 visit to Cuba, signals García's awareness of the connection between her own recuperation of Santería and the black-inspired literature produced by Europe's and Cuba's white intelligensia.[26] Lorca's *Gypsy Ballads*, hugely popular in Cuba, depicts Grenada's Gypsies (who migrated from India in the fourteenth century) as "more Andalusian than the Andalusians themselves."[27] Lorca's figure of the dusky, passionate Andalusian Gypsy plays a role similar to that of the Afro-Cubanists' negro/mulatto, a point that Lorca himself recognized when he described his first encounter with the blacks of Havana.[28] While in Cuba, Lorca made his own contribution to Afro-Cubanism, dedicating to Fernando Ortiz the poem "Son de negros en Cuba," after the Afro-Cuban music and dance form known as the *son*. Lorca explicitly linked the Andalusian Gypsy with blacks (and Jews), claiming, in perhaps too easy an identification with otherness, a "fellow feeling" for these persecuted peoples "whom all *granadinos* carry inside them."[29] In turning to the Gypsy as his source of inspiration, Lorca sees himself as illuminating a shadowy, officially repressed side of Spain that is nevertheless the origin of Andalusian culture. The heart of ethnicity is to be found in what has been denied but still haunts.

We see in Cristina García something of this tendency to locate in an oppressed minority's culture the defining characteristics of a country's identity. Yet there are significant differences between García's and the earlier Afro-Cubanists' approaches to black culture. Santería in *Dreaming in Cuban* is presented sympathetically, but it is not romanticized as the source of glamorously dangerous political and sexual forces. To a large extent this is due to the inclusion of Herminia Delgado's sane, perceptive, practical voice in the chapter "God's Will." Certainly compared to the del Pino family, with their penchant for "ruinous passion" (157), the Delgado family of *santeros* provides a picture of domestic normality. (Celia recalls her surprise when Salvador Delgado, the feared "witch doctor" (77), turns out to be "an unassuming, soft-spoken man" who serves her "tea and homemade cookies" [163] when Felicia brings her for a visit.) The only one outside the family to be given a narrative, Herminia offers a new perspective on Felicia's eccentricities and on Cuban race relations. She observes that Cuban racism was for many years "considered too disagreeable to discuss," and that the nation's history books reduced to "a footnote" "the Little War of 1912," when "our men were hunted down day and night like animals, and finally hung by their genitals from the lampposts in Guáimaro," including Herminia's grandfather and great uncles (185). She refers to what is often called "La Guerra de Razas" (the "Race War"), a political uprising against the government that resulted in the suspension of civil rights, the opening of concentration camps, and the slaughter of an estimated six thousand blacks.[30] Herminia learns to trust her family's oral history over recorded "official" history, a view that links her to Pilar, whose distrust of "history books" ("Who chooses what we should know or what's important?") provokes an interest in the unwritten lives of women and in her grandmother's stories (28). Santería, with its view of the world as infused by invisible spirits, represents in the novel that part of Cuba's history that has been rendered nearly invisible but that still haunts.[31]

Dreaming in Cuban lacks the strong element of anti-imperialist political criticism that characterizes much Afro-Cubanist literature (however much that literature may ultimately result in what Kutzinski calls "a depoliticized ethnographic discourse"); unlike the Afro-Cubanists, García does not look to black culture as an antidote to U.S. commercialism and cultural hegemony.[32] In the same paragraph in which Pilar describes the magical alchemy of Cuba, for example, she decides that she must return to New York, "where I belong—not *instead* of here,

but *more* than here" (236). Afro-Cuban culture provides not an indigenous antidote to America but a model for an American identity founded
on cultural translation—or, to borrow a term from Fernando Ortiz,
"transculturation." Ortiz, whose anthropological work inspired the Afro-
Cubanist movement, coined the term "transculturation" to describe the
process by which Cuba's syncretic culture emerged. Dissatisfied with the
term "acculturation," commonly used by sociologists and anthropologists as a synonym for a one-sided assimilation, Ortiz introduced transculturation to denote an active interchange, a give and take that results
in "a new syncretism of cultures." Ortiz describes this interchange, not
as a system of happy, unfettered pickings and choosings, but as a complex and disorienting series of readjustments on the part of peoples
"torn" from origin cultures. Ortiz defines transculturation as a concept appropriate to the history of Cuba's influxes of peoples (he names
the waves of Spaniards, Africans [Ciboneys, Tainos, Mandingas, Yolofes,
Hausas, Dahomeyans, and Yorubas], Genoese, Florentines, Levantines,
Berbers, Indians from the mainland, Jews, Portuguese, Anglo-Saxons,
French, North Americans, and Chinese). "This is one of the strange
social features of Cuba," Ortiz observes, "that since the sixteenth century [with the extermination of aboriginal peoples] all its classes, races,
and cultures, coming in by will or by force, have all been exogenous and
have all been torn from their places of origin, suffering the shock of this
first uprooting and a harsh transplanting."[33]

Ortiz's description of Cuba as a nation of exiles transplanting and
remaking themselves in alien soil has clear resonance for García's examination of Cuban exiles in the United States. Ortiz's agricultural metaphor helps to explain the sequence of episodes in which Pilar visits the
botánica and then, on her walk home, is assaulted by three boys who
hold her at knifepoint and suckle her breasts before fleeing. The *botánica*
owner is described as "long and straight, as if his ancestors were royal
palms" (200), a comparison that underscores his rootedness in both
nature and Cuban culture, despite his emigration. The novel associates
the palm with either the aboriginally or natively Cuban; "royal palms,"
for example, "dwarf a marble statue of Christopher Columbus" in Havana's Plaza de las Armas (43), while the del Pino house, Pilar's ancestral Cuban home, is located on Palmas Street. The image of the Cuban
tree returns when Pilar, leaving the *botánica* and entering Morningside
Park, remembers the royal palm just outside her bedroom window in

Cuba. In a thunderstorm the tree is struck by lightning, snaps, and crashes into the aviary. The fact that the birds "[circle] in confusion before flying north" links this memory of the snapped ancestral tree with Pilar's own severance from her Cuban family, and particularly from her grandmother. The sexual assault on Pilar that immediately follows this memory violently parodies the bond between children and their mothers; with their eyes "hot and erased of memory" (201), Pilar's young attackers represent the perversion of family connection. The assault may allude to Sethe's forced nursing by boys in *Beloved*, a scene also linked to the destruction of family ties. Sethe's attack is followed by a whipping that produces on her back a welter of scars resembling a "chokecherry tree."[34] The link in *Beloved* between a forced nursing and a "tree" on the victim's back finds an echo in García's novel: after her attackers flee, Pilar sits at the base of an elm tree, pressing her back against the tree and closing her eyes. Through her body, she "can feel the pulsing of its great taproot, the howling cello in its trunk. I know the sun sears its branches to hot wires" (202). At this moment of severe disorientation, Pilar "grounds" herself by imagining the rootedness of the tree. The hot "searing" of the branches evokes the lightning damage to her Cuban palm; the "howling" of the elm recalls the "whin[ing]" (201) fronds of the palm as it crashed to the ground. Uprooted from her original home, Pilar has in a sense replanted her felled Cuban tree in American soil. Although the royal palm is transformed into the American elm, Pilar's ability to hear the tree's living spirit reflects a Santerían perspective of the natural world as infused with spirit: the American tree speaks with an Afro-Cuban voice.[35] García will rework this imagery in *The Agüero Sisters*, further clarifying the connection of the lightning-struck tree to translation: "Lightning strikes a nearby cluster of palms. The tallest tree flares up in a plume of smoke. A black gash divides it in two. . . . Reina decides that this isn't an accident but an act of translation. Only she doesn't yet know the language" (230). The splitting of the Cuban tree provides a metaphor for the division of Cuban families through exile, a division that leads to the doubleness of bilingual, bicultural translation. In attempting to understand the translation that evades other characters, Pilar receives assistance from the spirit-infused perspective of Santería. That lightning—in both García's novels the metaphorical agent of family division—names the weapon of Changó, the Thor-like hurler of thunderbolts, casts Santería less as an expression of Cuba's

desk as she wrote *Dreaming in Cuban*.[39] Morrison's protagonist Milkman
Dead is, much like Pilar, young and adrift. The two novels share a basic
narrative trajectory: after much confusion about identity, a young protagonist must, toward the novel's end, recover an obscure family history
by making a trip south. Traveling to Virginia, where his father was
raised and where his slave ancestors labored, Milkman ends up in the
woods, sitting at the foot of a sweet gum tree. Here he lets go of all that
has hampered him; throwing off "the cocoon that was 'personality,'" he
is suddenly able to perceive the world around him with "some other
sense." He hears the "howl" of the hunting dogs, a "low *howm howm*
that sounded like a string bass," and realizes that he is hearing the pre-
verbal "language" that men once shared with animals. Like Pilar listening to the tree through her body, Milkman "sank his fingers into the
grass" at the base of the tree "to listen with his fingertips," a listening
that saves his life (because he senses an attacker approaching). The echoes in García's text are obvious: Morrison's "howl" of the "string bass"
becomes García's "howling cello" that harkens back to the "heirloom"
acoustic bass; the trees in both novels mark the site of an attack. More
importantly, both trees are associated with the recovery of ancestry. We
are told that "Down either side of his thighs [Milkman] felt the sweet
gum's surface roots cradling him like the rough but maternal hands of a
grandfather."[40] While Morrison performs a curious inversion of gender
roles (giving the maternal hands to a grandfather), García accomplishes
a different inversion of the "natural."[41] Returning to the description
of the elm, we note that the elm tree is described as casting shade with
its "aerial roots" (200). The youngest members of the "family tree,"
the spreading branches, are transformed into its elders, the "roots" or
origins. Pilar envisions the branches as roots because their form is similar, yet her metaphor depends on the crucial difference of element, air
rather than soil. In an alien element, transplanted onto American soil,
the youngest members of the Cuban family become, in a sense, their
own ancestors, an inversion of natural order necessary in order to make
sense of the new reality in which they find themselves. The new Cuban
Americans must refashion the cultural inheritance they receive in fragments, often from unreliable sources, so that it speaks to their experiences of a world so different from what their elders knew. Both Pilar's
visit to the *botánica* and her experience under the elm tree, connected
as they are to the worldview of Santería, anticipate her recovery of the

nation obviously sanctions Pilar's "bad-seed" rebelliousness, ironically making it an index to familial tradition (most family members, after all, can be considered rebellious outsiders in one form or another: Celia in her iconoclasm, for example, or Lourdes in her resistance to Cuban upper-class airs, or Felicia in her eccentricity and eventual madness). The fact that "recombinant light" must dissolve "hard lines" in order to get to "essences" gestures toward Pilar's rejection of the "hard line" politics of both island *compañeros* and exile anticommunists. The militant Lourdes's vision, for example, is marked by a preference for strong, divisive lines: she finds the view of New York from the Brooklyn Bridge comforting because the "grid of steel cables" divides the cityscape "into manageable fragments" (24). For Lourdes, stark lines provide definition: viewing a pale sky through the bridge's sooty "lattice," she finds the "black outlines [the sky], defines it" (195). Pilar's desire to find a special light that dissolves such severely defining lines also hints at her need to "disintegrate," in order to "rearrange," familial lines. The light in which she paints, which by disintegrating hard lines gives a ghostly indeterminateness to the world around her, illuminates Pilar's imaginative re-creation of her heritage. Excessively definite family lines have the unexpected effect of removing the heir from the "essence" of familial heritage; the distancing of exile, while painfully disorienting, gives Pilar license to recombine and rearrange familial givens. In "disintegrat[ing] hard lines and planes," Pilar draws close to Celia's "disregard for boundaries," which she comes to see as the "essence" of her grandmother's "legacy" (176). She also, rather surprisingly, draws close to Lourdes, whose severe dieting leaves her feeling "transparent, as if the hard lines of her hulking form were disintegrating" (167). The verbal echo, however, serves to underline the essential differences between these two disintegrations: whereas Pilar dissolves to prepare for new combinations, Lourdes loses her identity, becoming "transparent" or ghostly in a purely negative sense. Unlike her mother, who is so haunted by "Old sentences" that new words "refuse to form in her mouth" (237–38), Pilar will be able to "recombine" the old words to reframe the family's narrative of alienation and division.

Pilar's "recombinant" ethnicity stands in stark contrast to the model of identity offered by Felicia's twin daughters, Luz and Milagro, those "double stones of a single fruit" (38). García gives Luz, who speaks for both sisters, a brief first-person narrative, commanding comparison with Pilar, the novel's central first-person narrator. Luz exults in the strength her twinned identity with Milagro provides: "We're a double helix, tight and impervious. That's why Mamá can't penetrate us" (120). Defending themselves (quite understandably) against a dangerously erratic mother whom they often call "not-Mamá," the twins unintentionally ensure, on a purely biological level, familial continuity: they stand as a DNA spiral that will not split, the necessary first stage in recombination. Genetic mutations begin with a division of the DNA helix, each strand of which is then free to recombine with a new and different genetic configuration. That Felicia's children are, in a biological sense, more genetically hybrid than Pilar (the description of their father, Hugo, indicates he derives from black and Indian ancestry, whereas Felicia is identified as white) underlines the fact that García's genetic metaphors refer us to cultural, as opposed to purely biological, ethnic recombinations. Luz and Milagro remain impervious to translation, "speaking in symbols only they understand" (38). They are also the only family members to remain in Cuba after Celia's death. The novel implies that exile, while a condition of loss, provides a highly fertile "matrix" for new, syncretic identities. The splitting of exile, a temporary loss of identic wholeness, produces through transplantings new ethnic syntheses. García's "recombinant" ethnicity resembles formulations of "hybridity" we find in postcolonial thought. Salman Rushdie's observation that "mass migrations" create "radically new types of human being: people who root themselves in ideas rather than places, in memories as much as in material things," "people in whose deepest selves strange fusions occur, unprecedented unions between what they were and where they find themselves" works with metaphors quite close to García's own: "strange fusions" and "unprecedented unions" producing "new types of human being" strongly resembles *Dreaming in Cuban*'s "genetic" ethnic recombinations.[42]

For Rushdie, the "strangeness" of the new ethnic fusions derives in part from their being unhinged from "material things"; that is, ethnic identity for emigrants is, more so than for the unexiled, a product of memory's imaginative reworking of origins. García stresses the "immaterial" nature of strange ethnic fusions in another way, by linking "recombination" with ghostliness. Pilar mentions twice that her "recombinant light" is "violet" in color (178). A violet or blue light—like Pilar's "recombinant light"—marks the appearances of the novel's ghost: when

Jorge appears to Celia, his "blue eyes are like lasers" that turn the house "blue, ultraviolet" (5). Jorge, whom Lourdes buried with "a bouquet of violets" (64), returns regularly to Lourdes at dusk, when the "twilight falls in broad violet sheets" (72). On his final appearance, when he announces to Lourdes that she will no longer receive his ghostly visitations, the sky is appropriately a "near-absent blue" (195). García borrows from Wallace Stevens (who provides the novel's epigraph) the association between blue and the imagination; blue also, as García herself has pointed out, evokes Cuba's seascapes.[43] Cuba belongs to the blue, ghostly world of the imagination; it names for Pilar less a real than an imagined, magical place—this is true even when she returns to Cuba and comes to know her grandmother and the island in a much fuller way. Pilar cannot help but see her grandmother in her "recombinant," blue light: "So tell me how you want to be remembered," she teases Celia on a morning lit by "transparent blue" light; "I can paint you any way you like" (232). But although Celia asks to be painted young, slender, and in dramatic red, after a few obliging attempts Pilar settles on blue portraits: "Mostly, though, I paint her in blue. Until I returned to Cuba, I never realized how many blues exist. The aquamarines near the shoreline, the azures of deeper waters, the eggshell blues beneath by [sic] grandmother's eyes, the fragile indigos tracking her hands. There's a blue, too, in the curves of the palms, and the edges of the words we speak, a blue tinge to the sand and the seashells and the plump gulls on the beach. The mole by Abuela's mouth is also blue, a vanishing blue" (233).

Pilar's list tellingly ends in a "vanishing blue," a hint that Cuba's blue ghostliness results from its "fad[ing]" (138) as a real home for Pilar. The novel's Cuban-American ethnic "recombination" partakes of the ghostly because it operates largely in the absence of the material reality of Cuba. As the ethnic go-between traveling between death and life, the United States and Cuba, the ghost represents the force of ethnogenesis itself, constructing "new types of human being" out of the workings of memory. Even the words Pilar and Celia share are tinged with blue, reminding us of Felicia's ability to translate the languages of colors. Pilar has come to Cuba for the "truth" her mother denies her; what she finds is the inescapable filtering of her first homeland through the exile's blue imagination. Pilar leaves Cuba shortly after she has "used up most of her blue" paint (230). Refusing her mother's evasions of truth but seeing Cuba always in a blue, imaginative light, Pilar finally mediates between

Felicia, who madly relishes the colorful imagination's transformation of lies to truth, and Lourdes, who holds that truth is always a simple matter of "black and white."

In Cuba, Pilar finds her closest ally in the family's youngest member, Felicia's thirteen-year-old son, Ivanito, who in each of the novel's three sections delivers a first-person subchapter. Ivanito's attraction to the Russian language because it bespeaks a "colder world, a world that pre-served history," while in his native Cuba "everything seemed temporal, distorted by the sun," reveals his desire to escape not only Cuba's insu-larity but his adored mother's distortions (146). Yet Ivanito resists his twin sisters' reductive, unimaginative thinking; he vows he "will never speak his sisters' language, account for his movements like a cow with a dull bell" (86). Standing, like Pilar, between extremes, Ivanito chooses the path of translation: when Lourdes attempts to lure him north with capitalist success stories, Ivanito tells her that instead he dreams of be-ing "a translator for world leaders" (230). Already proficient in Russian, Ivanito learns English by picking up Key West stations on his radio, where he discovers the Wolfman Jack show. The popular American disc jockey becomes his idol; he wants to "talk," like the Wolfman, "to a million people at once" (191). The choice of Wolfman Jack returns us to some of the novel's central issues: a white man named, plainly enough, Robert Smith, Wolfman Jack accomplished his flamboyant self-transformation through a racial crossing. He launched his career as the Wolfman by assuming a growly black voice to host the Motown music he loved—a necessary strategy at a time when radio stations matched music to the ethnicity of DJs.[44] The "blackface" (or "blackphone") Wolfman, whose very name emphasizes transformation, points to the idea of ethnicity as assumed rather than inherited. That the mixed race Ivanito locates the liberation of his voice in an identification with a white man who began his career as a black impersonator certainly underlines the ironies of ethnic semiosis. It appears that Ivanito's sense of freedom derives from the abandonment of identity as biologically determined, an idea linked to the experience of exile: he becomes the Wolfman when, standing in the courtyard of the Peruvian embassy with the defectors who began the Mariel migration, he lets out the DJ's signature howl: "Crraaaazzzzy!" Imminent exile propels Ivanito into a new, enlarged world of communication (finally, like the Wolfman, he "[talks] to a mil-lion people at once" [241]). Yet the Wolfman's famous howl has a special significance for the son of a madwoman: mass communication in a non-native language allows Ivanito to channel the creative, imaginative aspect of his mother's craziness—particularly her ability to converse in the multiple "languages" of color—into a less dangerous form. He receives his radio as a gift while he mourns his mother's death, intimating that the many-voiced radio replaces his mother's polyvocal presence (he turns the dial "half expecting to hear Mom singing in her deep-throated way" [191]). In Ivanito, García depicts the possibility that the movement out of one's "mother tongue" (while maintaining memory of the mother) can liberate, a view that contrasts with Pilar's earlier belief that her second and now primary language pales in contrast to the emotional expressiveness of Cuban Spanish, leaving her at a loss for words.[45] The loss of roots through exile has its compensations, not the least of which for García is the freedom to redefine confining parental or ancestral models. Pilar decides that this redefinition is possible only outside a country that, as Celia explains to her, at present "can't afford the luxury of dissent" (235).

Such geographic, linguistic, and familial dissension is depicted, however, as a serious betrayal, something close to murder. "*Ay, mi cielo,*" sighs Celia mournfully, "what do all the years and the separation mean except a more significant betrayal?" Pilar listens in silence, the tortured awareness of her own imminent abandonment of her grandmother making her "thoughts feel like broken glass in [her] head" (240), a reaction that closely resembles the "spider headache" that afflicts Maxine Hong Kingston when she similarly wrenches herself free enough from family to shape her own life.[46] After years of flirting with suicide, Celia finally commits herself to the sea when her "nomad[ic]" (7) grandchildren choose to leave Cuba. Celia's death closes the novel in a scene of extraordinary ambivalence. Celia recalls, for example, her expulsion as a child from her family home when she is sent to live with an aunt in Havana, a memory obviously triggered by her abandonment by her grandchildren. Yet she also remembers how this aunt "*taught [her] to play piano, to make each note distinct from the others yet part of the whole*" (243), a comforting lesson about the possibilities of familial connection despite difference or separation. Earlier Celia's hands failed to reach the distant notes: when she learns of Ivanito's disappearance, her hands instinctively "stretch like she's doing piano lessons" and then "crumple in her lap like injured fans" (240). Although the attempt to restrain his departure proves futile, as Celia's crumpled hands presage, the returned memory of the piano lesson in the final scene, emphasizing music's potential "wholeness," renews the hopefulness of the image. Celia's piano playing, in fact, links the drives toward travel and rootedness at home. Debussy, her most beloved composer, is forbidden to her by doctors concerned that "the Frenchman's restless style" (8) would exacerbate Celia's nervous condition. Yet in her husband's absence, she obsessively plays *La Soirée dans Grenade*, a piece that reminds her of Gustavo, the Spanish lover who has abandoned her, and of her desire to join him in Spain, but that also significantly draws on the rhythms of the Cuban *habanera*.[47] Federico García Lorca, the poet who provides inspiration for Celia's romanticism, also much admired Debussy's *La Soirée dans Grenade*, which he felt captured his Grenada perfectly and which reminded him of the Cuban *habaneras* sung by his family.[48] Celia's musical "restlessness," reflected in her playing of a Frenchman's musical evocation of Spain based on the rhythm of Cuban song, takes her full circle, in an imaginative departure from her island exile that returns her to her home.

García Lorca plays a crucial role in Celia's final scene. At the end of her life, Celia walks toward the sea, removes her shoes, and "buries her feet in the sand until she is planted, rooted as the palms, rooted as the gnarled gardenia tree." In the sudden stillness, she thinks of Lorca's dark romanticism, of giving herself up to the *"black sounds"* of poet's music. She recalls a favorite passage from "Poema de la siguiriya" and hears through the poet's words about dark rains of cold stars the call of the *duende*, Lorca's figure of the earthy, erotic imagination. The *duende* bids her *"sing,"* an invitation to the transcendence through death that figures so largely in Lorca's poetry. She enters the water, removes the earrings given to her by the Spanish lover who abandoned her forty-five years earlier, and breathes water "through her wounds" (243). Celia chooses the death by water that Lorca frequently associated with transcendence. Earlier in the novel, Celia recites to her son, Javier, Lorca's "Gacela de la huida" (Ghazal of the flight), a poem that begins *"Me he perdido muchas veces por el mar"* (I have lost myself many times in the sea) and that ends (lines not quoted by García) "I go seeking / a death of light that would consume me" (156).[49] Like Lorca's speaker, Celia desires to lose herself in the sea's "blue waves of light" (242). Lorca scholar Andrew A. Anderson notes that a desired death by drowning appears repeatedly in

Lorca's work, often in contrast to "death in burial underground." The sea in Lorca "symbolizes liberty, immensity, solitude, mystery, a potent natural force, birth, regeneration and rebirth. Thus the poet's 'losing himself in the sea' may be read as seeking solace from the anguish of life on earth, seeking to avoid physical death and inhumation, seeking forgetfulness or oblivion in the hypnotic immensity of the ocean, seeking emotional freedom on the 'high seas' of passion, but also consciously seeking some kind of moral perdition, as well as finally some sort of transcendence in identification with an infinitely powerful natural element."[50] Clearly Lorca's sea resists simple definition but carries strongly positive connotations, a fact that invites us to read Celia's suicide as something other than pure defeat. The suicide is not motivated simply by despair over her grandchildren's defections, nor by a pathetic desire to "return" to her faithless lover (her removal of his earrings marks her permanent release from his memory's sway), but by a romantic yearning for transcendence long frustrated in Celia.[51]

As depicted in García Lorca's poetry, this transcendence is contrasted with burial in the ground. Celia has in the past associated her husband's burial in the United States (in the ground, but not on Cuban land) with her family's nomadic condition (7). She begins her last scene by digging in, burying her feet in the sand until she is "rooted as the palms" (243), but as she enters the sea she uproots herself, becoming the second del Pino to refuse burial on Cuban soil. Like Pilar's lightning-struck royal palm, Celia's uprooted palms betoken the loss of Cuba as home (and graveyard) to the del Pinos. Entering the "blue waves of light," Celia merges with the ghostly recombinant light of Pilar's exilic ethnic redefinition. The connection to Pilar is underscored by the fact that the Lorca poem Celia recalls at this moment appears in English, Pilar's language. This is the first time in the novel that a Lorca poem is translated; the same passage from "Poema de la siguiriya" appears in Spanish earlier in the novel when Celia remembers Lorca's visit to Cuba (94). As Celia gives her soul to the waters dividing Cuba and the United States, entering the in-between realm that metaphorically evokes the Cuban-American condition, Celia gives herself to the powers of translation.[52] At the moment of her death, she immerses herself in the blue waters, giving herself up to the recombinant energies of the sea. Celia's self-sacrifice sanctions Pilar's choice to leave Cuba to assume a translational identity.

Yet it also makes clear that translation is founded on a death: the unrecoverable loss of the original language and the original home. In embracing her "translated" identity as Cuban American, not Cuban, Pilar forever relinquishes Cuba as her true homeland. She will never again speak in Cuban, but always in what Celia describes as her tourist's Spanish (7), falling somewhat short of García's ideal of the "truly bilingual." She will, however, compensate by "dreaming in Cuban," recuperating a version of what was lost and reinventing her Cuban ethnicity through the ghostly realm of dreams and the imagination.

García's novel concludes by emphasizing continuity rather than death. Immediately following the scene of Celia's death, the last letter Celia wrote to her Spanish lover, dated 11 January 1959, appears as a kind of postscript: "The revolution is eleven days old. My granddaughter, Pilar Puente del Pino, was born today. It is also my birthday. I am fifty years old. I will no longer write to you, *mi amor*. She will remember everything" (245). The letter reminds us that Pilar has inherited Celia's memories along with her collection of unmailed letters. Earlier, as she held Celia's callused hands and listened to her stories, Pilar felt her "grandmother's life passing to me through her hands" like "a steady electricity, humming and true" (222), an image of electrical connection that returns us to the pulsing "hot wires" (202) of the elm tree. Electric charge, which in the form of lightning rends the family tree into translated halves, also conducts the family heritage. The letter confirms Pilar's position as inheritor and replacement of Celia. In giving, for the first time in the novel, Pilar's full name (which translates as "pillar of a wooden [pine] bridge"), the letter also hints that Pilar, as family historian and translator, will support the "bridging" of American and Cuban cultures. As William Boelhower has observed, a frequent technique of American literary ethnogenesis is the mining of an ethnic name's "signifying potential."[53] In *Dreaming in Cuban*, the nonrecombinant Luz and Milagro adamantly reject the meanings of their names: when Felicia explains their names' significance ("You're my little jewel, Milagro"; "You, Luz, you're the light in the night that guides our dreams"), Luz comments sourly, "Pretty words. Meaningless words that didn't nourish us, that didn't comfort us, that kept us prisoners in her alphabet world" (120–21). Unlike the twins, who are in no danger of losing their identity as Cubans, Pilar must learn to recombine the family's "alphabet world" to arrive at the ethnicity symbolically contained in her Spanish name. In doing so, she also realizes (and translates) the names of her cousins: *milagro/luz* ("miracle"/"light") describes the magical "recombinant light," the ghostly medium through which Pilar reforms her ethnic givens to become the family's "puente del pino." The image of the wooden *puente* surfaced earlier in the novel, when Celia in a playful divination game of I Ching receives the symbol "Ta Kuo" or "critical mass." Pilar, reading from an English translation of the Chinese chart (which itself translates or decodes symbolic hexagrams) and "translating into Spanish as she goes along" (230), explains the symbol's meaning as "having a piece of wood suspended between two chairs, but piled in the middle with too many heavy objects. The pressure will eventually break it" (231). While Celia desperately but unsuccessfully tried to hold together her dispersing family, Pilar will embody, as Cuban American, the disparate family elements, the different family languages. The novel's conclusion predicts that Pilar, as Celia's heir, will realize the ethnic significance of her name, assuming her role as the family's cultural "bridge."

With Celia's suicide, Ivanito's defection, Felicia's death, and Pilar's symbolic absorption of the identity implicit in Milagro and Luz's combined names, Cuba is, rather startlingly, emptied out by the end of the novel. The twins are the only family members to remain in Cuba, but they already plan to leave for Africa when they are older (121). The disturbing implication is that Cuban-American identity may in fact be purchased by the death of Cuba: a real place becomes *merely* a ghostly memory, whatever importance it has bestowed only by those who have left. Celia's death, moreover, remains at the novel's end unmourned, suggesting that Pilar's transformation has only begun. The proper conclusion of mourning involves the "translation" or incorporation of the past into the present, a positive "haunting" that contrasts with Lourdes's silencing possession by the past. The ritual of secondary burial that organizes so many stories of cultural haunting and that is introduced in *Dreaming in Cuban* by Jorge's haunting has yet to be fully performed; while we are assured that Pilar will guard Celia's memory, we never learn exactly how she will allow Celia's ghost to inspirit her American life. Not surprisingly then, García's next novel will turn on an unfinished mourning. Refusing to be so easily and so finally put away, Cuba continues to haunt her emigrants in unsettling ways. In *The Agüero Sisters*, a Cuban

Ethnic Memory, Ethnic Mourning

In Cristina García's *The Agüero Sisters*, Ignacio Agüero remembers the death of his father, Reinaldo, who emigrated to Cuba from
the hills of Galicia toward the end of the nineteenth century. Seeing
Reinaldo stiffen with fear as death overtakes him, Ignacio's mother leans
over her husband and gently assures, "*'Go, if you must,* mi amor. . . . *Your
memory is safe with us*" (151). Yet memory is far from safe in the world
of this novel. Both the content of memories and the process of remembering itself raise suspicion, leaving characters profoundly uneasy
about their relationship to the past and, by extension, the future. One of
Reinaldo's granddaughters, an emigrant to the United States, waits in an
airport for the arrival of her pregnant daughter and contemplates the
succession of generations: "When you give birth . . . you cede your place
to another. You say, in effect, when I'm gone, you will live, you will
remember. But what is it exactly they're supposed to remember?" (211).
Confronting her own suspect memories, another granddaughter wonders "if memory is little more than this: a series of erasures and per-
fected selections" (163). Reinaldo's great-granddaughter reexperiences
in Florida the forgotten taste of the Cuban sandwich called *medianoche*
and thinks, quite unlike Marcel over his *petite madeleine*, "how close we
are to forgetting everything, how close we are to not existing at all"
(288). She is dismayed, not by the unavailability of Cuban cuisine in the
United States—she could eat a *medianoche* in Miami every day if she
chooses—but by the knowledge that even before she left Cuba, this

particularly "Cuban" food disappeared. What troubles her as she negotiates a new country is that her Cuban self seems built on quicksand: for the exile, Cuban identity is fostered by the memory of a Cuba that no longer exists. The loss of faith in memory spells the erosion of ethnic identity: when we are "close . . . to forgetting," we are "close . . . to not existing" as a *we*.

Memory is the mirror that reflects ethnicity: to be Cuban, Irish, or Jewish is, to a large degree, to remember oneself as such, a memory of connectedness that carries with it certain privileges and responsibilities. Shared memories, whether "officially" broadcast or secretly transmitted, link the generations in history and make particular social orders legitimate. Even when strong political and social forces work to shape ethnicity from without—particularly in the case of visible ethnic difference—groups create meaningful identities through a negotiation with the past they claim as their own. Social or collective memory functions first and foremost to support the identity of the group; it accretes tradition by emphasizing almost exclusively resemblances between past and present that define the fundamental characteristics of the group. Memory confirms who we are. Yet collective memories, however stabilizing to group identities, are in fact repeatedly reinterpreted over time in answer to changing needs, so that the present is informed by a past that in turn is continually revised by present perspectives. In his groundbreaking work on collective memory, sociologist Maurice Halbwachs argues that individual memory can never be completely separated from social memory, which provides the framework within which personal memory, whether consciously or unconsciously, is configured. He also observes that most groups preserve their shared memories by spatializing them: they "engrave their form in some way upon the soil and retrieve their collective remembrances within the spatial framework thus defined." Individual memories are then mapped within the mental and physical spaces of the group.[1] But what happens when dramatic historical breaks in social continuity—such as the experiences of enslavement, exile, immigration, and colonization—fracture the familiar ways of mapping memory? Stories of cultural haunting attempt to remap an often fragmented and inevitably changed memory to its new coordinates by conjuring ghosts who pass from the past into the present, from the old territory into the new. The ghosts bear witness to the rift that necessitates their presence, even as they often function to transmit a tradition threatened by accelerated or violent change.

The experience of being cut loose, to varying degrees, from the embrace of an informing social memory results in a heightened anxiety about ethnic identity. This anxiety manifests itself in a variety of fears about ghosts and haunting, often finding narrative articulation in plots of possession. In some haunted tales, such as Maxine Hong Kingston's *The Woman Warrior*, separation from one's ancestral group can render one ghostly; while in others, such as Nora Okja Keller's *Comfort Woman*, reabsorption into only partially understood ethnic traditions is imagined as possession by potentially dangerous spirits. Keller's Korean-American Beccah, terrified of her mother's pantheon of Korean spirits and longing to be a "normal" (that is, unhaunted, un-Korean) American child, is pursued by "images of the resurrected dead" (194). García's Constancia, an exile to the United States in *The Agüero Sisters*, is similarly "appalled by the tenacity the deceased have for the living, by their ferocious tribal need for reunions" (259). At issue for these troubled characters is the role of ethnic memory: how to remember safely, what to remember, how to recollect group memories no longer handed down whole, how to connect memories of the past meaningfully to the present.

The ambiguity attaching to the ghost who might possess or liberate speaks of a deep uneasiness about the nature and functions of memory. The literature of cultural haunting strongly suggests that ethnicity is a function of memory, yet it also testifies repeatedly to memory's instability and capriciousness. "Ghosts have no memory" (184–85), Chinese immigrants in Maxine Hong Kingston's *The Woman Warrior* say of non–Chinese Americans, reluctantly consigning their own children, as Chinese Americans, to this nation of ghostly amnesiacs. These immigrant parents nevertheless attempt to draw their children back by populating their imaginations with another kind of ghostliness entirely, the "invisible world" of Chinese spirits. In William Kennedy's *Ironweed*, Francis Phelan must enter the ghostly underworld of his past before he can understand how his private demons intersect with Irish-American immigrant politics, yet he is hampered in his Dantean quest by "his own repetitive and fallible memory" (223). Listening in the night to the passing tread of her ancestral ghosts, Gloria Naylor's Mama Day strains to remember something she has never herself witnessed (118). Inheriting "only fragments of her family's past," Dulce Fuerte in *The Agüero Sisters* finds she cannot distinguish "all the false histories pressed upon us" from "our true history" (144). The haunted Beccah in Keller's *Comfort Woman* realizes that "not only could I not trust my mother's [multiple and contradictory] stories" of the past, "I could not trust my own" (34). When conflicting memories contend, each validating a different conception of family and group identity, the troubled heirs of uncertain histories must ask, What is it we should remember?

This question is linked inextricably to another: How should we remember? The use of the supernatural to gain access to an inadequately known past implicitly questions the ability of conventional historiography to capture what of that past is most valuable and necessary to the present. Supplementing documented history through the phantasmal, as we have seen, is never a simple act of addition. The turn to the supernatural—to what Morrison has called "discredited" cosmologies—inevitably unsettles conceptions of history as a neutral and (even hypothetically) complete accounting of the past. We have noted how Morrison opposes the inadequacy of mere documentation to the ghostly conjuring of the past. The aim in *Beloved*, as in other stories of cultural haunting, is not simply to provide more information about the past, valuable as that knowledge surely is, nor even to acquire different kinds of information than that found in most conventional histories, though this is certainly part of every haunted tale's project. Rather, what is centrally at stake in the literature of cultural haunting is the establishment by Americans of a different relationship to historical knowledge itself. Stories of cultural haunting aim less to record than to memorialize or commemorate.

The impulse to memorialize takes, of course, many different forms; we need to delineate carefully how commemoration operates in stories of cultural haunting, especially since some of these stories implicitly oppose their own rites of commemoration to others viewed as inadequate or even dangerous. Morrison's *Beloved* provides an especially clear example. The novel is set during Reconstruction, when memorials to the Civil War were first being erected amidst considerable controversy. In his study of Civil War monuments, Kirk Savage notes that of the various planned memorials, the monuments to be built in both the North and South elevate the idea of the soldier's "loyalty," whether to the Union or to the state, and displace the issues of slavery, the Emancipation, and black participation in the war. Recasting the war "as a struggle between two ultimately compatible 'principles' of union and state sovereignty," these monuments came to be generally perceived, though this perception was rarely articulated, as gestures of a whites-only reconciliation. Savage concludes that commemorations can be as much about forgetting as about remembering: "Public monuments are important precisely because they do in some measure work to impose a permanent memory on the very landscape within which we order our lives. Inasmuch as the monuments make credible particular collectivities, they must erase others; or more precisely, they erase the very possibility of rival collectivities. But the cultural contest that monuments seem to settle need not end once they are built and dedicated. Monuments can be reappropriated, combatted with countermonuments, or even . . . taken back down."[2]

Beloved can be read as such a "countermonument," responding directly and critically to the erasure of blacks in the monumentalizing of a reunited white national collective. The novel's first chapter introduces a headstone carved with the word "Beloved," an inadequate monument replaced by the countermonumental text of *Beloved* itself. Morrison has identified memorialization as the central impetus for the novel:

> There is no place you or I can go . . . to summon the presences of, or recollect the absences of slaves; nothing that reminds us of the ones who made the journey and of those who did not make it. There is no suitable memorial or plaque or wreath or wall or park or skyscraper lobby. There's no 300-foot tower. There's no small bench by the road. There is not even a tree scored, an initial that I can visit or you can visit in Charleston or Savannah or New York or Providence or, better still, on the banks of the Mississippi. And because such a place doesn't exist (that I know of), the book had to.[3]

The two alternative activities Morrison assigns to memorial sites—summoning presences and recollecting absences—are brought together in the present/absent figure of the novel's ghost, who makes visible an erased history and collectivity. Morrison's textual monument, however, differs from the war monuments Savage describes not only in honoring and thereby establishing the legitimacy of a "rival collectivity." The novel's conclusion, which refuses to resolve fully the ghost's haunting, works against the sense of finality and permanence that monuments typically are intended to project—an illusory permanence that, as Savage notes, derives from the attempted erasure of rival perspectives on the past. Moreover, by describing how the black community decides to "forget" what the ghost represents, the novel calls attention to how groups (even minority or oppressed groups) forge identities through selective erasures, a strategy that could be defined as "counter-monumental" since bringing the process of communal forgetting to the foreground makes visible what most monuments render invisible. *Beloved* thus suggests that commemorations, while chiefly designed to honor, may not entirely exclude ambivalence or critical perspective, though this potential is developed in cultural ghost stories to markedly varying degrees from author to author. The continued presence of the ghost at the novel's end, despite the black community's efforts to erase its existence permanently, also reminds us that the community's narratives about the past contain telling silences. The strong emphasis on storytelling and multiple perspectives in most stories of cultural haunting tends to undercut the idea that commemoration necessarily involves the imposition of a permanent and static memory.

In commemorating the past, stories of cultural haunting are always invested in, and in some cases are organized by, rituals of mourning. While ethnicity generally can be understood as a function of memory, which establishes the sameness of persons and groups despite changing time and circumstance, for the writers I describe as "heir-ethnographers," ethnicity is more specifically a function of mourning. Mourning represents a form of memory centrally marked by an awareness of a break with the past. The heir-ethnographer, the insider who also stands between cultures, recognizes both continuity with and distance from the collective traditions consolidated by social memory. That distance—whether construed temporally in the passing of generations or geographically in the movement away from the old country or, most often, both—is figuratively represented in the movement of the ghost from one realm to another. As restless or invasive spirits, the ghosts propel characters toward the completion of a mourning that, if properly accomplished, allows the past to be in some sense revised and incorporated into the present. We have already seen how Erdrich, Morrison, and García employ a thematics of mourning to represent the process by which ethnic identity can be redefined. In this final chapter, I want to return to the theme of mourning to illustrate how pervasively it struc-

of Cocoa's great aunt, whose childhood death by drowning in a well led Cocoa's grief-maddened grandmother to drown herself, an act that eerily echoes the plunge their enslaved African ancestor, Sapphira, takes off a cliff overlooking the Atlantic (a reworking of legends about slaves flying back to Africa). The violent history of slavery plagues the family by replaying itself in slightly different forms through the generations: memory, unacknowledged and secret, will embody itself in each generation until "exorcised." *Mama Day* suggests that the curse of endless repetition will be lifted only when the devastation of slavery is properly mourned. As the novel appears to be sliding toward yet another tragic repetition, a key turning point occurs: Cocoa's spiritual guide, Mama Day, tears off the wooden lid that sealed up the family well after Peace's death, releasing a collective "screaming" from the well's black cavity (284). The scene, recalling the classical maxim that truth is found at the bottom of a well, stages a symbolic exhumation, an intentional opening up of past pain necessary before the dead can be fully and properly mourned. The knowledge Mama Day draws from this well of past pain cannot save Cocoa's husband George, who, fully acculturated to mainstream society, persists in believing that "Only the present has potential" (23). Nevertheless it succeeds in lifting the family curse by bringing the past to light: once Mama Day connects the family's present predicament with its slave history, the family is released from the unconscious reenactment of past trauma. When at the novel's end Cocoa fully understands her family inheritance and her face has been given "peace" (312), she incorporates and thus continues the no-longer-dangerous dead.

The Charles family piano in August Wilson's play *The Piano Lesson* is both ancestral totem and tomb, a site of memory and mourning. In an interview, Wilson explained what the piano represented to him: "It provided a link to the past, to Africa, to who these people are. And then the question became, What do you [do] with your legacy? How do you best put it to use?"[5] The drama centers on the struggle between Berniece Charles, who keeps the piano as a silent altar to an unspeakable history, and her brother, Boy Willie, who wants to sell this family heirloom to buy himself farmland and a future. At issue is what American blacks are to make of the historical legacy of slavery. The piano was acquired by the slave-owning Sutter family through the trade of Berniece and Boy Willie's great-grandmother and grandfather. Their sale off the Sutter plantation severed the family, leaving behind Berniece and

Boy Willie's great-grandfather, who in his grief rebelliously cut his family history into the piano's legs—weddings, births, and funerals "carved in the manner of African sculpture . . . resembling totems" (xiii), according to Wilson's notes for the setting. In 1911 Berniece's and Boy Willie's father, furious that the Sutters still owned the emblem of the Charles family history, stole the piano, losing his life in the process. For the hardworking and grimly solemn widow Berniece, the piano represents generations of misery best forgotten. She remembers her widowed mother "polished this piano with her tears for seventeen years. For seventeen years she rubbed on it till her hands bled. Then she rubbed the blood in" (52). "When my daddy died seem like all her life went into that piano" (70). Seeing the piano as a tomb that could draw in her own life as it did her mother's, she refuses to touch the keys lest she "wake them spirits" (70), but she also refuses to give the piano to Boy Willie, whom she (unfairly it seems) blames for her husband's shooting by a white sheriff. Berniece's mourning takes the form of a frozen resentment that turns inward; the racial nature of her self-abnegation is evidenced in her fierce straightening of her daughter's hair and her refusal to pass on to the girl the family stories. The locked battle between Berniece and Boy Willie is upset by the appearance of Sutter's ghost, who hovers around his stolen piano and threatens Boy Willie's life. He is the spectral manifestation of Berniece's spiritual self-enslavement, her belief, in Wilson's own words, that "self-worth" comes from "denying her past."[6] Berniece saves Boy Willie's life by playing the piano, calling upon the family ghosts to exorcise the demonic Sutter. In doing so, she implicitly forgives Boy Willie for her husband's death. Through her ritualistic chanting of the family names, Berniece performs the commemorative ceremony that reconnects her to her ancestral spirits and lifts the palling shadow of Sutter's ghost from her own soul.

The link between mourning and ethnogenesis also centrally informs Maxine Hong Kingston's *The Woman Warrior*. Kingston dedicates her book to an aunt who died shamed and unmourned: the book itself represents the aunt's secondary or proper funeral, its pages, as Kingston explicitly claims at the end of the first chapter, replacing the origami funerary offerings the Chinese make to dead ancestors (16). Like her knowledge of China, Kingston's knowledge of her aunt is secondhand, limited to what her immigrant mother tells her. Yet, also like China, the aunt looms in Kingston's imagination as the secret key to her confusing bicultural identity: to understand her aunt's legacy would clarify "what things in [Chinese Americans] are Chinese" (5). We can say then that in mourning the "no-name" aunt—who as a ghost is both dead and alive, present and absent—Kingston mourns a China both distant and near, a China she has never seen but that is palpably present in the stories her mother tells, in the family home her mother creates, in the Chinatown of her youth. Through her commemorations of her dead aunt as an ancestral spirit, Kingston defines her own Chinese-American ethnicity.

The work of mourning for the heir-ethnographer is significantly double: Kingston attempts both to put the wandering spirit of the "no-name" woman to rest and to reanimate the dead aunt as a "forerunner" (8). To mourn China as *dead* would represent a purely assimilationist process. Mourning in Kingston's work, as in other stories of cultural haunting, centrally involves the recuperation of the dead through rituals of commemoration as living spirits. Contrary to Freud, who argues that the work of mourning ends only when survivors relinquish the dead as entirely lost, the completion of mourning may in fact recover what has been lost by incorporating the dead as memorialized presences into the present. The commemorative rituals that dominate stories of cultural haunting recuperate the dead through the process of mourning. The dead, however, are not simply "restored" by these rituals but are actively re-created.

Stories of cultural haunting suggest that the true purpose of commemoration is to make whom and what we mourn our own. Commemorations lay claim, an act that subtly changes both what is claimed and who does the claiming. Kingston's transformation of an unknown, outcast relative into "*my* forerunner" (8, emphasis added) certainly illustrates this understanding of commemoration. So also does Morrison's assertion that, having rescued Margaret Garner's child from "*the grave of time and inattention*" to memorialize her in *Beloved*, she has "*seen, named and claimed*" her spirit.[7] By claiming the dead girl as her own, Morrison transforms the child into a symbol of all historically nameless victims of the slave trade and positions herself as inheritor of a particular legacy. Commemoration involves placing oneself in a special relation to the past: those who memorialize establish a "kinship" with the dead that, to the degree that it is established first and foremost through ritual (rather than through blood), can be described as ghostly. Taking sociologist Paul Connerton's point that "commemorative ceremonies prove to be commemorative only in so far as they are performative,"[8] I argue that the commemorative rituals enscripted within the literature of cultural haunting *perform* ethnicity. By speaking of ethnicity as performance, I by implication understand ethnic identity not as a thing but rather as a process. What we call ethnic "identity," all too often as if indicating a bounded, homogenous, and natural entity, represents the manifestation, at any particular time, of the ongoing symbolic process of ethnic semiosis.[9] The ghosts conjured and, with varying success, put to rest (incorporated safely into the present) through rites of commemoration should be read as active agents of ethnogenesis.

Commemorative rituals take place when memory can no longer be taken for granted. The anxiety about memory more or less evident in all stories of cultural haunting points to a general awareness of disconnection from the past, even when that past is portrayed as invading the present in troubling ways. This estrangement from collective memory can be measured by how differently the authors of America's haunted tales imagine their own conjured ghosts from how they envision the spirits of unbroken tradition. In the very act of establishing a continuity between past and present, or old country and new, their own ghosts bear witness to the discontinuity that required their conjuring. For example, Kingston comments sadly on her loss of the ghost vision that the first-generation immigrants still maintain: "Now when I peek in the basement window where the villagers say they see a girl dancing like a bottle imp, I can no longer see a spirit in a skirt made of light, but a voiceless girl dancing when she thought no one was looking" (205). The ghost who opens *The Woman Warrior* is a very different creature from the villagers' dazzling "spirit in a skirt made of light." Just before her death, the "no-name" aunt is a vulnerable "bright dot in blackness, without home, without a companion," brutally cut off from the "roundness" of village life (14, 13). An anomalous "tribal person alone" (14), she reflects Kingston's fear that, as a Chinese American who publicly condemns the misogyny of Chinese culture, she may have inherited a tribal culture only to be cast out. The "no-name" ghost who "haunts" Kingston's book derives its power from Chinese tradition but represents the price of transgressing that tradition. For Kingston, the ghost is, as Thomas J. Ferraro has sharply observed, "the embodiment of a partially alien culture that justifiably seeks its revenge upon her, a revenge she experiences not as an assimilated colonial, for whom a ghost is but a cartoon, but as an American-born daughter who is Chinese enough to know what a ghost means in its own idiom."[10] "Chinese enough" but partially alienated, Kingston shapes a haunted textual memorial that gives evidence of both cultural rupture and persistence.

As memorials that testify at once to cultural continuity and discontinuity, stories of cultural haunting can be said to function as *lieux de mémoire*, historian Pierre Nora's term for "the embodiment of memory in certain sites where a sense of historical continuity persists" despite a "consciousness of a break with the past." For Nora, these memory-sites differ from true "environments of memory" (*milieux de mémoire*) in their awareness of an alienation or distance from the past; they speak of both cultural persistence and estrangement. *Lieux de mémoire*, which can take the form of places, objects, or texts, are not simply repositories of the past; these sites that serve to anchor collective memory are invested by the imagination with a symbolic aura, and they are always associated with ritual. They originate not as spontaneous memories but as deliberate, consciously willed attempts in a deritualized world to commemorate the past. Part of this self-consciousness is directed at the operation of memory: Nora points out that modern places of memory "complicate the simple exercise of memory with a set of questions directed to memory itself." The deliberate, studied nature of *lieux de mémoire* attests to an ineradicable distance from the ingrained and unthreatened memory of living tradition, a collective memory that seamlessly connects the past to the present.[11]

Nora's concept of the *lieu de mémoire* as a symbolic site that anchors a threatened collective memory depends upon a larger historical schema in which living social memory is supplanted by modern critical history, a development he sees beginning in the nineteenth century. Nora defines social or collective memory as living tradition, an unconsciously evolving dialectic of remembering and forgetting that creates a sense of unbroken continuity with the past; as such, it belongs to a time when traditions thrived without being interrogated. History, by which Nora means modern critical and analytic histories, inadvertently undermines social memory by questioning its central myths and by reminding us of the pastness of the past. For Nora, *lieux de mémoire* belong to this realm of history, harkening back to a collective memory that in fact no longer exists. I do not accept Nora's premise that social memory and history in all cultures belong to separate historical periods, with some point in the nineteenth century marking the fall into historical self-consciousness.

Different forms of memory, including those that Nora describes as the collective and the historical, can and do exist side by side.[12] Nevertheless, Nora's idea that certain places of memory—and the commemorative rituals associated with them—betoken an awareness of collective memory as fragile and threatened resonates with the anxiety underlying stories of cultural haunting. Central aspects of *lieux de mémoire* mark these haunted texts: the awareness of simultaneous continuity and rupture, the deliberate preservation by individuals of a collective memory seen as threatened, the sense that remembering is no longer a simple and unproblematic act. But in their plots of possession and exorcism, these texts diverge from Nora's considerably less troubled places of memory.

The authors of haunted ethnic stories, to greater and lesser degrees, share an awareness of some form of rupture: gone is the unproblematic, unquestioned, unthreatened inclusion in ancestral or old-world culture. In their negative aspects, the ghosts of haunted ethnic literature can remind us of a diminished sense of embeddedness in tradition: the ghosts come from *some other place* to the present, often bearing across the divide a piece of lost culture. In Gloria Naylor's *Mama Day*, for example, the novel's ghosts are associated with the environs of a house called the "other place" (225), the site of the Day family's ancestral slave history. The family head, Miranda, finds hidden in the rafters of this house a family ledger and her slave ancestor's documents of sale, but this "archive" fails to give her the full knowledge of the past she craves. This intimate knowledge comes only when the ghost of her African ancestor, Sapphira, appears to her. Undoubtedly a symbol of connection to an African past, and to an Africanist worldview in which the living and the dead remain in close connection, the conjured ghost also reflects Miranda's exclusion—without deliberate and sustained effort—from what historian Yosef Hayim Yerushalmi calls the "eternal contemporaneity" of social memory: Miranda desperately needs the ghost precisely because crucial parts of her past have been violently erased and are no longer available through any other means.[13]

In many haunted tales, the transmission of culture itself represents a form of departure. When, for example, Chippewa oral tradition is written down and revised by Louise Erdrich, tradition is not severed but is substantially changed. As we have seen, Erdrich's transmission of tradition contains within it an awareness of a rift, even as she asserts that revisionism is itself "traditional." For those writers inheriting strong oral traditions, the very act of writing family stories indicates a displacement of tradition, a deviation that in turn widens tradition (always, of course, already in a process of redefinition, but less consciously or less precipitately so). These authors use various strategies to recapture a collectively memorial consciousness: Erdrich, for example, typically relies on multiple narrators to convey the communality of Chippewa culture; Kingston, in *The Woman Warrior*, constructs her individual identity by narrating the stories of many women—living and ghostly, historical and legendary—thus recovering the Chinese sense of the self as collectively defined.[14] In doing so, however, Kingston is sharply, at times painfully, aware of how she violates what Yerushalmi, in his study of Jewish social memory, calls the "enchanted circle of tradition."[15] Her opening chapter evokes this circle: the "round moon cakes and round doorways, the round tables of graduated sizes that fit one roundness inside another, round windows and rice bowls," all "talismans" of a culture's wholeness (13). Kingston secures her inclusion in the "roundness" of Chinese tradition by seeking out within that tradition models of what she calls "extravagance," which in its root meaning of "wandering beyond" refers us to both the violation of cultural norms and emigration to America. The "roundness" of tradition's enchanted circle is thus simultaneously asserted and undermined, so that Kingston's deviations and displacements of tradition, anticipated by her ghostly ancestor, the "no-name woman," become at once marginal and central.[16]

Societies bolster their social memories by establishing memorial places that serve as public reminders of a shared history: memory, as Halbwachs notes, is deliberately mapped onto the terrain. When Nora discusses the purest form of *lieux de mémoire*, those associated directly with death, he names as examples specific places, such as the cemetery of Père-Lachaise or the battlefield of Douaumont, localizations of history to which pilgrimages can be made.[17] In the literature of cultural haunting, we sometimes find the past mapped onto the present in this topographical manner: Gerald's grave, for example, in *Ironweed* forecasts the exiled Francis's reentry into the Irish community by its placement in Saint Agnes's Cemetery, surrounded by Albany's collected Irish dead. We might think also of the haunted woods around Lake Matchimanito in Erdrich's *Tracks*, or the Day family graveyard at which the narrative of Naylor's *Mama Day* takes its final rest.

But more often such localized, physical sites are a luxury not to be afforded by a generation wrenched from its past. In Cynthia Ozick's *The Shawl*, for example, a Holocaust survivor mourns a daughter murdered in the death camps, her body never to be recovered and properly interred. Instead, the memory of this daughter returns to inhabit her mother, ghostly possession replacing ceremonial entombment. "There is no place you or I can go," Morrison laments, to summon the presences of dead slaves.[18] And so her ghost arises from a watery grave, an image certainly appropriate to the unrecorded, unmarked deaths of slaves on the Middle Passage. Strikingly, the association of the tomb with water abounds in American stories of cultural haunting, with the fluid element conveying the sense of unanchored memory. We have noted already how Celia in *Dreaming in Cuban* gives herself to the waters between Cuba and America. Beccah at the end of *Comfort Woman* sprinkles her mother's ashes over a Hawaiian river, hoping that these American waters may lead her mother's soul back to her native Yalu River in Korea. In Bharati Mukherjee's "The Management of Grief," Shaila mourns her husband and sons, who plunged to their deaths in the Irish sea on a fatal flight from Canada to India. Confused about whether she now belongs in the New World or the Old, Shaila stands "knee-deep in water," floating out to sea memorial objects (a model plane, a pocket calculator, a poem to her husband), hoping that if her family is not miraculously returned to her, their ghosts will at least give her guidance.[19] In *Mama Day*, missing graves in the family plot testify to the women who died or left by water: Mama Day's mother and Sapphira, the African ancestor who originated the Day family line in America.

What happens when descendants themselves become living tombs, when the ghosts of the past are not securely ensconced in memorial sites that can be visited—and left? In story after story of cultural haunting, protagonists negotiate a way to incorporate the living past safely by moving through—and concluding—a painful process of mourning. In the hands of different authors, of course, the work of mourning takes on different inflections, depending on the historical circumstances addressed and the particular cultural storehouses tapped. Yet in each case it is through rituals of mourning that ethnic identity is redefined. I close this chapter by suggesting how a reading that attends to the interrelationship of ethnogenesis and mourning might be developed for three haunted stories by American heir-ethnographers: Paule Marshall's *Praisesong for the Widow*, Nora Okja Keller's *Comfort Woman*, and

Cynthia Ozick's *The Shawl.* These works each present haunting in different ways, but together they illustrate well how centrally and how pervasively mourning ritual organizes the literature of cultural haunting. In concluding with these haunted tales, I return to key themes developed by Erdrich, Morrison, and García: the attempted shift from malignant to beneficent forms of haunting, the incorporation of the dead through rituals of secondary burial, ghostly possession as traumatic repetition, and the ghost as a figure of a past at once intractable and malleable, refusing to be "buried" but, if properly mourned, open to redefinition.

"Shadowy Forms" in Paule Marshall's *Praisesong for the Widow*

The idea that the ghosts conjured by heir-ethnographers function as "memory sites" that reestablish connection to the insider's social memory while, at the same time, testifying to outsiderhood and disconnection finds confirmation in Geraldine Smith-Wright's comment that the largely assimilated black protagonists of Paule Marshall's *Praisesong for the Widow* and Toni Morrison's *Tar Baby* "encounter ghosts mainly because they stand outside the collective experience of Black culture."[20] While Marshall's ghosts can be said to derive from an Africanist worldview in which the dead and living coexist in one spiritual continuum, they differ from ancestral spirits that evidence an unquestioned binding of each generation to all those that came before. Even as they labor to reconfirm such unbroken symbolic lineage, these ghosts also bear witness to what necessitates them: the loss of "Africa" as the mythic source of black American identity. By the novel's end, the ghost comes to represent the process of ethnogenesis itself; that is, the ghost signals the degree to which "Africa" as the ground of an African-American identity names an imaginary construct. *Praisesong* reminds us that its characters conjure perforce from a distance. Although the novel voices some ambivalence about this fact, its main thrust is to celebrate the compensatory power of the ethnic imagination, linking this imagination to a deeply spiritual "vision."

Praisesong, published in 1983, recounts the midlife ethnic crisis of Avey Johnson, who in her journey from a fifth-floor walk-up in a rundown neighborhood of Brooklyn to the affluent and aptly (if heavy-handedly) named North White Plains has sacrificed her vital connection to black culture. As the novel opens, Avey, who is with friends aboard an ocean liner in the Caribbean, plots her escape from this long-planned vacation. Seized in the middle of the night by an inexplicable sense of illness and dread, she stealthily and hastily packs her belongings for a hasty retreat to New York. The opening description of Avey dressed in a luminous "pale" nightgown and moving through the cabin's eerie half-darkness casts her as a ghost. Her ghostliness here, as Geraldine Smith-Wright has observed, works to "reinforce the hollowness of her life,"[21] but it also serves as a reminder of the ghostly or spiritual power that will soon be awakened in her, an ethnic strength that extends from "the subtle aura, unbeknown to her, which her dark skin had given off since birth" (11). Two kinds of ghosts emerge in this novel: ghostliness associated with *paleness* connotes the assumption by blacks of white mainstream culture's materialist values, while the ghostly light that comes from *darkness* signals the presence of African ancestral spirits among their new-world descendants.[22] Avey, however, would prefer to keep her ethnic ghosts under wraps: she "feverishly" zippers and latches her suitcases "As if sealing a tomb" (16). Yet she cannot so easily keep the dead in their place. Rising up from her grave in a "colored cemetery" (41), the novel's first ghost, Avey's great-aunt Cuney, functions as the return of the culturally repressed, recalling Avey through reawakened memories to a past denied in the quest for middle-class economic security and (white-bestowed) respectability. The ghost, in fact, has already appeared before the novel opens; we are significantly apprised of this haunting through Avey's memory. Barbara Christian has observed that Marshall's "entire opus focuses on the consciousness of black people as they remember" a "spiritual/sensual integrity" that stands "against the materialism that characterizes American societies."[23] While it is certainly true that in Marshall's work characters rely on memory, whether of a personal or mythic (African) past, to establish a specifically black identity, it would be more accurate to say that in *Praisesong* black identity is a function of mourning. More so than memory, which at least minimally acknowledges the pastness of the past, mourning represents a way of remembering that brings into relief a break in continuity. *Praisesong* is organized by two key mournings: the novel's first two sections, "Runagate" and "Sleeper's Wake," describe Avey's aborted cruise and her belated mourning for Jay, her dead husband. In the second two sections, "Lavé Tête" and "The Beg Pardon," Avey sails to the island of Carriacou, where she participates in a commemorative ritual honoring African ancestors. In each case, the scene of mourning is preceded by a water voyage and is introduced by the appearance of a ghost or ghostly figure. It is not simply in embodying memory or "bringing the past to life" that the ghosts in *Praisesong* become vehicles of ethnicity; they propel the protagonist toward rituals of mourning or commemoration through which she "performs" a newly redefined ethnic identity.

Avey's very presence on a cruise ship is linked to death. She initiated her annual cruise vacations in 1974, when her husband "had been dead only a little over a year." "It'll take your mind off Daddy" (15), her daughter Annawilda encourages, not understanding her mother's inability to grieve for her dead husband. Jay, whom Avey began to think of as the severe and distant "Jerome Johnson," in fact died in spirit years before his biological death. Determined to escape poverty and frustrated by the racism he encounters, the fun-loving, musical, sexual Jay commits spiritual suicide, becoming the grimly ambitious and acquisitive Jerome Johnson, whose economic journey to North White Plains requires that he and Avey spurn the African-American culture in which they were once immersed. Gone are the nightly dancing to "Flying Home," "Take the A-Train," "After Hours"; the recitations of beloved poems by Hayden, Dunbar, and Hughes; the ritual chicken and waffles at Dickie Wells; and the Sunday radio filling their Brooklyn apartment with the "black voices" of Wings Over Jordan and the Five Blind Boys of Atlanta, Georgia. These "black voices" that rose "like spirits ascending" (124) are banished from the Johnsons' middle-class existence, to be replaced by another, less positive (and less black) form of ghostliness. To Avey's eye, Jay's visage shows the "pale outline of another face superimposed on his, as in a double exposure" (131). This second, false face hovers "pale and shadowy" (132) over the face of Jay, "pale" because it is modeled on white middle-class respectability, "shadowy" because "Jerome" emerges as the insubstantial ghost of the once vibrant Jay. Formal and unemotional at Jay's funeral, Avey looks into the casket to see that same "joyless" mask still attached in death. Jerome Johnson's "sealed face" (133) reflects Avey's own emotional entombment, her need to close off memories of their Brooklyn life just as she locks her suitcases: "As if sealing a tomb."

Avey needs to mourn not Jerome, who is only a dead ghost, but Jay, and through Jay, the loss of her former self. She is moved toward this task by the appearance of her great-aunt Cuney, who rises up from the "colored cemetery" to haunt Avey vacationing on the all too obviously named *Bianca Pride*, bringing a denied blackness into the ship's metaphorical whiteness. In a dream, Cuney's ghost summons her great-niece to a spit of land called "Ibo Landing" on the South Carolina tidewater island of Tatem.[24] Here, according to Cuney's grandmother Avatara, after whom Avey was named, the family's enslaved African ancestors were first landed. During her childhood summers in Tatem, Avey regularly made the journey to Ibo Landing with Cuney, who always told the legend of the Ibos with "the voice that possessed her" (38), presumably the voice of the original Avatara. Cuney's possession echoes in turn the possession of Avatara by the Ibos who take one look at the New World and return to Africa, miraculously walking across the water: "*Her body she always usta say might be in Tatem, but her mind, her mind was long gone with the Ibos*" (139). To Jerome's possession by the false values of (white American) materialism, Cuney opposes the desirable possession by African ancestral spirits. The ritualistic pilgrimages to Ibo Landing and the retellings of Avatara's memory (a version of the popular African-American folktale about slaves walking or flying over the Atlantic to Africa) re-create history.[25] As Cuney stands "on the consecrated ground," her shadow is drawn by the afternoon sun "out over the water at their feet" (39), as if she herself—or rather the shadowy or spiritual aspect of herself—repeats the same action of the Ibos. Cuney's ghost provides the novel's first clue to Marshall's understanding of commemorative ritual. The performative aspect of ritual repeats the actions of ancestors or, to borrow Paul Connerton's description of commemorative ceremonies, "re-present[s]" the dead in the sense of "causing to reappear that which has disappeared."[26]

Avey, of course, resists this ghostly behest (she is too well dressed for the occasion, she reasons in Jerome-like fashion), but the disturbing dream nevertheless sets in motion the spiritual crisis that ultimately leads Avey to abandon ship. Feeling mysteriously ill (an uncomfortable gastrointestinal "fullness" clearly evoking her materialistic excess), Avey heads for Grenada, the nearest island, from which she plans to fly back to New York. She escapes one ghost, however, to confront yet another: in a Grenadian hotel room a business-suited Jerome appears to rebuke her for the wasted vacation money. The sight of her husband now brings back memories of Halsey Street in Brooklyn, memories denied for forty years (a biblical wilderness of emotional deadness). For the first time in the four years since his death, Avey "was mourning him, finally shedding the tears that had eluded her even on the day of his funeral" (134). Deciding that they "could have done both" (escaped their economic precariousness while retaining their sense of blackness), she mourns "not his death so much, but his life" (139, 134), a *black* life unnecessarily sacrificed to the pursuit of economic security. The mourning is described repeatedly in terms of water imagery: her grief is "the bursting forth of a river"; it is a "bewildering flood" that "inundat[es] her mind" (139). Avey's symbolic drowning prepares for her resurrection in the novel's second half. The section in which she mourns Jay is appropriately named "Sleeper's Wake": through her "wake" or mourning for Jay, she is awakened from her deathly state.

The title of the third section, "Lavé Tête" (referring to the washing of the initiate's head in voodoo ritual), picks up the potential baptismal implications of Avey's immersion in grief.[27] In this section Avey, wandering aimlessly along the beach, encounters Lebert Joseph, who convinces her to delay her return to New York in order to witness a Carriacouan Big Drum.[28] While not a literal ghost, Joseph has one foot in the world of ghosts. His "shadowed" eyes pierce Avey's soul, recalling the extraordinary vision of the Ibos who "could see in more ways than one" (161, 37). Just as Jerome's "double exposure" face marked him as a ghost, the lame Joseph's doubleness signals his ghostliness: the weight of his years "bent him almost double over [his walking] stick and turned him into an apparition that had come hobbling out of Shad Dawson's wood to frighten a child on a dark country road" (233). Avey refers here to the haunted wood on Tatem, next to which the ghost of Cuney appeared in her dream. Joseph fulfills in the novel's second half the ghostly function of Cuney in the first half: he annoys and provokes Avey into undertaking the work of mourning. The mild "duplicity" (253) he employs to get Avey to the nearby island of Carriacou, where the Big Drum ceremony is held, further connects him to the images of ghostly doubles, while also indicating his nature as a spiritual trickster. Hobbling on legs of different lengths, Joseph is a manifestation of the Dahomeyan trickster Legba, the lame god of crossroads and gateways.[29] As a mortal "shadowed" by his divine other self, Joseph, much like Cuney's ghost, mediates the natural and supernatural realms for Avey.

On the night of the Big Drum, Joseph's appearance as an "apparition" makes Avey suspect she has "been indeed seeing things" (233), hinting that, through Joseph's influence, Avey's vision is being broadened to approximate the special vision of the Ibos, who see the past and future in the present, ancestors and descendants participating in one atemporal reality. Time is nearly dissolved in the long, climactic scene of the ritual Big Drum. As Avey walks toward the ceremonies under a starless night sky, the darkened land cannot be distinguished from the sky, the convergence of elements hinting at a similar convergence of spirit and human worlds. "Walking the blacked-out countryside," Avey imagines "that every ha'nt in Shad Dawson's wood of cedar and live oak had escaped and was following hard on their heels. She would feel them reaching for her with their ghostly arms" (231–32). Avey's memory of Tatem's haunted wood is superimposed on the landscape of Carriacou, dissolving the passage of time between her childhood and the present: Avey feels herself "to be dwelling in any number of places at once and in a score of different time frames" (232). The dissolution of time and place also further establishes Marshall's implicit argument for an African diaspora culture.[30] After Cuney's appearance, Avey realizes that the ghost was summoned by a verbal memory: listening to the patois spoken on Martinique, she hears an echo of the "slightly atonal music underscoring" the Gullah dialect of Tatem (67). Both the language and the ghosts of South Carolina's tidewater islands and the Grenadines share a family resemblance that links them to a common African ancestry. Thus when Avey walks through the haunted "blacked-out" countryside, the blackness she encounters symbolically represents the African-based ethnicity she will come to realize in the Big Drum ceremony. As Joseph guides her "across a dark moat of a front yard" (233) toward the ceremony site, Avey continues the reverse Middle Passage begun by her cruise.

The Big Drum opens with the "Beg Pardon," a ritualistic petitioning of the "Old Parents" or ancestors, followed by a series of "nation dances" performed by those who can identify their specific African ancestry (generally only the very old). The ancestral spirits are invited to join the dancers until "Kin, visible, metamorphosed and invisible, repeatedly circled the cleared space together" (239). The circular dancing vividly recalls to Avey the Ring Shouts she witnessed but could not participate in at the Baptist church in Tatem. The step is the same: a shuffle that never allows the whole foot to lift off the ground. When Avey joins the dance, she feels as if "after all these decades [she] made it across" (248)—across the divide between herself and the Shouters, and also across the divide between the Americas and Africa. In his analysis of African slave culture, historian Sterling Stuckey notes that in the central and west African regions from which most slaves were brought, "an integral part of religion and culture was movement in a ring during ceremonies honoring the ancestors." In the Americas, slaves reasserted their continued oneness with ancestral spirits by performing some version of the ring dance, often in a counterclockwise direction with the feet never entirely lifting off the ground, so that an unbroken circle is traced on the ground by the dancers' tread.[31] In *Praisesong*, Avey eventually joins the dancers, who move in a "counterclockwise direction" (247), performing a "shuffle designed to stay the course of history" (250). To "stay" here should be read to mean both "to keep up with" and "to halt": ritualistic repetition of an ancient dance has the effect of symbolically stopping time, as the counterclockwise dancing—reversing the movement of clock time—also intimates.

Stuckey adds that the circle dance "is linked to the most important of all African ceremonies, the burial ceremony,"[32] and here indeed, as the Big Drum continues, Avey begins to notice that the ceremony takes on a funereal aspect. The head drummer signals the change by drawing his thumb sharply across the goatskin, producing a "single, dark, plangent note" that "sounded like the distillation of a thousand sorrow songs":

> The theme of separation and loss the note embodied, the unacknowledged longing it conveyed summed up feelings that were beyond words, feelings and a host of subliminal memories that over the years had proven more durable and trustworthy than the history with its trauma and pain out of which they had come. After centuries of forgetfulness and even denial, they refused to go away. The note was a lamentation that could hardly have come from the rum keg of a drum. Its source had to be the heart, the bruised still-bleeding innermost chamber of the collective heart. (244–45)

Again we see Marshall's emphasis on memory: the "subliminal memories," rather than the "history" itself, ground group identity. Tellingly, it is just at this moment, as the ritual dance becomes a ritual mourning, that Avey, after years of "forgetfulness and even denial," reconnects with the collective memory of the African diaspora.

In an echo of her mourning scene for Jay, which associated grief with flooding and drowning, Avey now finds herself "engulfed" (245) by the circling dancers. She feels "an arm made up of many arms [reach] out from the circle to draw her in" (247), recalling the "reaching . . . ghostly arms" (232) of Shad's haunted wood. Embraced by a collective ghostly presence, she moves into the dance "cautiously at first, each foot edging forward as if the ground under her was really water" (248), a "repetition" of the Ibos' miraculous return to Africa. When the dancing ends, Avey becomes "Avatara," an avatar or incarnation of the divine in the earthly. She embodies her ancestral spirits by commemorating them, becoming black by allowing herself to be possessed, in an entirely positive sense, by (ancestral) ghosts. Only by participating in a ritual of mourning in which she incorporates the spirits of the dead does Avey recuperate a denied past and redefine her own ethnic identity.

In the novel's final chapter, ghostliness takes on yet another meaning. As her plane lifts off from Carriacou, Avey surveys the swiftly receding coastline below her and thinks, "Everything fleeting and ephemeral. The island more a mirage rather than an actual place. Something conjured up perhaps to satisfy a longing and need. She was leaving Carriacou without having really seen it" (254). This is a startling observation, given how earnestly Avey's apotheosis into Avatara is depicted in the preceding chapter. Moreover, this earlier chapter repeatedly asserts that Avey's vision has magically sharpened, while in her last look back at Carriacou the accuracy of her sight is suddenly cast in doubt. The ghost now names the imaginative faculty that "conjure[s] up" what we need, regardless of the "actual." Marshall clearly acknowledges the degree to which "Africa" in her novel remains an imaginative construct and, I think, reveals some ambivalence about the substitution of the imagined for the real. To see this admission of ambivalence as fully subverting the authority of the earlier mourning scenes, however, would be to read against the grain of the novel. Looking back at Avey's description of the ring dance, we note a curious shift in her perspective. Her first impressions are not particularly positive: she notes the "feeble efforts of the elderly folk to dance their nation" (239), the substitution of rum kegs for real drums, the scrubby, lifeless landscape. "All that was left," she thinks, "were a few names of what they called nations which they could no longer even pronounce properly, the fragments of a dozen or so songs, the shadowy forms of long-ago dances." She is, nevertheless, powerfully drawn in. "It was the essence of something rather than the thing itself she was witnessing. Those present—the old ones—understood this" (240). The commemorative ceremony Avey witnesses could rightly be called a *lieu de mémoire*, a site at which collective memory is confirmed, even as a break with the past is acknowledged. The essence that replaces "the thing itself," much like the "memories" that replace "history," is a "shadowy form," the ghostly or imaginative substitute for what has disappeared. Ethnicity is, for Marshall, essentially "ghostly," but by defining her ghosts in terms of African ancestor worship, Marshall celebrates the work of imagining ethnicity by representing it as a spiritual act.

"Your Body in Mine": Shamanic Ethnicity in Nora Okja Keller's *Comfort Woman*

We have seen how Marshall establishes two opposed forms of ghostliness: bad haunting as the loss of connection to symbolic kin and acculturation to white mainstream society, good haunting as the indwelling of African ancestral spirits. This spiritual indwelling represents a desirable form of "possession," through which descendants in turn more firmly possess their past as a living legacy. In Nora Okja Keller's *Comfort Woman*, the theme of possession both more centrally structures the novel and receives more ambivalent treatment than in *Praisesong*. Both bad and good forms of possession in *Comfort Woman* are associated with the Korean heritage the novel attempts to recuperate. The novel centers on the relationship between the Korean emigrant Akiko and her Korean-American daughter, Beccah, who, like the first American generation in Kingston's *The Woman Warrior*, must "figure out how the invisible world the emigrants built around [her childhood] fits in solid America" (5). Torn between loyalty to her mother and the need for individuation, Beccah at first sees her mother's Korean ghosts as cannibals, spirits who possess in order to kill. As in Marshall's *Praisesong*, Keller's novel moves from negative to positive forms of haunting, but here the task is how to transform a dangerous and bewildering pantheon of spirits into a ghostly legacy that "fits in solid America," usefully informing the present. Once again, this process of ethnic redefinition takes the specific form of mourning: *Comfort Woman* performs a "secondary burial" in which ghosts of the old country are safely incorporated into America.

Born in Seoul to a Korean mother and a white American father and raised in Hawaii, Keller has spoken of her early repudiation of things Korean. Her mother, "so conscious of her own difference," would not teach Keller the Korean language lest she further weight her American daughter with the burden of otherness. Keller comments, "I know I went through a period of feeling really embarrassed and alienated from things that were Korean. So I write now, in part, to go back to that Korean perspective and try to reclaim what I denied for so long." That reclamation takes the form of the 1997 *Comfort Woman*, Keller's first novel, an account of a part-white, part-Korean daughter's relationship with her Korean mother, who (unlike Keller's own mother) served as a "comfort woman" to Japanese soldiers during World War II. Keller has located her decision to become a writer in her experience of hearing a Korean woman at a human rights symposium tell her story of being forced by the Japanese into sexual slavery during the war. The woman haunted Keller, appearing in her dreams, until she began to transcribe those dreams—producing the embryonic form of *Comfort Woman*.[33] The historical comfort woman Keller heard speak is transformed in her imagination into a ghost who, in calling the author to bear witness, re-calls her to a denied Koreanness. That authorial haunting finds reflection in the novel's double story of haunting: Akiko, a former comfort woman now working in Hawaii as a professional shaman, is repeatedly possessed by the spirit of an executed comfort woman named Induk. Akiko's Korean-American daughter, Beccah, is multiply haunted, by the ghost of the American father who died when she was five, by the cannibalistic demons of her mother's imagination, and by nightmares in which her mother either abandons her or, holding her too closely, suffocates her. Beccah eagerly imagines the ghost of her minister father "burning with his blue eyes the Korean ghosts and demons that fed off our lives" (2), but the fantasy of expunging the dangerous Koreanness her mother exemplifies represents only a half-desire. Torn between loyalty to her mother and the need for independence, between her mother's world of Korean spirits and her American youth, Beccah is herself something of a ghost who inhabits "the boundary between Korea and America, between life and death" (116).

Beccah's announcement of her mother's death at the end of the first chapter hints that the resolution of her haunting—a resolution that will define her ethnicity—must be accomplished through the process of mourning. Beccah works as the writer of obituaries, but although she has become adept at recording the lives of the dead, she discovers upon attempting to write her mother's death notice that she does "not know how to start imagining her life" (26). Beccah cannot properly mourn her

mother until she moves beyond the limitations of the loving but per-
plexed and resentful perspective she has held since she was a little girl.
Beccah's chapters, which recount her unusual childhood as the daughter of a shaman, establish a parallel between troubled mourning and
deep ambivalence about ethnic identity. As she struggles to understand
her mysterious mother in order to mourn her, Beccah must come to
terms with her confusing and contradictory inheritances. Interspersed
in Beccah's narrative are Akiko's chapters, describing her impoverished
Korean childhood, her imprisonment as a comfort woman, and her later
reincarnation as the wife of an American missionary who "saves" her
besmirched soul, takes her to the United States, and enjoins her to silence over her shameful (but, to him, also covertly sexy) past. In the final
two chapters, Beccah uncovers her maternal "inheritance," a cassette
tape on which her mother recorded her history as a comfort woman, the
secret past that Akiko's chapters have just unfolded. At this point, Beccah
is finally able to perform the proper rites of mourning for her mother
and accepts, through the internalization of her mother's ghost, a Korean
identity she had feared and resisted.

Keller's narrative, opening with the announcement of the mother's
death in the first chapter and closing with the funeral in the final chapter, is thus organized by the structure of secondary burial, the ritual
pattern present in both Morrison and García. The period from the first,
provisional funeral (or moment of death) to the final funeral designates
the period of mourning, during which the dead as restless ghosts invade
the lives of the mourners, who themselves take on aspects of ghostliness.
Beccah, as we have already noted, is described (by Akiko) as "Bloom-
ing in the boundary . . . between life and death." Akiko understands her
violation by soldiers as a death, rendering the rest of her life ghostly.[34]
In turn, her husband, her sisters in Korea, her neighbors, all become
ghosts: "What are living people to ghosts," she remarks, "except ghosts
themselves?" (18). Only Beccah remains real to her, because in Akiko's
mind her daughter shares her status as ghost (a conferred identity
Beccah naturally enough resents, since it alienates her from all but her
mother). Akiko's ghostliness results from her traumatization, but it can
also be said that both mother and daughter partake of the ghostly because, for most of their narratives, both inhabit the intermediary period
between first and final funerals. Two mournings occur simultaneously
in the alternating chapters: just as Beccah is haunted by her as yet im-

properly mourned mother, Akiko is haunted by Induk, a comfort woman in her camp murdered by the Japanese when she rebelliously violates their prohibition against all speech. Akiko realizes that Induk chose her death by provoking the soldiers to murder. She remembers how one night Induk (renamed "Akiko" by the soldiers, who assigned all comfort women numbers and Japanese names) began talking loudly and nonstop, "reclaiming her Korean name, reciting her family genealogy, even chanting the recipes her mother had passed on to her" (20). The soldiers leave Induk's skewered body in the open as a warning to the other comfort women, who are forbidden to prepare the damaged and decomposing body for burial.[35]

Induk's death has special significance for Akiko, who until this point worked in the recreation camps as a menial, retaining her real, Korean name of Soon Hyo. Upon Induk's death, the twelve-year-old Soon Hyo "dies" by becoming "Akiko 41," the replacement prostitute: "The corpse the soldiers brought back from the woods wasn't Induk," she declares. "It was Akiko 41; it was me" (21). This transfer of identity prepares for Akiko's later possession by the spirit of Induk. When the ghost returns to rebuke Akiko for her failure to perform the proper funereal rites ("Why did you leave me to putrefy in the open air, as food for the wild animals just as if I were an animal myself?"), Akiko offers secondary burial in her own body, giving the ghost "my own hands, my eyes, my skin" to inhabit. In turn, she says, the ghost "offered me salvation" (96). Akiko's interpretation of possession as "salvation" recalls her missionary husband's attempt at converting her many years earlier. Begging her to surrender herself to Christ (and, in marriage, to him), he encouraged, "His body will become your body; your flesh, His. Just give yourself to Him!" (94). The novel is, in fact, rife with varieties of possession, most of which are clearly not redemptive. Imperial Japan possesses the body of occupied Korea, for example, while the soldiers sexually "possess" the bodies of imprisoned prostitutes.

What distinguishes clearly evil or, in the case of conversion, suspect possessions is that they all require the relinquishing of language or voice. Akiko recalls that, because of the occupation, her "mother's generation was the first in Korea to learn a new alphabet, and new words for everyday things. She had to learn to answer to a new name, to think of herself and her world in a new way. To hide her true self" (153). The comfort women also receive new names and, forbidden to speak any language at

all, are reduced to communicating with each other through bodily gestures and humming; the experience leaves Akiko mute for a long time
after she escapes the camps. Feeling too sullied by her rapes in the military camps to remain in Korea, Akiko escapes via marriage and a purely
nominal conversion to the United States, but on pain of silence: she is
never to speak of her experience during the war to her daughter. Immigration "saves" Akiko, only to effect an occupation of her voice reminis-
cent of the more drastic silencing in the Japanese camps. Akiko acknowledges the connection: "Hiding my true self," she claims, "enabled me to
survive in the recreation camp and in a new country" (153). With the
price of speech seared into her mind, Akiko grows suspicious of all verbal
language, especially of her husband's multilinguality, and determines to
teach her daughter a purely bodily communication, the only "language
I know is true" (21).

Induk's possession of Akiko's body differs from these bad forms of
possession in being associated with Induk's reclamation of her Korean
name and tongue just before her death. Through Induk, Akiko regains
connection to her family dead left behind in Korea: walking behind her,
Akiko observes that the ghost's form "would blur until it doubled, then
quadrupled," shape-shifting into Akiko's mother, grandmother, and ancestors (53). In the wave of postwar migrations and division of Korea by
a now uncrossable border, many people left behind their dead, who become, Akiko observes, "restless spirits" (104) unhonored by descendants
in the annual *chesa* or funereal ceremony. Induk's complaints to Akiko
can be read as referring to these abandoned dead, as much as to the
comfort women: "No one performed the proper rites of the dead. For
me. For you. Who was there to cry for us in kok, announcing our death?
Or to fulfill the duties of yom: bathing and dressing our bodies, combing
our hair, trimming our nails, laying us out? Who was there to write our
names, to even know our names and to remember us?" (38). Remembering her family dead by mourning Induk, Akiko performs their proper (or
"secondary") funeral. These rites of mourning reconfirm her Koreanness despite her permanent loss of Korea as home.

Akiko's surrender of her body to Induk also brings Korea to the
United States by reproducing a central component of Korean shamanic
ritual. Akiko's frequent fits of possession, though easily viewed as only
expressions of trauma-induced madness, identify her as a traditional Korean shaman. In Korean folk belief, *sinbyŏng*, or "possession sickness,"

afflicts "those whose souls have been 'fractured'" by personal tragedy or abuse; those who survive the sickness become powerful shamans, able to interpret the thoughts of the dead to the living by becoming temporary vessels for the spirits.[36] The spirits who regularly claim Akiko's soul—the Birth Grandmother, the Seven Stars, Saja the Death Messenger—are all familiar figures in Korean shamanic ritual; also traditional to shamanic practice are *honyaek*, the "Red Disaster" Akiko fears for Beccah when she reaches womanhood (77, 76); *sal*, the evil arrowheads Akiko believes have pierced her daughter's body (82); and the ballad of Princess Pari, the myth through which Beccah is taught her proper filial role. In Korea, shamans are hired to resolve domestic disruptions caused by the family's unquiet dead; allowing themselves to be possessed by these restless spirits, shamans transmit the messages of the dead to the living. One of their chief functions is to propitiate the restless dead by properly mourning them. According to anthropologist Laurel Kendall, shamans in Korea do not perform normal funereal rituals (the responsibility of ancestor worship belongs to male household heads); rather, they are called upon in times of extraordinary trouble, when "war and social upheaval" sever family ties: "These ruptures imply a moral breach in the ritual continuity of generations and expose the family to supernatural danger. A *mansin* [shaman] confirms the deaths of relatives lost in the North or separated during the war. Through a cathartic ritual confrontation and by subsequent offerings, family members alleviate grief and guilt as they draw lost kin back into the home for periodic family feasting."[37] Akiko's mourning for Induk and for her own lost youth in Korea takes the form of possession because the severe "ruptures . . . in ritual continuity" caused first by war and then emigration call for extraordinary, shamanic treatment. In Hawaii, Akiko generally works as a hired mourner for immigrants who worry about dead ancestors left behind in the old country. Akiko's mourning has centrally to do with the process by which immigrants become Americans: in her fits of possession, she reconnects the grieving living with their dead, bringing together old country and new, so that the living may "alleviate [their] grief and guilt" as they construct new lives far from natal homes. Akiko's shamanic rituals help new immigrants negotiate shifting identities and loyalties by at once confirming ancestral ties and safely distancing the living and the dead. Through her mourning, Akiko's troubled clients redefine their relationships to both the old country and the new.

In Korea, shamans are almost exclusively women who serve a largely female clientele; the rare men who practice shamanism dress as women. Several scholars who have studied Korean shamans have noted that shamanic activity, though often viewed in Korea as an embarrassment, gives many women a domestic and public authority otherwise unknown. Anthropologist Youngsook Kim Harvey, whose book on shamanism Keller mentions in her acknowledgments, argues that "possession sickness," while socially stigmatizing, allows women to "transcend the natural (culturally defined) limits of being a woman."[38] Keller's seizing upon the powerful but "outcast" shamanism as the medium through which Korean-American ethnicity is shaped can be compared to García's use of the marginal Santería to define a Cuban-American identity. In Keller's case, however, the complex implications of cross-racial (white from black) borrowing do not apply; the marginalized culture that comes to the foreground is marked by gender rather than race. In her study of Korean shamanism, Kendall notes that while women in Korea's patrilineal society are severed from their natal families upon marriage, the female client's relationship with her natal gods and ancestors, who ordinarily would have no place in the married woman's ancestral worship, often undergirds shamanic ritual.[39] Nevertheless, Kendall observes that despite this inclusion of a woman's natal kin in rituals, shamanism reflects the patrilineal bias of Korean society by more often conjuring the husband's dead relatives.[40] Here we see Keller's revision of traditional shamanic practice in *Comfort Woman:* keening for the abandoned dead, Akiko reestablishes the exclusively female (and Korean) line of ghostly ancestry that passes through her to her daughter. Her surprising inclusion of Induk, who is not a family member, in this line underscores the ghostly rather than blood ties that link the members of Akiko's "family" of female spirits. If Beccah is to be an American, as Akiko desires, it will evidently not be through her American father's line; incapable of trusting men after her disastrous war experience, Akiko shapes a Korean-American identity for her daughter by transplanting almost exclusively female Korean ghosts to America.[41]

Beccah does not see, at least until the novel's resolution, this maternal legacy as a privilege. Wanting her daughter to feel grounded in her native land, Akiko smears a bit of American dirt on her nipples before nursing her newborn. Beccah will be, Akiko determines, "an American girl" (119), but by virtue of America being fed to her through her mother's

Korean body. Beccah, however, grows up to feel swallowed by her over-protective mother and, echoing the bad forms of possession Akiko herself has known, silenced by her: she cannot speak her real thoughts lest she insult or anger Akiko. When she hears her mother's tape (a recording of a funereal ceremony for Induk and all the family women who have come to be associated with the ghost), she comes to understand both the causes of her mother's crazy behavior and the ways in which the frightening possessions have in fact preserved Korea for her. Beccah's new understanding leads her to imitate her mother's "secondary burial" for Induk by inviting the very possession by her mother she has long feared. "Your body in mine," Beccah chants during the death ritual she finally performs for Akiko (212). Earlier Beccah described her mother as a *yongson*, the "ghost of a person who traveled far from home and died a stranger" (140). By inviting her mother to live on within her, she gives her mother's *yongson* spirit a home and, at the same time, gives herself a newly imagined Korean identity. She internalizes not only her mother but the whole line of female Korean ancestors that Akiko herself internalized in her shamanic possessions. Beccah's funereal ceremony accomplishes for Akiko the recovery of ethnic self for which Induk died: the reclamation of her Korean name, language, and identity. "This is for your name, Omoni [mother]," she sings, "so you can speak it true: Soon Hyo. Soon Hyo. Soon Hyo" (209). As she chants, Beccah wraps her mother's body in strips of bed-linen upon which she has transcribed her mother's (disembodied) taped voice. The image of Akiko's body arrayed in this shroud of writing suggests a healing of the division of body and language that characterizes trauma.[42] Through Beccah's funereal ritual, Akiko is finally—although only in death—reconciled to the language she had learned to distrust.

Beccah's aloneness at this moment—she is accompanied only by her mother's body and the spirits she mourns—raises a troubling question. At the same time that Beccah performs her solitary commemoration, another funeral for Akiko is being staged to a packed audience. The financial opportunist "Auntie" Reno, who managed Akiko's shaman business, with Beccah's reluctant permission has organized a false funeral for Akiko's devoted clients, many of them Korean immigrants. Unaware that the coffin is empty, Akiko's multitude of mourners, "crammed shoulder-to-shoulder" (210), pay their respects and drop off envelopes stuffed with money, a customary practice at Korean funerals.

Beccah's mourning ceremony in effect performs her newly defined ethnicity, but she has not at the same time acquired a living ethnic community. Akiko's possession of Beccah is described as an impregnation: a "small seed planted" by Akiko waits "to be born" (213). Beccah will presumably "reproduce" her mother if she gives birth to a daughter (as Akiko felt her own mother returned to her through Beccah), but we are left with the image of Beccah alone, anticipating a purely spectral offspring. At the close of *Comfort Woman*, we can only imagine how Beccah might translate her ghostly ethnicity into living community.

Imagining the Past in Cynthia Ozick's *The Shawl*

Cynthia Ozick's inclusion in the category of American heir-ethnographer may seem at first surprising, given that Ozick has so thoroughly defined herself as the heir of Jewish tradition. Perhaps no other Jewish-American author has insisted so vehemently and articulately on the importance of being fully a cultural insider. Ozick has decried assimilated American Jews, "illiterates" in Jewish culture "who have maintained, generally via 'ethnic' food, something called 'Jewish identity' that is utterly without mental content—metaphysically and historically empty."[43] She has challenged Jewish-American writers to shun what she calls the Hellenism of Western literature, rebuilding Judaism by producing what she intends her own fiction to exemplify: a "centrally Jewish" literature, characterized by its resistance to the idolatrous and its aspirations to the liturgical.[44] In her essays and interviews, Ozick has stressed cultural continuity, almost to the point of denying that discontinuity can play any positive role in the production of Jewish (or any) culture. When asked in an interview whether "disruption and doubt" could possibly "reinvigorate a culture," in light of Irving Howe's argument that Jewish tradition "should be thought of as discontinuity," Ozick is quick to dismiss the possibility. While she acknowledges that art can be made out of discontinuity, she denies that this art can in turn reinvigorate culture on the grounds that culture depends on "heritage, received tradition, continuity." "That would apply both to culture and agriculture," she adds, "a farmer learns from the practices of his forebears, a child inherits—doesn't have to reinvent—the alphabet."[45]

Ozick's belief that culture derives strictly from inheritance, not from inventions in the face of discontinuity, distinguishes her from writers

moment of most violent rupture, the Holocaust, the subject of the short story ("The Shawl") and novella ("Rosa") published together in 1988 as *The Shawl.* Like an unwanted ghost, the subject of the Holocaust arrives, in Ozick's words, "unbidden, unsummoned," forcing its way into her writing despite her concurrence with Theodor Adorno's dictum: "after Auschwitz, no more poetry."[49] Although Ozick views remembering the Holocaust as an ethical necessity, she agonizes over the difference between historical witnessing and fictional imagining. The daughter of Russian emigrants to the United States, Ozick must imagine what she herself never witnessed, though that imagination is well fueled by extensive reading of documents and memoirs. In the fourteen years between her first published novel and "The Shawl," Ozick returns repeatedly to the theme of the Holocaust, but for the first time in "The Shawl" she sets her story directly in the death camps. When the story first appeared in 1980 in the *New Yorker,* Ozick received letters of protest from Holocaust survivors who questioned her authority to imagine the Shoah. Ozick responded by arguing that it is her duty as a Jew "to incorporate . . . into my own mind and flesh" the events of Jewish history.[50] For Ozick, mourning the Holocaust constitutes an imaginative act of empathy that affirms Jewish identity. Incorporating the losses of others into her own mind and body, Ozick makes an other's history her own; Jewish identity emerges out of this imaginative identification with an other who becomes oneself. While never relinquishing the idea of imaginative identification as a moral imperative, Ozick in a 1993 interview criticizes the identification she accomplished in "The Shawl," arguing that only the "true witness" who directly experienced the Holocaust should record it: "I don't admire that I did it. I did it because I couldn't help it. It wanted to be done. I didn't want to do it, and afterward I've in a way punished myself, I've accused myself for having done it. I wasn't there, and I pretended through imagination that I was."[51] Clearly Ozick's thinking is marked by contradiction, the sign of a strongly religious and literary mind struggling with a deep ambivalence about the nature of the imagination. Ozick approaches the Holocaust as both insider and, to the degree that vicarious suffering is never the same as real suffering, outsider: as a Jew who understands the Jewish victims "were surrogates for us," and as a Jewish-American writer who should not dare, but is nevertheless compelled, to imagine an experience of that order not directly her own.[52] In thinking about Ozick's literary treatment of the Holocaust, I want to underscore two points: first, that for Ozick mourning the Holocaust is a central and centrally defining activity for the Jew; and second, that as a Jewish-American writer who did not experience the Holocaust firsthand, Ozick, with powerful ambivalence, assumes the heir-ethnographer's position of commemorating in order to make a history that is simultaneously hers and not hers more fully her own.[53]

The Shawl diverges from the model of mourning developed by Marshall and Keller. In *Praisesong* and *Comfort Woman*, the protagonists' situations more or less mirror those of their authors: the novels' scenes of ritual mourning illustrate Marshall's and Keller's own recuperations of nearly forgotten or denied cultural legacies. I argue that, although their particular manifestations are shaped by African or Korean folk religions, the ghosts in these novels do not simply emerge from retained old-country worldviews; rather, they are symbols of both cultural continuity and rupture: their presence is made necessary by the distance of the protagonists from a living collective memory. Ozick's motivation in writing *The Shawl* similarly connects to her awareness of the failure of collective memory. Writing for an audience she sees as composed largely of de-Judaized Jews and Gentiles, Ozick has spoken passionately of "the necessity of memory in a time when memory begins to melt into history and history is discarded."[54] *The Shawl*, however, does not depict a character in search of a lost or rapidly disappearing past; Holocaust survivor Rosa Lublin is instead haunted by a history all too mercilessly present. Ozick's strategy here may be compared to Morrison's in *Beloved*, which like *The Shawl* dramatizes how traumatic memory perpetuates the damage it remembers through the haunting of a mother by her dead daughter's ghost. *Beloved*'s recuperation of the past through fantasy can be said to reflect the extraordinary measures the author must take to "remember" a nearly obliterated history, yet on the level of plot, the haunting illustrates the dangerous subsumption of the present into the past. Morrison and Ozick both tell haunted tales to commemorate the past, a commemoration that, borrowing Ozick's idea of "incorporating" Jewish history into her "own mind and flesh," mourns the past in order to establish a living connection between past and present. Each does so by describing a pathological form of "incorporation": interminable mourning as possession. Like *Beloved*, *The Shawl* is a meditation on the proper uses of memory.

In the small space of seven pages, "The Shawl" recounts the events leading to the death of Rosa's infant daughter, Magda. On the march to the camps, Rosa protects Magda by hiding her under her shawl. When her mother's milk dries up, Magda begins to suck the edges of the cloth, miraculously surviving for three days and nights on the "shawl's good flavor, milk of linen" (5). The shawl, now viewed as magical by Rosa, also protects Magda by keeping her quiet; as long as she has the shawl, Magda's silence keeps her presence in the camps unknown to the German guards. When Stella (Rosa's niece, as we learn later in "Rosa") steals the shawl from Magda to warm herself, the child wanders into an open area loudly "grieving for the loss of her shawl" (8). Rosa runs to fetch the silencing shawl but returns too late; before her horrified eyes, Magda is seized by a soldier and hurled to her death against an electrified fence. The story ends with Rosa stifling "the wolf's screech ascending now through the ladder of her skeleton" (10) by stuffing the shawl in her mouth. To cry out, attracting the soldier's attention, would mean joining Magda in death.

First published in 1983, three years after "The Shawl," "Rosa" picks up with Rosa's life in America some thirty-five years after Magda's death. Having left behind an antiques shop in New York that she herself demolished, Rosa now lives alone in Miami in a small hotel room, spending her days lost in wartime memories or in writing letters—to Stella, who now lives in New York and whom Rosa has secretly never forgiven for Madga's death, and to Magda, whose ghost periodically materializes "like an electric jolt" before Rosa's eyes. Magda's electrifying appearances, so powerful that "Rosa's ribs were knocked on their insides by copper hammers, clanging and gonging" (62), recall the child's death on the electric fence, suggesting that through Magda's haunting Rosa repeatedly relives Magda's death as her own. In her unending grief, both for Magda and for her lost Warsaw life, with its high-culture elegance and erudition, Rosa has herself become unreal, ghostly. Never in her mind having left the death camp, she lives a living death; the smashing of her store was a "kind of suicide," she admits: "Where I put myself is in hell" (46, 14). The Miami before her eyes, with its streets "a furnace," its blazing sun "an executioner" (14), is filtered through Rosa's memory of the camp. The aging retirees filling the Miami hotels, libraries, and coffee shops suffer Rosa's projections: "Everyone had left behind a real life. Here they had nothing" (16). She despises Stella's decision to move on with her life by becoming "an ordinary American," as "if innocent," Rosa growls, "as if ignorant, as if *not there*" (33). The implicit verb tense gives away Rosa's atemporal perspective: Stella offends not because she behaves "as if she hadn't been there," but "as if [now, even in New York, she is] *not there*." "There"—the construction of a memory so relentlessly vivid as to displace much of present reality—is where Rosa still lives, much as Sethe never leaves the "there" (36) of which she warns Denver in *Beloved*. As Rosa tries to explain to Simon Persky—a Jew, like Rosa, from Warsaw, but who escaped her fate by emigrating before the war—a Holocaust survivor has three lives: "The life before, the life during, the life after." For her, "Before is a dream. After is a joke. Only during stays. And to call it a life is a lie" (58). Rosa's eternal "during," reflected in Miami's hellishly scorching "Summer without end" (28), is the product of mourning gone awry. Horrific as it is, Rosa cannot exit this "lie" because to do so would expose another lie, one that sustains Rosa in her arrested life: that Magda, as Rosa fantastically asserts, survived to flourish in New York as a professor of philosophy at Columbia University. Rosa inhabits a kind of ghostly afterlife rather than relinquish her daughter as dead. When Rosa stuffs the shawl into her mouth after witnessing Magda's murder, she symbolically internalizes Magda, burying the child in the mother's body to keep her, in some sense, alive. Thirty-five years later, Rosa's incorporation of Magda has left her a walking tomb, a "shell," as Rosa puts it, with no real life inside.[55] The story's suspense lies in whether, through Persky's unwanted but persistent encouragement, Rosa can conclude her long, deathly mourning and join the living. To do so would entail an exorcism of the ghost—exhuming Magda from Rosa's own body and, ideally, reburying her in a less dangerous fashion.

Ozick complicates this mourning plot by making "Rosa" as much a story about the dangers of Jewish assimilation as about the Holocaust. "The Shawl," in its stark spareness, focuses exclusively on the present anguish of the death camp. In the novella, Rosa's memories of her Warsaw life before the war, often taking the form of letters to Magda, provide a portrait of upper-middle-class Jewish assimilation in prewar Poland:

> The Warsaw of her girlhood: a great light: she switched it on, she wanted to live inside her eyes. The curve of the legs of her mother's bureau. The strict leather smell of her father's desk. The white tile tract of the kitchen

floor, the big pots breathing, a narrow tower stair next to the attic . . . the house of her girlhood laden with a thousand books. Polish, German, French; her father's Latin books; the shelf of shy periodicals her mother's poetry now and then wandered through, in short lines like heated telegrams. Cultivation, old civilization, beauty, history! . . . Her father, like her mother, mocked at Yiddish; there was not a particle of ghetto left in him, not a grain of rot. (20–21)

The assimilation of the Lublin family in Poland is echoed by the new generation of Jewish Americans, who, if less cultivated and refined in their tastes, abandon their Jewishness with as much alacrity.[56] Florida's aging immigrant Jews, "in love with rumors of their grandchildren, Katie at Bryn Mawr, Jeff at Princeton" (17), receive letters from miraculously affluent offspring who now seem, through their acculturation, the real emigrants: "dim children who had migrated long ago, to other continents, inaccessible landscapes, incomprehensible vocabularies" (29). The retirees attempt to compensate for this cultural discontinuity between the generations by finding solace "in the seamless continuity of the body." Rosa ridicules their fantasy of eternal youth, belied by the drawn lips, the dewlaps, and the legs "blue-marbled" with veins—a mockery of the "immortal," statuesque bodies they see in their mind's eye. Yet Rosa's pitiless assessment thinly veils self-commentary. For Rosa, much as for the old Jews of Miami, "Everything had stayed the same" (28); she too imagines her youth as fantastically immortalized, not in her own body, but in Magda's. Rosa conjures Madga's ghost to recreate (and partly reinvent) her own stolen youth. Magda appears to Rosa as a girl of sixteen, near Rosa's age before the war, full of the intellectual and artistic potential that the war prevented Rosa from realizing. Rosa writes Magda literal letters, but she is also able to compose missives to her daughter "inside a blazing flying current, a terrible beak of light bleeding out a kind of cuneiform on the underside of her brain" (69). Clearly deriving its "terrible" charge from Magda's death on the fence, Rosa's "blazing" writing "on the underside of her brain" recalls, in nightmarish intensification, the "great light" of old Warsaw that Rosa switches on "to live inside her eyes": through her communication with Magda's ghost, Rosa returns to her youthful world of (non-Jewish) cultivation and gentility. The writing itself is described tellingly as "a kind of cuneiform," an alphabet of ancient Sumerians, Babylonians, Persians, and other Middle Eastern peoples, but not that of the Jews. Although

Rosa tells her ghostly daughter that she is free to be either Jewish or Gentile, the blond-haired, blue-eyed Magda—sired perhaps, as Rosa insists, by a Polish lover of Gentile and converted Jewish parentage; perhaps, as Stella contends, by one of the S.S. officers who raped Rosa—in part represents an Aryan fantasy. I read Magda's ghost not just as the traumatic representation of Rosa's maternal bereavement but also as an embodiment of Rosa's own self-denial. This view of the ghost as an "Aryan" self-projection suggests that Ozick places on a continuum Jewish assimilationism and the anti-Semitism that made possible the camps. In "The Shawl," Stella looks at the fair child and hisses "Aryan," which to Rosa sounds "as if Stella had really said 'Let us devour her'" (5). But it is Rosa who incorporates or "devours" Magda when she eats the shawl, internalizing her in the form of an Aryan version of herself. Rosa's description of Madga's face in "The Shawl" as a "pocket mirror" (4) forecasts the way Magda's ghost will reflect Rosa to herself—not exactly as she was, but partly as she aspired to be.

Rosa was schooled in her anti-Semitism by her assimilated Jewish parents, who saw themselves first and foremost as Poles of distinction, and who looked down with "a certain contempt" on the "swarm" of dirty and ignorant Jews in the ghetto (52). The outrage that breaks Rosa's cultivated, poet-mother's heart is that she should be taken by the Germans along with "them." This mother "despised" the sounds of her own mother's Yiddish cradle-croonings to the infant Rosa. All that Rosa recalls of this grandmother from Minsk is one sentence: "*Unter Reyzls vigele shteyt a klorvays tsigele. . . . Under Rosa's cradle there's a clear-white little goat*" (19). The lullaby is an adaptation of the Yiddish folk song "Unter Yankeles Vigele," in which a mother, rocking her son to sleep, tells him that like the white "kid" that "has been to market," he too will go to market as a trader in raisins and almonds. The memory of the embarrassingly Jewish grandmother and her lullaby bears ugly fruit: as an adult, Rosa derogatorily associates Jews with lowly trade. Persky's career as a seller of buttons and notions is dismissed as "trivial" (55). By contrast, Rosa's family belongs to Poland's intellectual elite, her mother a refined poet and her father, though the director general of the Warsaw bank, "a natural nobleman" (40) trained in philosophy and the classics. Even those Miami Jews who reveal intellectual interests are dismissed because they are, after all, buyers and sellers of the mundane: "She saw them walking with Tolstoy under their arms, with Dostoyevsky. They knew good material. Whatever you wore they would feel between their fingers and give a name to: faille, corduroy, herringbone, shantung, worsted, velour, crepe" (16). The shift in the meaning of "good material," which at first seems to refer to the classic Russian novels, subtly removes the Jews from the erudite world that Rosa claims as her non-Jewish legacy.[57]

The "little goat" may have another anti-Semitic connotation for Rosa. Although there is, to my knowledge, no association in Jewish tradition between the goat and lust, the novella arguably makes this connection (and certainly Ozick can count on this association being made by many of her readers).[58] Rosa remembers the line from her grandmother's lullaby when she fears the Jewish (and Yiddish-fluent) Persky, whom she has just met in a laundromat, might "touch her underpants" as he helps with her laundry (19). From her mother, Rosa comes to associate Jewishness with a lusty animality that lurks "under" innocent surfaces (and particularly under Rosa's own apparent innocence). The mother's desire to purge her Jewishness also motivates her flirtation with conversion to Catholicism. Rosa remembers, as a sign of her mother's exquisitely aesthetic sensibility, a little poem she composed about a statue of the Virgin Mary that she allowed a maid to keep in their kitchen (41). Later, Rosa wants to show Persky Magda's shawl as evidence that she is a mother, to "prove herself pure: a madonna" (59). By imagining herself as the virginal Madonna, and by implication Magda as a Christ, Rosa attempts to erase the memory of her violation in the camps. Yet Rosa's association of motherhood with the Madonna effectively connects ghostliness not with a denied Jewishness (as it would in most stories of cultural haunting) but with the Aryan and Christian. Mary's insemination by the Holy Ghost, a divine act that guarantees Mary's purity, finds reflection in Rosa's belief that Magda's "other strain," the paternal strain that produced the silken yellow hair, "was ghostly, even dangerous" (65). Both Magda's purity and her dangerousness are associated with her yellow hair: "It was as if the peril hummed out from the filaments of Magda's hair, those bright narrow wires" (66).[59]

Rosa's sense of the ghost's dangerousness, an admission made late in the novella, hints that at least unconsciously Rosa has begun to make the connection between anti-Semitic violence (evoked by the description of the hair as humming "wires," referring back to the camp's electrified fence) and the idealization of the ghost as "My purity" (42), uneasily recalling Rosa's parents' view of themselves as uncontaminated by "a grain of [the ghetto's] rot." The search Rosa undertakes for a pair of her missing underpants, which she madly believes to be stolen and "buried" (47) somewhere on the beach, suggests that she needs to find a closed-off part of herself—a part that she has associated with her sexuality, a part not returned to her by the splendid Magda's visitations. At Magda's last appearance in the novella, Rosa has covered the telephone with Magda's shawl, an obvious metaphor for the way ghostly communications keep Rosa exiled from living society. When she "unshawls" the phone to receive a call announcing Persky, a visit Rosa accepts, the ghost is temporarily banished: "Magda was not there. Shy, she ran from Persky. Magda was away" (70). The unshawling of the phone suggests the Jewish practice of unveiling tombstones a year after the death; Rosa indicates here the conclusion of this intense and dangerous phase of her mourning for Magda, a development that connects *The Shawl* to the many stories of cultural haunting that link the redefinition of ethnicity to rituals of secondary burial. In accepting the English- and Yiddish-speaking Persky, Rosa symbolically allows back into her life her grandmother's Yiddish voice, the voice her parents had banished from their refined Polish home. Rosa is, for the moment at least, released from her disastrous Demeter-like mourning for her lost Persephone. Magda last springs to life when Rosa, holding the phone described as a "grimy . . . god" (70), hears Stella say the words "long *dis*tance" (64). When the ghost leaves, she returns to the underworld, taking with her, we might hope, Rosa's infernal perspective that transforms even the innocent flirt Persky into one of the "Persecutors," a "criminal capable of every base act" (49, 45). Although Ozick darkens the story of Persephone by linking the rape by Dis (which Persephone survives to be reunited, for a season, with her mother) to Magda's horrific death, "Rosa" concludes with allusions to an agricultural myth that links death and burial with future rebirth.[60] We do not yet know how Magda will return to Rosa, but the presence of Persky, who calls Rosa back to life and recalls her to the once denied Yiddish voice of her grandmother, gives hope for a less dangerous haunting.

Rosa's removal of Magda's shawl from the telephone marks her de-idolization of the shawl, which Stella accurately if cruelly described as Rosa's "idol," her holy relic: "You're like those people in the Middle

Ages who worshipped a piece of the True Cross, a splinter from some old outhouse as far as anybody knew" (31–32). Magda's shawl has been described by some critics as a symbolic *tallit* or traditional prayer shawl, but Ozick can only intend this allusion to work ironically in "Rosa": though it temporarily saves Magda's life by silencing her, the shawl after the war becomes an iconic object of self-suppression.[61] Rosa's "worship" of the dead past as her only reality shrivels her soul: she has performed a false Kaddish, magnifying and exalting not God's name but the dead's (and given how Rosa re-creates Magda through self-projection, Rosa's own name).[62] The proper function of memory, Ozick implies, is not to idolize the dead but to connect the living and the dead properly, allowing the past to inform but not overwhelm the present. Rosa's unshawling of the phone, now "animated" and "ardent with its cry" (70), signals a possible newborn life for Rosa through renewed connection to others. The conclusion of Rosa's idolatrous, spiritually suicidal mourning tellingly occurs with the arrival of a man who brings back memories of a repudiated Jewish past. The conclusion of mourning in *The Shawl*, as in other stories of cultural haunting, places in a vital and newly defined relationship past and present, the Old World and the New.

THOUGH THEY DRAW on the symbols of disparate cultural storehouses and give somewhat different inflections to ghostly haunting, Marshall's *Praisesong for the Widow*, Keller's *Comfort Woman*, and Ozick's *The Shawl* share with other stories of cultural haunting two fundamental assumptions: that ethnicity is grounded by memory, and that ethnic memory, unsettled by dramatic and sometimes violent dislocations and challenged by confusing new realities, no longer moors present experience as securely as it once did. We have seen again and again this sense of threatened memory: in *Tracks*, young Lulu returns to the reservation alienated from her mother and in danger of losing connection to tribal life, while for García's Pilar, Cuba "fades a little more" each day. Even those stories in which the past menacingly or unhealthily invades the present are predicated upon some form of threatened memory: though Sethe is tormented by a past she cannot forget, *Beloved* addresses a "national amnesia" about American slavery and its insidiously continuing effects. Similarly, though Rosa lives in the past, *The Shawl* takes as its subject the erasure of Jewish memory in the diaspora. The centrality of commemoration in stories of cultural haunting testifies to this strong sense of discontinuity, a perception of historical and cultural rupture that sparks ritualistic recuperations of the past. Cultural continuity is not assumed in these haunted tales but is achieved through the medium of ghosts. When dangerous possessions give way to more beneficent forms of haunting, the past is revised and continued as a living memory that usefully informs present action.

I argue that for heir-ethnographers, those who stand both inside and outside traditions, ethnicity should be construed not just in terms of memory but more specifically as a function of mourning, the form of memory that most directly confronts loss. The work of mourning is perhaps always paradoxical: mourning ritual confirms the separation of the dead and the living even as it reasserts their bond. "You gotta bury your dead," a minor character advises *Ironweed*'s Francis Phelan, but in this literature the dead are only put to rest when they are, in some fashion, safely incorporated into the present.[63] In tale after tale of cultural haunting, mourning is an essentially incorporative process through which the living struggle to integrate the dead in the new reality (and the new identities) they construct. These stories work to reconnect experience to memory by redefining the legacy bequeathed by earlier generations. Once dangerously possessed by a denied, forgotten, or otherwise sheared-off past, the protagonists of haunted texts come newly into possession of their reimagined histories. The exorcism of threatening ghosts yields to the more benign if weighty haunting of historical consciousness, an awareness not just of the pastness of the past but of how the past lives on in the present. Often taking the form of commemorative rituals in which ghostly "kinship" is claimed, this reconfiguration of the past spawns newly redefined ethnicities that both displace and continue older understandings of who "we" collectively are. Thus while the ghosts bear witness to the cultural rift that necessitates their existence, they also, in their refusal to be put away and forever forgotten, stand as figures for the mystery of cultural persistence in the face of powerful incentives to forget. Moving between past and present, this world and another, the ghosts that haunt so much of contemporary American literature are agents of the fluid, never completed process of ethnic redefinition.

Notes

1. Haunted Tales of Heirs and Ethnographers

1. On Africanisms in the New World, see Joseph E. Holloway, ed., *Africanisms in American Culture*.

2. Rodriguez, *Days of Obligation*, xv.

3. Hijuelos, *Our House*, 213, 98.

4. Tan, *Hundred Secret Senses*, 159.

5. Cristina García changed the spelling of her surname from Garcia to García between the publications of *Dreaming in Cuban* and *The Agüero Sisters*. I use the more recent spelling throughout.

6. Maso, *Ghost Dance*, 221. Note that I provide original publication dates in the text. Later dates may appear in the bibliography if I have quoted from later editions. In the case of plays, I give first performance dates in the text and publication dates in the bibliography.

7. There are, of course, many important studies focusing on writers from a particular ethnic group; this scholarship provides a usefully detailed understanding of the coherence and variety of writing within the group. To name just two recent, valuable studies of discrete traditions, see Fred L. Gardaphé, *Italian Signs, American Streets*, and Sau-ling Cynthia Wong, *Reading Asian American Literature*. In thinking about how to address connections between ethnic groups, I have found illuminating Thomas J. Ferraro's important and beautifully written book on the "immigrant mobility genre," *Ethnic Passages*, as well as William Boelhower's probing *Through a Glass Darkly*. In *Supernatural Forces*, a study of recent ethnic literature by women, Bonnie Winsbro makes the case that ethnic boundaries are maintained by spiritual beliefs, a position that has some relevance

for my argument about cultural haunting. Winsbro, who does not focus specifically on the subject of haunting, examines several of the authors discussed in this book, though our readings move in quite different directions.

8. Kingston's adulterous "no-name woman" in *The Woman Warrior*, for example, shows a family resemblance to Hawthorne's Hester Prynne; Kingston's conjuring of her outlaw ancestor from the merest scrap of information in her opening chapter recalls Hawthorne's preface to *The Scarlet Letter*, in which the author is exhorted by the "ghostly voice" of his "ancestor" to imaginatively re-create Prynne from an old document and a rag of cloth (33). Morrison's haunted house in *Beloved* looks back to Faulkner's haunted house in *Absalom, Absalom!* Ralph Ellison saw his own metaphor of racial "invisibility" as linked to Faulknerian ghostliness: "what is commonly assumed to be past history is actually as much a part of the living present as William Faulkner insisted. Furtive, implacable and tricky, it inspirits both the observer and the scene observed . . . and it speaks even when no one wills to listen" (*Invisible Man*, xvi).

9. A more proximate model for the handling of the supernatural in contemporary American fiction may be found in Latin American magical realist literature, a significant but, I think, not major influence on the literature of cultural haunting. Toni Morrison, for example, points out that she incorporated the magical into her novels before she discovered Gabriel García Márquez (see Morrison, "Toni Morrison: New Novel," 68), while Cristina García, acknowledging some influence of Latin American authors, nevertheless observes that American-raised Hispanic writers see their ethnicity differently because their "experiences are so different" (see García, "Fish Swims in My Lung," 66).

10. Although in the United States the term *ethnic* is often reserved for members of minority groups, I do not accept what Werner Sollors has described as the "ethnicity minus one" perspective, which defines ethnicity against the non-ethnic standard of white Anglo-Saxon Protestants. Literary criticism has yet to come up with a satisfactory replacement for the vexing term *ethnic literature*, which at least has the merit of distinguishing literature that brings to the foreground issues of ethnicity, assimilation, and cultural transmission.

11. I have found no better term than *genre* to describe the congruence of thematic and structural elements I examine here. Generic classification (particularly in regard to multigeneric literary forms) has been subject to considerable redefinition in recent years. I rely on Tzvetan Todorov's suggestion that genre is defined by shared form and function (see Ducrot and Todorov, *Encyclopedic Dictionary*).

12. Mark S. Greenberg and Bessel A. van der Kolk, "Retrieval and Integration of Traumatic Memories with the 'Painting Cure,'" in *Psychological Trauma*, ed. Bessel A. van der Kolk, 191–215; quoted in Cathy Caruth, ed., *Trauma*, 152.

13. Morrison, *Beloved*, 35–36.

14. Morrison, *Beloved*, 274.

15. See Janet, *Psychological Healing*, 661–63. For an illuminating discussion of Janet's work, see Bessel A. van der Kolk and Onno van der Hart, "The Intrusive Past," in Caruth, *Trauma*, 158–82.

16. Marshall, *Praisesong for the Widow*, 239, 240, 255.

17. Van der Kolk and van der Hart, "Intrusive Past," 163.

18. Keller, *Comfort Woman*, 2, 85.

19. Kingston, *Woman Warrior*, 108, 101.

20. Morrison, *Beloved*, 250.

21. Erdrich, *Tracks*, 6.

22. Erdrich, *Tracks*, 7.

23. J. Holloway, *Africanisms in American Culture*, 16. The terms *acculturation* and *assimilation* carry confusingly different meanings in both popular and scholarly usage (a confusion that in part reflects the different origins of these terms in anthropology and sociology respectively). The *American Heritage Dictionary* (3d ed.) defines *acculturation* neutrally as a "modification" in one culture "as a result of contact with a different culture," while it reserves *assimilation* for the more thorough *absorption* of groups into "the prevailing culture." The New College Edition of this dictionary defines *assimilation* similarly but underlines the unsavory moral connotations sometimes attached to *acculturation* by defining it as the "modification of a primitive culture by contact with an advanced culture," the implication being that some groups, having no real culture of their own, *come to culture* (*ad-cultura*) when "civilized" by European or Western cultures. Jules Chametzky, however, in his level-headed essay "Some Notes on Immigration," defines *acculturation* positively as the adaptation of traditional ways of life to new circumstances, an adaptation that he contrasts to the whole-hog abandonment of pre-American or pre-Columbian cultures represented by the term *assimilation*. By contrast, in his introduction to Fernando Ortiz's *Cuban Counterpoint*, Bronislaw Malinowski uses the words interchangeably (xi), a practice the *Concise Oxford Dictionary of Sociology* confirms as widespread in the field. I follow sociological practice in using acculturation and assimilation interchangeably to designate the process by which subordinate cultures voluntarily or under duress adapt to the dominant culture. I reserve "reciprocal acculturation" or Fernando Ortiz's useful coinage "transculturation" to refer to a process not of single-sided adaptation but of a more complicated give-and-take, through which all cultures in contact with each other are in some (not necessarily equal) measure altered.

24. Sollors, *Beyond Ethnicity*, 27–28. The passage is from Barth's introduction to *Ethnic Groups and Boundaries*, 38.

25. This view of ethnicity as continually reinvented has received support from the work of historians Terence Ranger and Eric Hobsbawm, who argue that many national traditions thought to be venerably ancient (and therefore

"authentic") are in fact modern inventions. Some of the contributors to Hobsbawm and Ranger's *Invention of Tradition* conflate invention with inauthenticity, a view not shared by the authors discussed here. As anthropologist Nicholas Thomas points out, "it is now emphasized that created identities are not somehow contrived and insincere, that culture is instead inevitably 'tailored and embellished in the process of transmission,' and that that process is 'dynamic, creative—and real'" (see "Inversion of Tradition," 213). See also Benedict Anderson's highly influential *Imagined Communities*.

26. Morrison, "Toni Morrison Now," 136.

27. Ward Churchill discusses one example of this phenomenon—the New Age expropriation of Native American spirituality by nonnatives—in *Fantasies of the Master Race*.

28. Gans, "Symbolic Ethnicity," 193, 201. See also Mary C. Waters, *Ethnic Options*. Waters demonstrates that many white ethnics now enjoy the satisfactions of "belonging" while avoiding group obligations and responsibilities perceived as burdensome.

29. Hollinger, *Postethnic America*, 119. On the difficulty of determining literary authenticity by the standard of the author's race, see Henry Louis Gates Jr., "'Authenticity,' or the Lesson of Little Tree." See also Salman Rushdie's attack on what he calls the "bogy of Authenticity" ("'Commonwealth Literature' Does Not Exist," in *Imaginary Homelands*, 67).

30. Rosaldo, "Others of Invention," 27. For other criticisms of the approach to ethnicity developed in Sollors's scholarship, see Alan Wald, "Theorizing Cultural Difference"; Curtis C. Smith, "Werner Sollors' *Beyond Ethnicity*"; Ward Churchill, "Beyond Ethnicity" in *Fantasies of the Master Race*; Michael Awkward, "Negotiations of Power"; Lawrence J. Oliver, "Deconstruction or Affirmative Action"; and Ramón Saldívar, *Chicano Narrative*.

31. Noting that "the social world can rarely be neatly divided into fixed groups with clear boundaries," anthropologist Thomas Hylland Eriksen cautions that "the existence of ethnic anomalies or liminal categories should serve as a reminder that group boundaries are not unproblematic. These are groups or individuals who are 'betwixt and between,' who are neither X nor Y and yet a bit of both. Their actual group membership may be open to situational negotiation, it may be ascribed by a dominant group, or the group may form a separate ethnic category" (see *Ethnicity and Nationalism*, 156).

32. De Beauvoir, *Second Sex*, xvii.

33. Sociologist Stuart Hall has observed that in the Jamaica of his birth he was not black, but he *became* black when he emigrated to England. Blackness for Hall is a political and social construction that, although imposed from without, can certainly be redefined (see Hall, "Ethnicity"). For a more extended discussion of the social forces that create ethnicities, see Stephen Steinberg, *Ethnic Myth*.

34. Ellison, introduction to *Invisible Man*, xv. Du Bois, *Souls of Black Folk*, 40.

35. Mukherjee, "Management of Grief," 185.

36. The differences between how ghostliness is manifested in Erdrich and in immigrant authors like Kingston and García illuminate the limitations of post-colonial theory—with its emphases on migrancy, nomadism, and diaspora—for the study of America's colonized native peoples, some of whom still live on ancestral soil. Postcolonial scholarship has only very recently begun to make a significant impact on American ethnic studies. For discussions of the applicability of postcolonialism to Native American studies, see Arnold Krupat, "Postcolonialism, Ideology," 30–55. On the postcolonial and the indigenous generally, see "Theory at the Crossroads" in Bill Ashcroft, Gareth Griffiths, and Helen Tiffin, *Empire Writes Back*, 116–54.

37. See de Certeau, *Writing of History*; and Hunt, "History as Gesture," 102–3.

38. Keller, *Comfort Woman*, 32.

39. Fischer, "Ethnicity and the Post-Modern Arts of Memory," in Clifford and Marcus, eds., *Writing Culture*, 195–96.

40. Rodriguez, "American Writer," 9, 8.

41. Fischer, "Ethnicity and the Post-Modern Arts," 195, 197.

42. See Michael White and David Epston, *Narrative Means*; and James L. Griffith and Melissa Elliott Griffith, *Body Speaks*. The Griffiths elaborate on the theory and clinical methods developed by White and Epston; their discussion labeled "Deliverance from a Haunted Body" employs the metaphor of ghostly possession to explore the distress of individuals who have unconsciously inherited "binding" family stories (117–20).

43. Freud, "Thoughts for the Times," in *Complete Psychological Works*, 14:294.

44. Kingston, *Woman Warrior*, 16, 8.

45. Freud, "Totem and Taboo," in *Complete Psychological Works*, 13:65–66.

46. For an excellent overview of research on the concept of immigrant "generations," see Donald Weber, "Reconsidering the Hansen Thesis." Hansen propounded the now well known and highly influential idea that the "third generation" American attempts to recoup the old-world legacy that the second generation worked hard to forget. In his review of recent reassessments of Hansen's thesis, Weber argues that "we need to rethink 'generations' as cultural construction, as a trope through which various ethnic writers could mediate the dominant culture and yet critique (in the process) the subculture which they straddle" (327).

47. For an analogous revision of gender identity, see Judith Butler's argument in *Gender Trouble* that gender is "performatively produced" (24).

48. Hall, "Ethnicity," 19. In this 1989 essay on the "new ethnicity," the Jamaican-born Hall offers up as an example his son's complex relation to his Jamaican heritage: "If you ask my son, who is seventeen and who was born in

London, where he comes from, he cannot tell you he comes from Jamaica. Part of his identity is there, but he has to *discover* that identity. He can't just take it out of a suitcase and plop it on the table and say 'That's mine.' It's not an essence like that. He has to learn to tell himself the story of his past. He has to interrogate his own history, he has to relearn that part of him that has an investment in that culture. For example, he's learning wood sculpture, and in order to do that he has had to discover the traditions of sculpturing of a society in which he has never lived." Hall's son's predicament, that he must "discover" what is his own, is shared to greater or lesser degrees by all American authors of cultural ghost stories, whether or not they, like Hall's son, are the offspring of immigrants.

49. Geertz, *Works and Lives*, 143–44.

50. Geertz, *Works and Lives*, 133, 145.

51. Although no ghosts appear in Yezierska's *Bread Givers*, a kind of metaphorical haunting arguably emerges at the novel's close, when Sara feels pressed by the burdensome "shadow" of her father's orthodox Jewish beliefs. The sense of burden results from Sara's need to be loyal to her father despite her anger at his oppressive misogyny and tyrannical nature; although this burden is felt and resented by Sara throughout her story, it is described as a "shadow" only at the novel's end, when Sara reconnects with her father after having won some measure of independence. For Yezierska, to be ethnic is to be shadowed by a past that one can never entirely escape.

52. Wharton, *Backward Glance*, 207.

53. Kingston, *Woman Warrior*, 45, 44.

54. Erdrich, *Tracks*, 12.

55. Kingston, *Woman Warrior*, 8.

56. Boelhower, *Through a Glass Darkly*, 142, 89.

2. Ghost Dancing

1. See Erdrich, "Whatever Is Really Yours," 83. "Chippewa" and "Ojibwa" are white-invented names for the people who called, and for the most part continue to call, themselves the "Anishinabe" (itself a phonetic transcription variously spelled). In *Tracks*, the older, more traditional Nanapush uses "Anishinabe"; Pauline, who attempts to reject her tribal heritage, refers to the "Chippewa" or the "Indians." While Erdrich herself uses all three terms, she favors "Chippewa" in interviews (apparently adhering to the general preference of the Turtle Mountain band to which she belongs). I follow Erdrich's choice in using the term "Chippewa." On the politics of tribal naming, see Gerald Vizenor, *People Named the Chippewa*, 13–21.

2. Rodriguez, *Days of Obligation*, 4.

3. Erdrich, "Where I Ought to Be," 23.

4. Christopher Vecsey, *Traditional Ojibwa Religion*, 65.

5. Momaday, *Names*, 26.

6. Welch, *Winter in the Blood*, 159.

7. Erdrich and Dorris, "Bangs and Whimpers," 1.

8. Erdrich and Dorris, "Interview with Louise Erdrich and Michael Dorris," 98–99.

9. Erdrich, "Where I Ought to Be," 1.

10. Erdrich, *Love Medicine*, 367, and *Bingo Palace*, 256–59.

11. On this subject see Robert M. Nelson, *Place and Vision;* and William Bevis, "Native American Novels," 15–45.

12. Erdrich, "Where I Ought to Be," 1.

13. Erdrich, "Where I Ought to Be," 24.

14. Dinesen, *Out of Africa*, 387.

15. Erdrich, "Where I Ought to Be," 24.

16. Erdrich's subtle unfixing of "home" can be read as reflecting a postcolonial perspective. Numerous critics have emphasized the importance of migration, boundary crossing, travel, displacement, and the fluid definition of home as central to postcolonial literatures. For a recent discussion of the idea of "home" in postcolonial texts, see Rosemary Marangoly George, *Politics of Home*. Considerable disagreement has surfaced about the applicability of postcolonial criticism and theory to Native American literature. In "How(!) Is an Indian? A Contest of Stories," Jana Sequoya argues that the postcolonial emphasis on travel and diaspora is fundamentally at odds with Native American understandings of identity and culture as essentially "geocentric" (in Arnold Krupat, ed., *New Voices*, 459). Krupat, on the other hand, finds postcolonial theory useful to the study of Native American culture and literature (see "Postcolonialism, Ideology"). Krupat warns, however, that postcolonial criticism must be applied with careful qualification, because contemporary Native American literature only partially fits under the rubric of the postcolonial. One obvious difference, as Krupat and others have noted, is that "there is not yet a 'post-' to the colonial status of Native Americans" [30]). For examples of Native American literary criticism influenced by postcolonialism, see David L. Moore, "Myth, History, and Identity in Silko and Young Bear," in Krupat, *New Voices*, 370–95; and Gloria Bird, "Searching for Evidence of Colonialism."

17. Erdrich is careful to note that when sacred reservation land such as Black Mesa is violated, the loss cannot be so readily recouped ("Whatever Is Really Yours," 80, 79).

18. I borrow the term "narrative transaction" from Barbara Herrnstein Smith. Rather than focusing on narrative as text or structure, Smith asks us to investigate the function of storytelling relative to the social conditions in which the telling occurs, a view particularly useful when considering the different roles

of Nanapush's and Pauline's narratives (see "Narrative Versions, Narrative Theories").

19. Erdrich, "Whatever Is Really Yours," 83.

20. Krupat, *Voice in the Margin*, 226, 216. Murray, *Forked Tongues*, 3, 6. Krupat, "Postcolonialism, Ideology," 32, 36, 38. James Ruppert's view of Native American writers as cultural "mediators" parallels Krupat's argument about translation (see Ruppert, "Mediation and Multiple Narrative"). Krupat models his idea of "anti-imperial translation" on the ideal of translation forwarded by Walter Benjamin in "The Task of the Translator." In that essay, Benjamin cites Rudolph Pannwitz's view that the "basic error of the translator is that he preserves the state in which his own language happens to be instead of allowing his language to be powerfully affected by the foreign tongue" (W. Benjamin, "Task of the Translator"; quoted in Krupat, "Postcolonialism, Ideology," 35). The idea that in translation the source language should "powerfully affect"—even strain, stress, and deform—the target language has been embraced particularly by scholars concerned about the appropriative violence of translation. See, for example, Eric Cheyfitz, who discusses translative violence in colonial contexts in *Poetics of Imperialism*, and the valuable essays collected in Brian Swann's *Translation of Native American Literatures*. Tzvetan Todorov's *Conquest of America* and Talal Asad's "The Concept of Cultural Translation" (in Clifford and Marcus, *Writing Culture*, 141–64) have been influential in the ongoing dialogue about translation. In thinking about cultural translation, I have found useful Sanford Budick and Wolfgang Iser's collection entitled *Translatability of Cultures*, particularly the essays by Jan Assmann and Karlheinz Stierle. I have also found illuminating Lawrence Rosenwald's discussion of translation theory in "Buber and Rosenzweig's Challenge," his introduction to his translation of Martin Buber and Franz Rosenzweig's *Scripture and Translation*. In "Lost in Translation" Rosenwald discusses Benjamin's similar challenge to translators.

21. Silberman, "Opening the Text: *Love Medicine* and the Return of the Native American Woman," 111, and Kroeber, "Technology and Tribal Narrative," 18; both appear in Gerald Vizenor, ed., *Narrative Chance*.

22. Sequoya, "How(!) Is an Indian," 453, 455, 472. Sequoya is particularly troubled about the implications of some Native American writers wrenching sacred and (to outsiders) secret oral stories out of their communally sanctioned tribal contexts. She refers specifically to N. Scott Momaday's and Leslie Marmon Silko's use in their novels of sacred Pueblo stories that, according to Paula Gunn Allen, are "not to be told outside of the clan" (quoted in Sequoya, 467). See also Sequoya-Magdaleno, "Telling the *différance*."

23. See Erdrich, "Interview with Louise Erdrich," 231, an interview conducted by Allan Chavkin and Nancy Feyl Chavkin. For discussions of the ways

in which Erdrich's narrative strategies evoke the oral tradition, see James Flavin, "Novel as Performance," and Joni Adamson Clarke, "Why Bears Are Good."

24. De Certeau, *Writing of History*, 46.

25. Boelhower, *Through a Glass Darkly*, 104.

26. Vecsey, *Traditional Ojibwa Religion*, 26.

27. Russell Thornton, *American Indian Holocaust*, 175.

28. Janet A. McDonnell, *Dispossession of the American Indian*, 100.

29. Francis Paul Prucha, *Great Father*, 2:848.

30. Van Gennep, *Rites of Passage*, 147. Van Gennep's work on rites of passage closely parallels the argument of his contemporary Robert Hertz about death rituals and "secondary burial."

31. Turner, "Death and the Dead," 24–39.

32. This rejection of food in favor of consuming spirits bears superficial resemblance to the Chippewa vision quest, in which adolescents fast in order to induce hallucinations. The purpose of the vision quest is to empty oneself as an invitation to the spirits. One is not possessed by the spirit that appears, but takes that spirit's name (a name regarded thereafter as an individual's true name and held in secrecy) and acquires some of its attributes. In the vision quest, starvation leads to identity. Fleur and Nanapush's starvation, however, is pure possession, a possession that silences and kills, that erases personal identity through radical identification with the dead. Morton Teicher collects windigo folklore and accounts of actual cannibalism (most of which have since been discounted as uncorroborated rumor) in *Windigo Psychosis*, 1–129. See also Victor Barnouw, *Wisconsin Chippewa Myths and Tales*, 120–31. Lou Marano usefully summarizes the anthropological research on the subject in "Windigo Psychosis," 385–412. John Robert Colombo collects windigo stories in *Windigo*.

33. On windigo belief as a response to ecological stress, see Charles A. Bishop, "Northern Algonkian Cannibalism," 237–48. Marano argues that "the windigo belief complex was the Northern Algonkian manifestation of the collective witch fear that is predictable in traumatized societies" ("Windigo Psychosis," 397). William Asikinack, himself Anishinabe, complains that nonnative scholars overemphasize the cannibalistic aspect of the windigo and fail to understand that windigo stories belong to "the genre of the *contrary* for the Anishinabe. The role of the *contrary* in the Anishinabe world was to teach the proper roles for people to follow" ("Anishinabe (Ojibway) Legends," 5). He notes that windigo stories are used to warn against greedy excess (3–8). This view of the windigo finds confirmation in Basil Johnston, *Manitous*, 222–23. On the role of evil spirits in Chippewa culture, see Theresa S. Smith, *Island of the Anishnaabeg*.

34. The windigo also appears as a seductive figure in Erdrich's poem "Windigo," from her collection *Jacklight*.

35. For a more elaborate description of trauma's reenactments, see chapter 3. Eduardo and Bonnie Duran discuss trauma in the specific context of Native American communities in *Native American Postcolonial Psychology*.

36. For information about the trickster Nanabushu (variously spelled "Nana'b'oozoo," "Nanabozho," "Nehnehbush," "Wenebojo," among other versions), see Vecsey, *Traditional Ojibwa Religion*, 84–100; and Johnston, *Manitous*, 51–95. Nancy J. Peterson perceptively notes that Nanapush is like the trickster Nanabushu in "adopt[ing] the techniques of the oppressor to even the score and to balance the distribution of power" ("History, Postmodernism," 990). On trickster figures generally in Native American literature, see Andrew Wiget, "His Life in His Tail."

37. Stewart, *Nonsense*, 62.

38. Hertha D. Wong has observed that while the novel's mothers tend to abandon their children, "it is Nanapush . . . who 'mothers' most consistently throughout the novel," by nursing Fleur and later Lulu through illnesses ("Adoptive Mothers," 185). It is important, however, to recognize that Nanapush's mothering takes the form of both physical caretaking and storytelling.

39. Pauline's identity as a consumer takes other forms. Bonnie Winsbro has noted that Pauline, as the reservation's undertaker, recalls the windigo by metaphorically "feeding off the scraps of her dying neighbors" (*Supernatural Forces*, 71–72).

40. Monica Furlong, *Thérèse of Lisieux*, 111.

41. Steiner, *After Babel*, 316.

42. Susan Stanford Friedman points out the parallels between Nanapush's Anishinabe religion and Pauline's Catholic mysticism (for example, the importance of fasting and visions). Friedman persuasively argues that the novel advocates a syncretic, as opposed to fundamentalist, view of Native American identity. Although I also see parallels between Nanapush and Pauline, I do not follow Friedman in positing that the two narrators' views exist in a necessary "symbiosis." I argue for a parodic rather than symbiotic relationship between Pauline's and Nanapush's cultural translations. Presenting the tribe with an "unknown mixture of ingredients" (39), Pauline, in her mixing of traditional Chippewa religion and Catholicism, can be seen as a negative version of the syncretism Erdrich admired in her grandfather at Turtle Mountain: "My grandfather has had a real mixture of old time and church religion—which is another way of incorporating. He would do pipe ceremonies for ordinations and things like that. He just has a grasp on both realities, in both religions" (see Erdrich, "Whatever Is Really Yours, 81). The "necessity" of having both narrators is better understood in historical terms, as Peterson argues: "Because historical events caused intact tribes and bands like the Turtle Mountain Chippewa to become split at the root, Nanapush's and Pauline's points of view are both necessary to provide an 'in-

digenous' account of what happens in *Tracks*." See Friedman, "Identity Politics," 126; and Peterson, "History, Postmodernism," 989.

43. Catherine Rainwater argues that Pauline produces a "marginal and aberrant" Christianity by grafting elements of Chippewa religion "deformed away from their shamanic matrix" onto a Christian framework ("Reading between Worlds," 409). For an excellent discussion of Misshepeshu in Ojibwa myth and in Erdrich's fiction, see Victoria Brehm, "Metamorphoses of an Ojibwa *Manido*," 677–706.

44. Several distinct though related Ghost Dances have been identified, the two largest being the 1870 movement led by the Paviotso visionary Wodziwob and the 1890 movement led by Wovoka (Jack Wilson), the son of a Wodziwob disciple. Black Elk describes the tragedy at Wounded Knee in *Black Elk Speaks*. *The Sixth Grandfather*, edited by Raymond J. DeMallie, a collection of the interview transcripts from which John G. Neihardt composed *Black Elk Speaks*, makes clear Black Elk's continued belief in the Ghost Dance after Wounded Knee, despite his position as catechist for the Catholic church. Erdrich's own knowledge of and interest in the Ghost Dance is evident in the introduction of her essay on postnuclear catastrophe novels. See Erdrich and Michael Dorris, "Bangs and Whimpers," 1. Erdrich and Dorris also discuss the Ghost Dance in a 1989 interview with Bill Moyers (see Erdrich and Dorris, "Louise Erdrich and Michael Dorris: Writers").

45. James D. Stripes makes this connection in "Problem(s) of (Anishinaabe) History," 26–28.

46. The Ghost Dance was known to the Chippewa since 1889 (Vecsey, *Traditional Ojibwa Religion*, 195). Erdrich speaks approvingly of the pan-Indianness developed by Native American literature in an interview with Laura Coltelli (Erdrich and Dorris, "Louise Erdrich and Michael Dorris," 47). In the same interview, she cautions that "Writing is different from tribe to tribe, the images are different from tribe to tribe" (48).

47. Weston La Barre, *Ghost Dance*, 230.

48. Mooney, *Ghost-Dance Religion*. Thornton argues that the Ghost Dances of 1870 and 1890 "were deliberate attempts to respond to a threatening situation rather than a phenomenon of mass hysteria" (xi), and that their ultimate goals were a demographic revitalization of diminished populations (through incorporation of the dead into the living population) and reaffirmation of aboriginal cultures (see *We Shall Live Again*).

49. Erdrich and Dorris, "Bangs and Whimpers," 1.

50. Mooney, *Ghost-Dance Religion*, 1061.

51. Mooney, *Ghost-Dance Religion*, 1047.

52. Thornton, *We Shall Live Again*, 5.

53. Mooney, *Ghost-Dance Religion*, 1028. For another song that refers to a

humming that precedes the apocalyptic reordering of the world, see Mooney, *Ghost-Dance Religion*, 1035.

54. Mooney cites several songs in which dancers anticipate gambling with ghosts of dead friends (see, for example, *Ghost-Dance Religion*, 962, 994, 995, 1002, 1036).

55. On the significance of the winds in traditional Chippewa religion, see T. Smith, *Island of the Anishnaabeg*, 47.

56. Mooney, *Ghost-Dance Religion*, 1034. For other songs that mention the whirlwind, see 970, 1054, 1055.

57. Mooney, *Ghost-Dance Religion*, 1028. Mooney notes that the literal meaning of the line "rendered 'when you meet your friends again' is 'when you are living together again'" (1028), referring to the reunion of the living and the dead. The trembling of the earth appears in Arapaho and Kiowa Ghost Dance songs (958, 973, 1082).

58. See T. Smith, *Island of the Anishnaabeg*, 65–94.

59. Although the more spectacular claims of the Ghost Dance prophets did not materialize, the movements succeeded to some extent in revitalizing tribal cultures and populations (see Thornton, *We Shall Live Again*). Although on a smaller scale, the Ghost Dance survived the massacre at Wounded Knee.

60. Erdrich and Dorris, "Bangs and Whimpers," 1, 24, 1–24, 25, 1.

61. Rothenberg, "We Explain Nothing," in Brian Swann, ed., *Translation of Native American Literatures*, 68. Swann, in his introduction to that volume, argues that "any translation of a Native American text will always partake of the unknowable" and that, "Given the history of this hemisphere, to settle for the dignity of mystery is far preferable to any claims of definiteness." This argument is demonstrated by Fleur's continuing elusiveness, despite the efforts of two narrators to capture her verbally (see Swann, xvii). Fleur reemerges as a figure of substantial shamanic power in *The Bingo Palace*, where she lives in the woods on the outskirts of the reservation, reminding the increasingly assimilated Chippewa of another way.

62. La Barre, *Ghost Dance*, 232.

63. Vizenor, *Manifest Manners*, 105.

64. Vizenor, *Manifest Manners*, 106.

3. Getting Back One's Dead for Burial

1. James, *Sense of the Past*, 49.

2. James, *Sense of the Past*, 48.

3. The clipping appears in *Black Book*, a miscellany of African-American memorabilia that was compiled by Middleton A. Harris and on which Morrison worked during her time at Random House (10). Information about Margaret

Garner can also be found in Gerda Lerner, ed., *Black Women in White America*, 60–63.

4. The slave-owning Schoolteacher, of course, stands as the novel's paradigm of the nefarious "recorder" of black life.

5. Morrison somewhat overstates her case when she says she sees little evidence of an interior life in the writings of authors such as Frederick Douglass. Nevertheless, her point about the conforming of slave narratives to white literary conventions remains valid and important.

6. Morrison, "Site of Memory," 109, 110, 111, and 113. Much of the criticism of the novel deals with the issue of historical recovery, though with different emphases. Morrison's treatment of the Margaret Garner story has been examined by several critics (for the most extended analyses, see Cynthia Griffin Wolff, "'Margaret Garner,'" and Avery F. Gordon, *Ghostly Matters*). Marilyn Mobley ("Different Remembering"), Lynda Koolish ("Fictive Strategies"), Sally Keenan ("'Four Hundred Years'"), Molly Abel Travis ("Speaking from the Silence"), and Avery F. Gordon (*Ghostly Matters*) discuss Morrison's revisions of the conventions of the slave narrative in the effort to represent the formerly unrepresented. Others raise the question of the text's assumption or contestation of postmodern conceptions of history, language, and the self (see, for example, Valerie Smith, "'Circling the Subject'"; Andrew Schopp, "Narrative Control and Subjectivity"; William Handley, "House a Ghost Built"; Rafael Pérez-Torres, "Knitting and Knotting"; Barbara Frey Waxman, "Changing History"; and Kathie Birat, "Stories to Pass On"). Linda Krumholz takes a path more congruent with mine in considering the novel's recuperation of history in the context of ritual, but she is not interested in specifically funerary ritual, nor she does see the novel's ritual "resolution" of historical trauma as incomplete or problematic (see Krumholz, "Ghosts of Slavery"). Though our readings of the novel take us in very different directions, I find instructive Sally Keenan's remark in a footnote that *Beloved* should be viewed "less as a reconstruction of history than as a symbolic evocation of the burden of memory" ("'Four Hundred Years of Silence,'" 79).

7. Morrison, "Pain of Being Black," 120.

8. Morrison, "Site of Memory," 112.

9. For the reclamation of lost black history as a process of reanimation, in which dead predecessors are summoned, see interviews with Morrison by Christina Davis ("Interview with Toni Morrison," 143), by Gloria Naylor ("Conversation: Gloria Naylor and Toni Morrison," 586), and by Marsha Darling ("In the Realm of Responsibility," 6).

10. Morrison, "Conversation: Gloria Naylor and Toni Morrison," 593.

11. Morrison, "Conversation: Gloria Naylor and Toni Morrison," 585.

12. Hertz, "Contribution to the Study," 29, 36, 29–86.

13. For Richard Huntington and Peter Metcalf in *Celebrations of Death*, "death throws into relief the most important cultural values by which people live their lives and evaluate their experiences. Life becomes transparent against the background of death, and fundamental social and cultural issues are revealed" (2). They note that for Arnold van Gennep, a theorist of transitional rituals and a contemporary of Hertz, "of all the rites of passage, funerals are most strongly associated with symbols that express the core of life values sacred to the society at hand" (19). See also Jack Goody, *Death, Property and the Ancestors*. Goody draws out the sociological implications of Hertz's work in his study of West African funereal rituals.

14. Freud, "Mourning and Melancholia," in *Complete Psychological Works*, 14: 244–45. For Freud, the refusal to relinquish connection to the dead constitutes a "turning away from reality . . . through the medium of a hallucinatory wishful psychosis" (244). From this perspective, the conjured ghost represents the externalization of a regressive wish fulfillment, an evasive strategy that postpones the acknowledgment of final loss.

15. Hertz's paradigm helps to explain the odd disjunction between the dangerous, vampiric nature of the novel's ghost and Morrison's many references in interviews to "benevolent" ancestral spirits (see, for example, Morrison, "Conversation with Toni Morrison," 86; "Interview with Toni Morrison," by Nellie McKay, 415; "Interview with Toni Morrison," by Christina Davis, 145; "Toni Morrison Now," 137). The novel attempts, though it does not fully succeed, to translate the one to the other. The oddity of casting the ancestral ghost as a daughter is, however, striking. Carolyn Rody's reading of the return of Beloved to Sethe as a reflection of Morrison's role as a "daughter" in search of a lost maternal ancestry offers a possible explanation. Rody suggests that the jealous possessiveness of Beloved for Sethe could be read as the author's "agonistic struggle—or better, an ambivalent 'female affiliation complex'" with her literary foremothers, the female authors of slave narratives (see Rody, "Toni Morrison's *Beloved*," 108). A more likely explanation for casting the daughter as ghost may be that Morrison wants to emphasize how slavery robbed blacks of their *future* as well as their past. Sethe views the theft of her milk—and of her ability to nurture the future—as a far more horrific crime than her beating. On the topic of African ancestor worship and its retention in African-American culture, I have found useful Melville J. Herskovits, *Myth of the Negro Past*; Sterling Stuckey, *Slave Culture*; Joseph E. Holloway, *Africanisms in American Culture*; and Janheinz Jahn, *Muntu* and *Neo-African Literature*.

16. Morrison, "Bench by the Road," 4.

17. For Morrison, the necessary revision of the past works on two levels: the "obfuscation and distortion and erasure" of black experience in white historiography must be addressed by revisionist historians. But the job of recovering

the past also requires an imaginative response to recorded facts. In considering the moral "consequences" of past action, the artist searches for a "truth" that lies beyond "the province of the natural or social sciences." Although aware of the complexities of any historical representation, Morrison clearly distinguishes between what she calls historical "research" and her own imaginative recuperation of the past: "It's not the historians' job to do that," she flatly asserts. (See Morrison, "Interview with Toni Morrison," by Christina Davis, 142, and "Toni Morrison: New Novel," 68.) Perhaps it needs to be observed that Morrison's historical recuperation differs from nefarious forms of historical revisionism not only in its status as self-declared fiction but primarily in its intent. Her revision of the few recorded details of Margaret Garner's life is not obscurantist in purpose but aims to counter what historian David Blight calls "a "willfully narrow history" ("W. E. B. Du Bois," 53). It moves toward acceptance rather than evasion of responsibility for the past.

18. Morrison, "Pain of Being Black," 120.

19. Morrison, "Conversation: Gloria Naylor and Toni Morrison," 586, 593. Morrison rather confidently speaks of calling the dead "by their names," but in fact the name of Garner's child was never recorded. The name Morrison chooses—"Beloved"—is a memorial name (derived from her fictional child's eulogy), not the name either the historical or the fictional child was known by when alive. The name "Beloved" thus reminds us of what is irrevocably lost and, at the same time, underlines the ghost's representative function: she stands in for all the unnamed, improperly buried dead. The name also establishes the ghost's identity through and for others; in the novel, the different qualities of each character's haunting arise from the identification each makes with the ghost. Finally, the name reminds us that Morrison's novel intends to substitute for the inadequate eulogy delivered over the grave. "Dearly Beloved," of course, addresses the gathered mourners, not the dead. I argue that Morrison positions her readers as mourners who claim Beloved as their own.

20. Even the house assumes a ghostliness. Sethe remembers "Years ago— when 124 was alive" (95). Regarding Sethe's exchange of clothes with Beloved, I note that Jack Goody describes the exchange of clothing with the dead as one of the "reversal" rituals that mark secondary burial (see *Death, Property and the Ancestors*, 242). Denver also sometimes wears Sethe's clothes (11), but Sethe does not in turn wear Denver's. Sethe's relationship with the ghost, unlike her relationship with Denver, involves a dangerous exchange of identities.

21. Mae Henderson makes a similar observation, reading "this is not a story to be PASSED ON—not in the sense of being retold, but in the sense of being forgotten, repressed, or ignored" ("Toni Morrison's *Beloved*," 83). Earlier in the novel, when Sethe uses the words "pass on," she explicitly means "pass away": "Some things go. Pass on" (35).

22. Hamacher, "Journals, Politics," 459; Caruth, *Trauma*, 5.

23. Morrison, "In the Realm of Responsibility," 6.

24. I have found several works on trauma to be especially helpful: Cathy Caruth's *Unclaimed Experience* and the excellent multidisciplinary collection of essays she edited and introduced, first appearing in 1991 in *American Imago* and republished in 1995 as *Trauma: Explorations in Memory*. Also informative are Judith Lewis Herman's lucid and moving *Trauma and Recovery* and a collection of essays edited by Bessel A. van der Kolk entitled *Psychological Trauma*. An essay by van der Kolk and Onno van der Hart in Caruth's volume introduced me to the important work of Pierre Janet, whose conceptions of the "subconscious" and "dissociation" anticipated Freud's more elaborate formulations of the "unconscious" and "repression" (see van der Kolk and van der Hart, "Intrusive Past"). Herman also discusses Janet's work, as well as his fascinating rivalry with Freud (*Trauma and Recovery*, 11–12). Trauma research began in earnest during World War I, when soldiers returned from the front shell-shocked. After World War II, studies of trauma expanded to include civilian victims. On the specific context of the Holocaust, I have found illuminating the many volumes of Lawrence L. Langer, including *Admitting the Holocaust* and *Holocaust Testimonies;* Saul Friedlander, "Trauma, Transference and 'Working Through'"; Dominick LaCapra, *Representing the Holocaust;* James E. Young, *Writing and Rewriting the Holocaust;* and Edward T. Linenthal, *Preserving Memory*. Not surprisingly, the language of haunting enters most discussions of trauma. Henry Krystal, for example, describes the inability of posttraumatic patients to integrate traumatic events into their present lives as "an internal war against the ghosts of one's past" ("Trauma and Aging: A Thirty-Year Follow-up," in Caruth, *Trauma*, 78). Langer cites a camp survivor who finds that "it's very difficult to strike a balance between consciously remembering these things and being possessed by them" (*Holocaust Testimonies*, 173–74). Summarizing recent research on trauma, Caruth succinctly observes, "To be traumatized is precisely to be possessed by an image or event" (*Trauma*, 4–5). In her Lacanian reading of *Beloved*, Jean Wyatt suggestively observes in a footnote that theories of trauma might illuminate the novel's disturbances of memory; she does not, however, develop the point (see "Giving Body to the Word," 486).

25. Greenberg and van der Kolk, "Retrieval and Integration," 191; quoted in Caruth, *Trauma*, 152.

26. Van der Kolk and van der Hart, "Intrusive Past, 177.

27. Freud, "Uncanny," in *Complete Psychological Works*, 17:237, 241.

28. Paul D understands that "more important than what Sethe had done was what she claimed." This usurpation of the master's right to own and destroy "scared him" (164).

29. Marilyn Mobley has noted the novel's fragmentation of the linearity of

the slave narrative, arguing that "Morrison's text challenges the Western notion of linear time that informs American history and the slave narratives" (see
"Different Remembering," 192). Philip Page suggests that the novel's narrative
fragmentation and circularity have "affinities with African folklore and specifically with the traditional structure of oral narratives" (see "Circularity in Toni
Morrison's *Beloved*," 35).

30. Langer, *Holocaust Testimonies*, 173, 72, 174.

31. The only word Stamp Paid can make out is the repetition of "mine," a
word that surely expresses Sethe's, Beloved's, and Denver's joy at their reunion.
Yet, as David Lawrence has pointed out, it also uncomfortably echoes white
slave-owning possessiveness (see "Fleshly Ghosts and Ghostly Flesh," 196).

32. These syntactic dislocations occur most obviously in the ghost's speech
and are related to her self-dissociation and identic fragmentariness. The odd
phrasing of "he hurts where I sleep" (212) or "she is my face smiling at me"
(213), for example, from her description what is at once the afterlife and the
Middle Passage, reflects her tenuous relation to her own body. Rebecca Ferguson similarly reads Beloved's "profound fragmentation of the self" as registering
the traumatic "*effects* that slavery had" ("History, Memory and Language," 114).
For an entirely different reading of what I am describing as "traumatic language," see Karla Holloway, who argues that the monologues of the women
isolated in 124 represent a "liberation" of language. For Holloway, repetitiveness and the "suspension of time and place" signal the entrance into "freedom"
and the mythic. The wintry imagery associated with this language (Holloway
cites the sentences "Outside, snow solidified itself into graceful forms. The peace
of winter stars seemed permanent" [176]) marks the mythic timelessness that the
novel offers as an alternative to history. I would argue that these same wintry images are also suggestive of death. For example, the description of snowfall ("all
around 124 the snow went on and on and on. Piling itself, burying itself. Higher.
Deeper" [134]) feels ominous to me, hinting at live burial. I agree with Holloway
that the strategy of reclaiming a lost history through the supernatural challenges
conventional understandings of history as empirical recordkeeping and at the
same time offers an opportunity to reclaim "spiritual histories," but I find that
the novel also reminds us of the potential dangers of being haunted by history.
See K. Holloway, "*Beloved*: A Spiritual," 521, 518, 521, 518, 523.

33. Janet, *Psychological Healing*, 663, 661, 662.

34. Emily Budick also stresses the dangers of literality in the novel, pointing
out that parents who seek to replicate or construct themselves in their children
create a future that merely reproduces the past; instead of remembering the past,
they "re-remember or re-member it in some bodily fashion." See "Absence,
Loss," 122.

35. Traumatic faithfulness as a rite of mourning arises in other circum-

stances as well. Judith Lewis Herman, who notes that "In the absence of a socially meaningful form of testimony, many traumatized people choose to keep their symptoms," cites Wilfred Owen: "I confess I *bring on* what few war dreams I now have. . . . I have my duty to perform towards War" (*Trauma and Recovery*, 184).

36. Anne E. Goldman has observed that in being whipped, "Sethe has her body written upon at the behest of the man who owns her." Establishing a contrast between the "white ink" of mother's milk and the black ink Schoolteacher uses to commodify his slaves as his own "texts," Goldman argues that Sethe escapes being textualized and becomes an author in her own right when she speaks "a maternal language" (of storytelling) to her children. Sethe does indeed need to move toward authorial control, but I read the novel's "mother-child bond" as much more conflicted than Goldman does, and I argue that trauma repeatedly disrupts the scenes of storytelling. See Goldman, "'I Made the Ink,'" 323, 324, 325, 328.

37. Morrison, "Toni Morrison Now," 58.

38. Morrison, "Toni Morrison: New Novel," 68.

39. Henderson, "Toni Morrison's *Beloved*," 80–81. Lawrence, "Fleshly Ghosts and Ghostly Flesh," 198.

40. Henderson, "Toni Morrison's *Beloved*," 81.

41. Christ is repeatedly called "Beloved" in the Bible (see, for example, Ephesians 1:6).

42. Sethe's mother is branded by her owner with the sign of the cross (61), linking the master's Christianity with his slave ownership.

43. Henderson, "Toni Morrison's *Beloved*," 81, 80. Henderson's emphasis on Sethe's ability "to fashion a counternarrative" (77) to the master's narrative is shared by some other critics. See Goldman, "'I Made the Ink'" and Horvitz, "Nameless Ghosts."

44. Bereft of meaningful language and lying in Baby Suggs's deathbed, Sethe's position as Paul D arrives recalls the photograph of a dead young woman that provided inspiration for *Beloved*. Morrison has cited two sources for the novel: the story of Margaret Garner and *The Harlem Book of the Dead*, a collection of James Van der Zee's photographs of Harlem funerals. One picture in particular struck her: a photograph of a dead young girl who had been shot by someone she loved and who had refused to reveal what had happened to her. According to the accompanying story, she kept repeating, until she died, "I'll tell you tomorrow." This story eventually made its way into *Jazz*, but Morrison has said that the story of Sethe did not become clear until she linked Garner's story with this photograph of the dead girl who would not narrate. See Morrison, "Conversation: Gloria Naylor and Toni Morrison," 584.

45. Scarry, *Body in Pain*, 4. For Elaine Scarry, it is specifically physical pain

that destroys language; she argues that psychic pain finds no similar bar to verbal representation. Nevertheless, I find Scarry's comments about physical pain's resistance to language relevant to Morrison's treatment of the trauma of slavery, which is, of course, hardly limited to physical pain. Karen Remmler's analysis of Jean Améry's and Mali Fritz's post-Holocaust writings provides an interesting counterpoint, by focusing on how these writers use metaphor to "defy the breakdown between language and material reality" caused by physical and psychological torture (217). See Remmler, "Sheltering Battered Bodies in Language," 216–32.

46. In a key scene in *Song of Solomon*, Milkman Dead hears "what there was before language. Before things were written down. Language in the time when men and animals did talk to one another, when a man could sit down with an ape and the two converse" (278), a prehistoric "prelanguage" that might be compared to the women's return to a time when "there were no words" in *Beloved*. In her compelling reading of the novel, Deborah L. Clarke argues that the turn to prehistoric communication and later to children's language "offers a communal identity distinct from textual authority and written discourse," but that while this move "decenters the written text," it does so "without eradicating it as a form of discourse." Written language is rejected so that language can be made anew. The breaking of language in *Beloved* can be read similarly as a precondition for what Clarke calls "a fuller language" ("'What There Was before Language,'" 276), but the novel, unlike *Song of Solomon*, turns at its close not to a new discourse but to silence. I argue this is because the community's destruction of the master's language is predicated upon the erasure of the ghost, that is, of part of the community's own still unspeakable history. See "'What There Was before Language,'" 265–77.

47. As Emily Budick notes, the "way of remembering dramatized through the story is not the way of remembering that the text embodies" ("Absence, Loss," 117).

48. Another example appears when Baby Suggs's neighbors begin to resent her talent for abundance: "Loaves and fishes were His powers—they did not belong to an ex-slave" (137).

49. It is not clear, however, that Morrison ever thought of the reunion scene between Paul D and Sethe as a conclusion proper. When she gave Bob Gottlieb her manuscript, she was still thinking of the text of *Beloved* as possibly an installment of a much longer work. Morrison, "Toni Morrison: New Novel," 68.

50. Morrison, "Unspeakable Things Unspoken," 11, and *Playing in the Dark*, 48.

51. Turner, "Death and the Dead in the Pilgrimage Process," 24ff. Patterson, *Freedom in the Making*, 10, 17. See also Patterson, *Slavery and Social Death*.

52. Morrison uses the term "master narrative" in a 1989 interview with Bill

Moyers ("Toni Morrison: Novelist," 54). In his discussion of W. E. B. Du Bois's Reconstruction historiography, David Blight notes Nathan Huggins's use of the term in *Black Odyssey* to describe what Blight calls "the oldest and most enduring conception of the American past: the providential view of America as a chosen nation, a people of progress who ultimately solve their problems, and offer the world a model of an omniscient society thriving above threat or conflict." See "W. E. B. Du Bois," 48–49.

53. Young, *Writing and Rewriting the Holocaust*, 15–16.

54. Claude Lanzmann, director of *Shoah*, a film of Holocaust testimonies, has expressed this view: "There is an absolute obscenity in the very project of understanding. Not to understand was my iron law during all the eleven years of the production of *Shoah*. I had clung to this refusal of understanding as the only possible ethical and at the same time the only possible operative attitude" (quoted in Caruth, *Trauma*, 154–55). Peter Weiss, on the other hand, takes the view that understanding is a moral imperative. One of the witnesses in his play *The Investigation* makes the point: "We must drop the lofty view / that the camp world / is incomprehensible to us / We all knew the society / that produced a government / capable of creating such camps" (Weiss, quoted in Langer, *Admitting the Holocaust*, 97).

55. Werner Hamacher, "Journals, Politics," 458–59. I first came upon this passage from Hamacher in Eduardo Cadava's "Haunted Ethics of Paul Celan," an exquisite reading of Celan's "*Mit Brief und Uhr*" that reads verbal indeterminacy as the poet's moral response to historical catastrophe.

56. Pratt, *Imperial Eyes*, 7.

57. Rosenman and Handelsman, "Rising from the Ashes," 197–98.

4. From Exiles to Americans

1. Olson and Olson, *Cuban Americans*, 88, 74. The Olsons note that "More than 98 percent of the Cuban immigrants during the 1960s were white," and at the year the Mariel boatlift began, "Miami's Little Havana was 99 percent white" (84). According to George Brandon, the "racial composition of the exiles and refugees is not representative of the population of Cuba. In 1970, the last year for which racial data were available on Cuban Americans, the group was 96 percent white. . . . Seventeen years earlier, Cuba's island population was 27 percent mulatto, nine times that of the later Cuban-American population" (*Santería from Africa*, 104). The fact that "more than 40 percent of the Marielitos were Afro-Cubans," and that they came from poorer socioeconomic backgrounds (although higher than Cuban society in general), left the already established Cuban exiles ambivalent for the first time about Cuban emigration. When Congress late in 1980 passed the Refugee Act, which severely restricted Cuban

immigration, most Cuban Americans did not complain. The unpopularity of the new immigrants may have led to the gross exaggeration in the American media of claims that the Marielitos were largely Cuba's rejected criminals and mental patients. It is now estimated that only 6 percent of the Mariel emigrants had serious criminal records or histories of mental illness. See Olson and Olson, *Cuban Americans*, 84, 83, 88, 81. Wolfgang Binder claims, in what I suspect is an exaggeration that is nevertheless telling, that "For the already existing Cuban community [in the United States] the mere sight of black Cubans was shocking: 'La otra Cuba!'" ("American Dreams and Cuban Nightmares," 225).

2. "More than 83 percent of Cubans in Miami in 1966 said they would return to Cuba once Castro was overthrown," but in "the mid-1970s less than 25 percent of Cuban immigrants living in the United States expressed any desire to return to Cuba." The Olsons add that once Cuban emigrants "had children born in the United States, the desire of the family to return to Cuba declined dramatically" (*Cuban Americans*, 74). In an essay on Cuban-American fiction, Isabel Alvarez Borland includes a brief discussion of *Dreaming in Cuban*, noting that the novel "treats the experience of exile from the perspective of an ethnic writer." She refers to Eliana Rivero's observation in her essay on Cuban authors in the United States, "From Immigrants to Ethnics," "that a writer's transition from exilic to ethnic concerns entails coming into a personal awareness of biculturalism and takes for granted the reality of permanence in a society other than the one existing in the country of birth" ("Displacements and Autobiography," 46, 47). In *Dreaming in Cuban*, Cuban-American Pilar finally makes the decision that the United States is her permanent home. Wolfgang Binder argues that the "fear of passing from a nation to an ethnic group within North American society is . . . tangible in all [Cuban-American literary] texts" ("American Dreams and Cuban Nightmares," 252). For a comparison of themes in Cuban and Cuban-American literature, see Eliana Rivero, "Cubanos y Cubanoamericanos." Silvia Burunat statistically compares both themes and language choice (loanwords, anglicisms, etc.) in "A Comparative Study." In an essay published (like Rivero's and Burunat's) before the appearance of *Dreaming in Cuban*, Carolina Hospital examines the literature produced by children of Cuban exiles ("Los Hijos del Exilio Cubano").

3. García, "And There Is Only," 612, 606, 608. García was born in Havana in 1958 and emigrated with her family to New York in 1961. She changed the spelling of her name from "Garcia" to the more ethnic "García" between the publication of her two novels; I use the more recent spelling of her surname throughout.

4. Although Pilar is the only central family member to speak in the first person, García gives three other characters brief first-person subchapters: Pilar's Cuban cousins Ivanito and Luz, and the Afro-Cuban daughter of a Santería

priest, Herminia. As discussed later in this chapter, these characters, linked by the first-person voice, offer similar or opposing positions on cultural translation to the chief translator, Pilar. García may have learned the strategy of shifting the narration among members of a close group from Erdrich, a writer she is on record as admiring. See García, "Fish Swims in My Lung," 65.

5. In Lourdes's business and Celia's fieldwork, García contrasts capitalist and socialist economies. The direct connection between labor and profit is weakened in the United States: we never actually see Lourdes bake—she sells pastries that she takes out of boxes, delivered and baked by unseen hands.

6. García does not attempt to dramatize this difference in her English rendering of Spanish dialogue. Linguistic difference remains largely symbolic in her novels.

7. In *The Agüero Sisters*, the extermination of much of Cuba's indigenous bird population is explicitly linked to Spain's colonial destructiveness.

8. When Lourdes arrives in New York, she briefly indulges in the new American cuisine of "instant foods": the "mashed potatoes she whipped up from water and ashen powder, the chicken legs she shook in bags of spicy bread crumbs then baked at 350 degrees, the frozen carrots she boiled and served with imitation butter" (173).

9. The poem is marked by other slippages in identity. The sun and moon speak as if they still have the bodies of birds (hence their "tail" and "throat"). Later in the poem these celestial bodies merge with each other: "One was the other." After a "naked girl" briefly appears, the doves take on her defining quality: they are no longer "dark doves," but "naked doves." The laurel tree may refer to yet another metamorphosis, that of Daphne. See García Lorca, *Obras completas*, 1:598. All translations of García Lorca's poetry in this chapter are my own.

10. Olson and Olson, *Cuban Americans*, 85.

11. Brandon adds, that "At one end of the continuum were Santeria houses, the majority of whose rites imitated Catholic ceremonies complete with our fathers, hail marys, candles, incense, and the appropriate ritual gestures and material symbols. At the other end were houses where these Catholic elements never appeared" (*Santeria from Africa*, 99).

12. Brandon, *Santeria from Africa*, 97, 98.

13. Joseph M. Murphy, *Santería*, 32.

14. See Brandon, *Santeria from Africa*, 75; and Murphy, *Santería*, 113.

15. Brandon, *Santeria from Africa*, 136.

16. The "bead necklaces" refer to Felicia's involvement in Santería. The symbolically colored necklaces are worn by initiates to indicate their affiliation with various *orishas*.

17. Lourdes's rejection of the imagination attaches to her traumatic exit from

Cuba. As she breathes in the wintry air of New York, feeling its crystals "scraping and cleaning her inside," Lourdes "decides she has no patience for dreamers, for people who live between black and white" (129). The "scraping" air recalls the "scraping" knife during her rape, while the conjunction of scraping and "cleaning" of the insides evokes both the miscarriage and the saline abortion afterwards to rid her body of "her baby's remains" (174). The irony here is that in "scraping away" her bad memories of Cuba, New York only repeats the traumatic memory: Lourdes's vision of her new world is haunted by her unspeakable nightmares of the old. Her impatience with dreamers as she imagines her self-purification suggests that Lourdes's intolerance for the imagination really constitutes an intolerance for Cuba.

18. Ironically, as Pilar becomes daughter to a ritual parent, she also draws closer to her biological mother. The chapter titled "Daughters of Changó" includes narratives by both Pilar and Lourdes. In her fiery temper, Lourdes is unwittingly a child of Changó, the warrior *orisha* known for impetuous, passionate behavior and quick anger. Celia, of course, raised Lourdes "as if for war" (222). Lourdes also resembles Changó in having suffered a maternal rejection that initiates an existential condition of exile: thrown out of his home by his mother Obatalá, Changó "had no past. Without roots . . . he wandered the world" (Núñez, *Santeria*, 57).

19. García reveals in an interview that she learned about Santería from books (García, "And There Is Only," 610).

20. I think particularly here of the ghostly Africa conjured by Caribbean dancers in Paule Marshall's *Praisesong for the Widow* and of the China culled from her mother's stories by Maxine Hong Kingston in *Woman Warrior*.

21. Mageo and Howard, eds., *Spirits in Culture*, 4.

22. Brandon, *Santeria from Africa*, 113.

23. Brandon, *Santeria from Africa*, 104.

24. Kutzinski, *Sugar's Secrets*, 142.

25. Brandon, *Santeria from Africa*, 93; Kutzinski, *Sugar's Secrets*, 143. I thank Marianella Belliard-Acosta for informing me that in Cuba before independence the word "nation" (*nación*) originally referred specifically to a subgroup of free and enslaved blacks who came from a particular area of Africa (for example, both slaves and slave owners referred to the Ibo nation, the Lucumi nation, the Arara nation). The idea of Cuban "nationality" itself is inseparably tied to Afro-Cuban culture.

26. García Lorca's poetry also leaks into García's prose. For example, Lourdes's vision of her dead son's face as "blank as an egg" (174) echoes Lorca's "child with the blank face of an egg" in "Vuelta de paseo" (Back from a walk). Celia's decision to raise Lourdes to interpret the "columns of blood and numbers in men's eyes" (42) borrows Lorca's "columns of blood and numbers" in

"Danza de la muerte" (Dance of death). See García Lorca, *Obras completas*, 1: 447, 470. Steeped as she is in Lorca's poetry, it is not surprising that Celia would absorb his language. Her children in turn "learned her florid language" (110).

27. Gibson, *Federico García Lorca*, 29.

28. "And here come the Blacks with their rhythms, which I suddenly realize derive from our great Andalusia—friendly Blacks, with no anguish, who show the whites of their eyes and say: 'We are Latins. . . .'" Gibson, *Federico García Lorca*, 283.

29. Quoted in Gibson, *Federico García Lorca*, 29.

30. Olson and Olson, *Cuban Americans*, 35. Jules Robert Benjamin puts the number killed in the repression at "three to five thousand" (*United States and Cuba*, 22). For a detailed account of the race massacre of 1912, see Aline Helg, *Our Rightful Share*, 193–226; and Louis A. Pérez Jr., "Politics, Peasants, and People of Color."

31. Interestingly, García Lorca associated the Gypsies with the "invisible" Andalusia: he described *Gypsy Ballads* as a "book in which the *visible* Andalusia is hardly mentioned but in which palpitates the invisible one" (Gibson, *Federico García Lorca*, 135). The connection between repression and haunting in *Dreaming in Cuban* is made explicit when Celia runs into two stepbrothers from her father's second, unacknowledged family and, hurrying away, thinks of them as "twin ghosts." Celia's inability to "trust the clandestine rites of the African magic" that she sometimes dabbles in because "both good and evil may be borne in the same seed" (91, 90) hints at a possible connection in her mind between Santería and illegitimacy (her stepbrothers are, in a sense, her father's "bad seed").

32. Kutzinski, *Sugar's Secrets*, 145.

33. Fernando Ortiz, *Cuban Counterpoint*, 98, 100–101, 100. More recently, Cuban-American critic and poet Gustavo Pérez Firmat has argued that since "Cuban culture is composed entirely from exogenous ingredients," it "subsists in and through translation." Pérez Firmat's assertion of Cuba's "translation sensibility," as he acknowledges, is influenced by Ortiz's concept of "transculturation" (*Cuban Condition*, 2, 4, 1, 13).

34. Morrison, *Beloved*, 16.

35. Trees have special significance in Santería. Shrines are often set up near large trees (see Brandon, *Santeria from Africa*, 75), and many trees, particularly the ceiba, are considered holy sites of communication with the gods. The ceiba grows outside the del Pino house in Havana: "Celia knows that good charms and bad are hidden in the stirred earth near its sacred roots. Tía Alicia told her once that the ceiba is a saint, female and maternal" (43). Olson and Olson note that Santería believers "viewed the world from a unique perspective, uniting all nature into a cosmic whole. Animals, plants, minerals, sun, moon, stars, and the earth were alive, imbued with a measure of knowledge, individual consciousness, and an awareness of the things around them. . . . All of creation had a spiritual

essence, and there was a balance and solidarity to nature that people had to care-fully respect." See Olson and Olson, *Cuban Americans*, 85.

36. On Changó's association with storms and "deadly thunderbolts," see Núñez, *Santeria*, 46.

37. With the exception of Lourdes's close bond with her father, Jorge (and Herminia's with her father), the relationships between men and women in this novel are at best unhappy and, more often, disastrous. Felicia, for example, maims the brutal husband who gave her syphilis, later nearly kills her son, and successfully murders another husband. Celia is driven mad by the abandonment of a lover and then is punished for that love by the man who persuades her to marry him. One of Pilar's lovers is unfaithful to her, as is Pilar's father, Rufino, to Lourdes, much to Pilar's disgust. However, the relationships between women are hardly idealized: only Pilar's relationship with Celia and perhaps Felicia's with Herminia are not in some measure antagonistic, and Pilar will, of course, leave Celia.

38. See García Lorca, "Vuelta de paseo" (Back from a walk) in *Obras comple-tas*, 1:447.

39. See the interviews with García by López (García, "'And There Is Only,'" 614) and Vorda (García, "Fish Swims in My Lung," 65).

40. Toni Morrison, *Song of Solomon*, 277, 278, 279.

41. On Morrison's treatment of gender in this scene, see Deborah L. Clarke, "'What There Was before Language,'" 275–76.

42. Salman Rushdie, "Location of Brazil," in *Imaginary Homelands*, 124–25.

43. García, "Fish Swims in My Lung," 70.

44. In his autobiography, *Have Mercy!* Wolfman Jack confesses:

> I'm a guy who was born white, but soon got captivated heart and soul by black American culture. That culture, especially the musical and verbal sides of it, has made all the difference in my life. "Have Mercy!" stands for the vibrancy and all-out expressiveness of African-American culture: how it points people toward the happy-go-lucky, good-times side of life; how it creates music that is sexy, funny, crazy, and wise all at the same time; how that music has the power to even make you feel *good* about feeling *bad*. . . .
>
> The one thing I've learned . . . is that people in every country of the "civilized" world wish—either secretly or openly—that they had the ex-pressiveness, the flair, the I'm-so-glad-to-be-me spirit that black folks have made a part of American life. (xvi–xvii, xviii)

Wolfman Jack can be seen as a U.S. pop-culture version of Afro-Cubanism, though he makes no similar claim that black culture defines the "authentically" American. His celebration of African-American culture, at least in the above passage, uncomfortably downplays the political implications of visible blackness in racist America (though as the victim of a Klan cross-burning himself [for establishing a multiracial nightclub], he knew at least something of the nation's politics of race).

45. For example, Pilar "[envies Lourdes] her Spanish curses," which "make [Pilar's] English collapse in a heap" (59). Pilar and her Peruvian boyfriend speak in Spanish during lovemaking because "English seems an impossible language for intimacy" (180).

46. Kingston, *Woman Warrior*, 108.

47. On Debussy's use of the *habanera*, see Ian Gibson, *Federico García Lorca*, 282.

48. Gibson, *Federico García Lorca*, 33, 282.

49. See García Lorca, *Obras completas*, 1 : 583.

50. Andrew A. Anderson, *Lorca's Late Poetry*, 80, 100.

51. Celia's suicide in the sea, especially occurring as it does at the novel's end, may allude to Edna Pontellier's watery death at the close of Kate Chopin's *Awakening*. Both deaths are linked to an unfulfilled, perhaps unfulfillable, romantic yearning; both women relinquish former lovers at this moment. In each case the sea is a luminous siren. Edna notices that the Gulf is "gleaming with the million lights of the sun," its "voice . . . seductive." To Celia, the "sea beckons with its blue waves of light," its voice that of the *duende* who sings "*in throaty seduction*" (242–43). Celia gives herself to a sea whose blue light has been associated with ghostliness; Edna appears to those who see her just before her death as "an apparition." What is strikingly different is their connection to family. Edna sees her death as an evasion of her family's enslavement of her soul, while Celia in her last moments remembers fondly the aunt who raised her, recalling the piano lesson about family connection despite difference. See Chopin, *Awakening*, 999, 998.

52. The novel's opening sentence locates Celia's town on "the north coast of Cuba" (3). She is therefore entering the waters between the United States and Cuba, with Cuba to her back and the United States, and Pilar's future, before her. Pilar anticipates Celia's seaward walk in her *santera* coronation dream (33–34); the echo further strengthens the connection between Santería and translation.

53. William Boelhower, "Ethnographic Politics: The Uses of Memory in Ethnic Fiction," in Singh, Skerrett, and Hogan, eds., *Memory and Cultural Politics*, 26. Boelhower also discusses the significance of ethnic names in *Through a Glass Darkly*.

5. Ethnic Memory, Ethnic Mourning

1. Maurice Halbwachs, *Collective Memory*, 156. See also Halbwachs, *On Collective Memory*. I borrow the term "mapping" from Paul Connerton's discussion, in *How Societies Remember*, of the relationship of individual to collective memory

in Halbwachs. My understanding of collective memory has been influenced by a number of excellent historical and sociological studies on the subject. In addition to Connerton's book and the enormously influential work of Halbwachs, see Raphael Samuel and Paul Thompson, eds., *Myths We Live By;* Thomas Butler, ed., *Memory;* David Thelen, ed., *Memory and American History;* Michael Kammen, *Mystic Chords of Memory;* David Lowenthal, *Past Is a Foreign Country;* and James Fentress and Chris Wickham, eds., *Social Memory.* Group memory is the subject of two strong collections of literary essays edited by Amritjit Singh, Joseph T. Skerrett Jr., and Robert Hogan: *Memory, Narrative, and Identity* and *Memory and Cultural Politics.* See also George Lipsitz, "Myth, History, and Counter-Memory."

2. Savage, "Politics of Memory" in Gillis, ed., *Commemorations,* 131–32, 143. Savage notes that Boston's Shaw memorial is an exception, though the tension between the panel's foreground (with Shaw mounted) and background (the black soldiers marching) "inevitably takes on a racial charge because it springs from the competing claims to memory of the officer and the troops" (136). In thinking about the relationship between commemoration and ethnic memory, I have found informative a number of studies on the history and social psychology of public memorials: Gillis, *Commemorations,* a valuable collection of essays on the formation of national identities; Jay Winter, *Sites of Memory, Sites of Mourning,* on commemorations of World War I; James E. Young, ed., *Art of Memory,* on Holocaust memorials; Edward T. Linenthal, *Preserving Memory,* on the U.S. Holocaust Museum in Washington; Barry Schwartz, "Social Context of Commemoration," on the American Capitol; John Bodnar, *Remaking America,* on American commemorations of its national history; and Edward S. Casey's phenomenological study of commemoration in *Remembering,* 216–57.

3. Morrison, "Bench by the Road," 4.

4. Liam Kennedy astutely notes that as the hero of Edward Daugherty's play about the Irish strikers, Francis has been "interpolated as a mythic figure in the ethnic narrative of Irish-American progress," becoming, in the process, something of a ghost himself. "Francis may be viewed," he argues, "as a ghost of an ethnic, not just a familial, past, and as a ghost who refuses to be 'buried,' he reveals how aspects of that past have been idealized or willfully obscured." See L. Kennedy, "Memory and Hearsay," 75–76.

5. Wilson, "Round Five," 8.

6. Wilson, "Round Five," 8.

7. Morrison, "Conversation: Gloria Naylor and Toni Morrison," 593.

8. Connerton, *How Societies Remember,* 5.

9. On the dangers of reifying "identity," see Richard Handler, "Is 'Identity' a Useful Cross-Cultural Concept?" in Gillis, *Commemorations,* 27–40. See also Gillis's introduction to this collection of essays on social memory and national identity.

10. Ferraro, *Ethnic Passages*, 167. For a valuable essay focusing specifically on ghosts in Kingston's book, see Gayle K. Fujita Sato, "Ghosts as Chinese-American Constructs in Maxine Hong Kingston's *The Woman Warrior*," in Carpenter and Kolmar, eds., *Haunting the House of Fiction*, 193–214.

11. Nora, "Between Memory and History," 7, 21. Not surprisingly, the metaphors Nora employs to convey the doubleness or "in-betweenness" of memory-sites frequently associate these sites with ghostliness. *Lieux de mémoire* bring into the present for peoples "haunted by the need to recover their buried pasts" (15) a history that has become "invisible" (17). They represent "moments of history torn away from the movement of history, then returned; no longer quite life, not yet death" (12). They are "mixed, hybrid, mutant, bound intimately with life and death"; they "materialize the immaterial" (19).

12. Kirk Savage has pointed out that the American Civil War was remembered in the nineteenth century in a wide variety of ways, including the establishment of public memorials along the lines of Nora's *lieux de mémoire*, as well as "less formal activities of remembering in the home, church, or street." He concludes that these "various memory networks were not necessarily mutually exclusive and may in certain ways have been mutually reinforcing" ("Politics of Memory," in Gillis, *Commemorations*, 146).

13. Yerushalmi, *Zakhor*, 96.

14. Erdrich makes clear the connection between her multiple narration and Native American collective identity in a conversation with Deborah Stead. Observing that "The tale [of *Tracks*] was unlocked only when [Erdrich] finally found the right way to tell it," Stead quotes Erdrich: "Michael [Dorris] started talking about the Athapaskin Indians who live around Tyonek, Alaska, where he once hunted. In their language, there is no word for 'I'—only 'we.'" Stead adds, "So she used two narrators in 'Tracks,' spinning out the story from their contrasting points of view." See Stead, "Unlocking the Tale," 41. Strikingly, even the dangerous Pauline can be subsumed into the "we."

15. Yerushalmi, *Zakhor*, 96. Yerushalmi argues that the "collective memories of the Jewish people were a function of the shared faith, cohesiveness, and will of the group itself, transmitting and recreating its past through an entire complex of interlocking social and religious institutions that functioned organically to achieve this. The decline of Jewish collective memory in modern times is only a symptom of the unraveling of that common network of belief and praxis through whose mechanisms . . . the past was once made present" (94). He connects the movement from Jewish memory to Jewish historiography to the assimilation following the dissolution of the ghetto. The need for history arises from (and contributes to) "the decay of Jewish memory" (99).

16. Kingston was surprised—and enormously delighted—when, on a trip to China years after the publication of *The Woman Warrior*, certain Chinese au-

thors, feeling that the Cultural Revolution cut off "their roots to the past," greeted Kingston as a model for how to conserve Chinese cultural "roots": "they were saying," Kingston remembers, "that I was their continuity. And they wanted help in figuring out where to go. . . . they were telling me I was part of a Chinese canon. And here I was writing in English!" The "extravagant" and marginal indeed becomes central. See Kingston, "Interview," 790, and "*MELUS* Interview," 65.

17. Nora, "Between Memory and History," 23.

18. Morrison, "Bench by the Road," 4.

19. Mukherjee, "Management of Grief," 180.

20. Smith-Wright, "In Spite of the Klan: Ghosts in the Fiction of Black Women Writers," in Carpenter and Kolmar, *Haunting the House of Fiction*, 146.

21. Smith-Wright, "In Spite of the Klan," 160.

22. See, for example, "the darkness [that] contained its own light" (232) and "the darkness that is light" (250) in the culminating scene of the novel, when the ancestors are invited to join the circle of the living.

23. Christian, "Ritualistic Process," 74.

24. Brita Lindberg-Seyersted points out the appropriateness of Marshall's choice of a South Carolina sea island as the location for the Ibo legend: "This state was the key importer of slaves in the period before the American Revolution, and although most of the slaves were brought directly from Africa, some were shipped via the British West Indies. The first slaves brought to South Carolina in the seventeenth century came via Barbados. . . ." See *Black and Female*, 45. Marshall's parents emigrated from Barbados to New York.

25. Walking on water obviously alludes to Christian myth as well. On the novel's biblical imagery, see Mary Lederer, "Passage Back." Brita Lindberg-Seyersted notes that the Ibo myth appears in Lydia Parrish's collection of slave songs from the Georgia sea islands (*Black and Female*, 46).

26. Connerton, *How Societies Remember*, 69.

27. On Marshall's allusions to voodoo ritual, see Brita Lindberg-Seyersted, *Black and Female*, 39–61. Marshall consistently merges Africana and Christian imagery.

28. On Carriacou's Big Drum ceremonies and on Carriacouan culture generally, see M. G. Smith, *Kinship and Community in Carriacou*.

29. On Lebert Joseph as Legba, see Velma Pollard, "Cultural Connections," 289–90.

30. Abena P. A. Busia discusses Marshall's novels as diaspora literature in "Words Whispered over Voids." See also Busia, "What Is Your Nation?" and Gay Wilentz, "Towards a Spiritual Middle Passage."

31. Sterling Stuckey, *Slave Culture*, 11–12.

32. Stuckey, *Slave Culture*, 11.

33. My biographical information about Keller comes from Christopher John Farley's review, "No Man's Land," 101.

34. "That girl was dead" (93), she says of her earlier self as Soon Hyo, explaining why even in the United States she has retained the Japanese name imposed on her in the camps.

35. The novel includes other references to improper burials. Early in the novel Reno, Akiko's business manager, admits she did not do her mother justice: "But—and I stay shame for dis—I nevah put my maddah's remains where she asked, and now the city moving all dah graves where my maddah stay. Tractahs digging em up now" (9).

36. Youngsook Kim Harvey, *Six Korean Women*, 238.

37. Laurel Kendall, *Shamans, Housewives*, 149. See also Kendall's *Life and Hard Times*.

38. Harvey, *Six Korean Women*, 237. Harvey observes that "possession sickness" brings women oppressed by difficult family situations an escape route: "Inasmuch as only the shaman has direct access to the spirits, in any disputes between the shaman and other family members, the spirits are likely to be in coalition with the shaman. Thus, *sinbyŏng* ["possession sickness," also spelled *singbyŏng* and *sinbyong*] functions as a pathway out of an impasse in the relationships which can no longer be tolerated, and the assumption of the shaman role serves as a mechanism for stabilizing and maintaining the altered power positions in the family social structure. In other words, *sinbyŏng* provides a mechanism whereby the oppressed can turn the table on the oppressors with the latter's cooperation and support" (238–39). Certainly Akiko uses *sinbyŏng* (before she has become an official shaman) to turn the tables against her oppressively moralizing husband, the minister Bradley, though certainly not with his cooperation. Akiko guiltily attributes his death to her willing it.

"Ancestor worship is still esteemed as an expression of filial piety," Laurel Kendall points out, "while the ritual practices of women and shamans are disparaged as an embarrassing superstition" (*Shamans, Housewives*, 176). This view finds confirmation in Youngsook Kim Harvey's observation that "Koreans clearly regard shamans and their families as social deviants—as outcastes." Yet curiously Harvey also notes that shamanism is often regarded by scholars as "the only indigenous religion of Korea," embodying "the enduring core of Korean religious thought since the Three Kingdoms period" and, despite its outcast status, retaining "a potent political force." See *Six Korean Women*, 5, 7.

39. Kendall, *Shamans, Housewives*, 27.

40. Kendall, *Shamans, Housewives*, 159–60.

41. The male spirits she conjures, like Saja the Death Messenger, tend to be diabolic.

42. On traumatic memory as a bodily reenactment that resists verbalization, see Janet, *Psychological Healing*, 657–63.

43. Ozick, "Interview with Cynthia Ozick," 375, 387.

44. Ozick, "Toward a New Yiddish," 169.

45. "Interview with Cynthia Ozick," 385–86.

46. Ozick, preface to *Bloodshed and Three Novellas*, 9, 11, and "Toward a New Yiddish," 47.

47. See Ozick, "Toward a New Yiddish," 151–77. Ozick has qualified her early advocacy of English as the New Yiddish. While not rejecting the value of a Judaized English, Ozick writes, "I no longer believe that the project of fashioning a Diaspora literary culture . . . can be answered by any theory of an indispensable language—i.e., the Judaization of a single language used by large populations of Jews" (152).

48. Powers, "Disruptive Memories," 84, 88, 82. The phrase "a world without a past" quoted by Powers appears in the short story "Puttermesser."

49. Quoted in Lillian S. Kremer, *Witness through the Imagination*, 219. Ozick mentions Adorno's dictum in "Roundtable Discussion," 284.

50. Ozick's letter is quoted in Sarah Blacher Cohen, *Cynthia Ozick's Comic Art*, 148.

51. "Interview with Cynthia Ozick," 391.

52. Ozick, "Contraband Life," 92.

53. In true heir-ethnographer's fashion, Ozick describes herself as a "Jewish autodidact," noting that she learned nothing from her childhood Hebrew studies. But she does credit a grandmother "who told me lots of stories and read to me and was a great source of information" (see Eve Ottenberg, "Rich Visions of Cynthia Ozick, 62).

54. Ozick, "Interview with Cynthia Ozick," 380.

55. Rosa refers to the retirees as "shells like herself," hollowed-out people who left their real lives in the past, and who now appear as "[o]ld ghosts" (16).

56. Although the Lublins would detach themselves from all things Jewish, their name points to the terrible fate that even assimilated Jews could not escape. Lublin, Poland, was the site of the extermination camp of Majdanek, where 350,000 people, mostly Jews, were executed. In choosing the name of Lublin for her protagonist, Ozick may also have had in mind Isaac Bashevis Singer's *Magician of Lublin*, a novel (written in the Yiddish language the Lublins despise) that examines the contest between Jewish faith and assimilation. One of the Jewish protagonist's non-Jewish mistresses is named Magda.

57. Rosa sees as a measure of her own high-culture background her girlhood reading of the poet Julian Tuwin: "such delicacy, such loftiness, such *Polishness*" (20), she remembers. The lower-class, unassimilated Jews, by contrast, "couldn't read one line of Tuwim" (69), a damning indication to Rosa of their lack of (civilized) culture. Tuwim was an assimilated Polish Jew who, until the Second World War, rejected a Jewish identity. Learning about the Holocaust in 1944 while living in New York, Tuwim wrote "We, Polish Jews," in which he em-

braces a Jewish identity. Interestingly, the essay, dedicated to the "Shadow" of his mother, who was murdered in Poland, portrays ethnicity as a kind of haunting. Tuwim rejects a racial basis for ethnicity: he claims his Jewishness by blood—not the blood "inside of veins," he clarifies, but the spilled blood ("not Jewish blood") of Poland's destroyed Jewry. Haunted by the dead, Tuwim writes, "perhaps I should not say 'we Polish Jews,' but 'we ghosts, we shadows of our slaughtered brethren, the Polish Jews.'" Ozick clearly wants her readers to think of the Tuwim work Rosa appears not to know; Rosa has yet to make the change of heart that Tuwim passionately describes in "We, Polish Jews," but the allusion to Tuwim both suggests the possibility of such a turnaround and hints that if Rosa does come to embrace her Jewishness, it will likely happen as the result of her redefining the nature of her haunting. See Tuwim, *My, Żydzi Polscy*, 17, 18, 19, 20.

58. The "kid" in the children's Seder poem "The One Kid" is sometimes glossed as an allegorical figure for Israel. Ozick's translation of *tsigele* as "little goat" instead of the more likely "kid" may also indicate her desire to draw on non-Jewish associations with the "goat." I thank Lawrence Rosenwald for supplying me with information about "The One Kid" and "*Unter Yankeles Vigele*," as well as for pointing out the more familiar translation of *tsigele*.

59. On the Holy Ghost's role in Mary's conception, see Luke 1:35.

60. I am cautious, in light of Ozick's repudiation in her essays of "Hellenism" in favor of "Hebraism," about proposing a Greek myth as Ozick's figure of resolution. Yet Ozick's Hebraic and Hellenic symbols do not fall so neatly into good and bad camps, as the treatment of Magda's shawl as a misused *tallit* (traditional prayer shawl) suggests. The use of Greek myth at the close of *The Shawl* gives the resolution a tentativeness that does not, however, completely undermine the myth's positive implications. For a different reading of the Demeter/Persephone allusion, see Elaine M. Kauvar, *Cynthia Ozick's Fiction*, 199–200.

61. On the shawl as *tallit* in "The Shawl," see Alan L. Berger, *Crisis and Covenant*, 53. Sarah Blacher Cohen points out that what was *tallit* in "The Shawl" becomes fetish in "Rosa"; see *Cynthia Ozick's Comic Art*, 159.

62. The Kaddish, beginning with the words "Exalted and sanctified be God's great name," does not mention the dead. My information of Jewish mourning observances comes from Maurice Lamm, *Jewish Way in Death and Mourning*. I have also consulted Rabbi Harry A. Cohen, *Basic Jewish Encyclopedia*, and that classic heir-ethnographer's manual, Siegel, Strassfeld, and Strassfeld, eds., *First Jewish Catalog*, a how-to guide for Jews wanting to Judaize their lives.

63. W. Kennedy, *Ironweed*, 68. Though Francis finally banishes the scarily multiplying spectres of his past, he has already internalized the knowledge of self and community they brought him.

Bibliography

Abraham, Nicolas, and Maria Torok. *The Shell and the Kernel: Renewals of Psychoanalysis.* Vol 1. Ed. and trans., Nicholas T. Rand. Chicago: Univ. of Chicago Press, 1994.

Alvarez Borland, Isabel. "Displacements and Autobiography in Cuban-American Fiction." *World Literature Today* 68, no. 1 (winter 1994): 43–48.

Anaya, Rudolfo A. *Bless Me, Ultima.* Berkeley: TQS, 1972.

Anderson, Andrew A. *Lorca's Late Poetry: A Critical Study.* Leeds UK: Francis Cairns, 1990.

Anderson, Benedict. *Imagined Communities: Reflections on the Origin and Spread of Nationalism.* Rev. ed. London: Verso, 1991.

Ashcroft, Bill, Gareth Griffiths, and Helen Tiffin. *The Empire Writes Back: Theory and Practice in Post-Colonial Literatures.* London: Routledge, 1989.

Asikinack, William. "Anishinabe (Ojibway) Legends through Anishinabe Eyes." In *Contemporary Native American Cultural Issues: Proceedings from the Native American Studies Conference at Lake Superior State University, October 16–17, 1987,* ed. Thomas E. Schirer, 3–12. Sault Ste. Marie MI: Lake Superior State Univ. Press, 1988.

Awkward, Michael. "Negotiations of Power: White Critics, Black Texts, and the Self-Referential Impulse." *American Literary History* 2, no. 4 (winter 1990): 581–606.

Barnouw, Victor. *Wisconsin Chippewa Myths and Tales and Their Relation to Chippewa Life.* Madison: Univ. of Wisconsin Press, 1977.

Barth, Fredrik, ed. *Ethnic Groups and Boundaries: The Social Organization of Cultural Difference.* Boston: Little, Brown, 1969.

Benjamin, Jules Robert. *The United States and Cuba: Hegemony and Dependent Development, 1880–1934*. Pittsburgh: Univ. of Pittsburgh Press, 1977.

Benjamin, Walter. "The Task of the Translator." In *Illuminations*, ed. Hannah Arendt, trans. Harry Zohn, 69–82. New York: Harcourt, Brace & World, 1968.

Berger, Alan L. *Crisis and Covenant: The Holocaust in American Jewish Fiction*. Albany: State Univ. of New York Press, 1985.

Bevis, William. "Native American Novels: Homing In." In *Critical Perspectives on Native American Fiction*, ed. Richard F. Fleck, 15–45. Washington DC: Three Continents Press, 1993.

Binder, Wolfgang. "American Dreams and Cuban Nightmares; Or, Does Cuba Exist? Some Remarks on Cuban American Literature." In *Voix et Langages aux Etats-Unis*, vol. 2, ed. Serge Ricard, 223–58. Aix-en-Provence: Univ. de Provence, 1993.

Birat, Kathie. "Stories to Pass On: Closure and Community in Toni Morrison's *Beloved*." In *The Insular Dream: Obsession and Resistance*, ed. Kristiaan Versluys, 324–34. Amsterdam: VU Univ. Press, 1995.

Bird, Gloria. "Searching for Evidence of Colonialism at Work: A Reading of Louise Erdrich's *Tracks*." *Wicazo SA Review* 8, no. 2 (fall 1992): 40–47.

Bishop, Charles A. "Northern Algonkian Cannibalism and Windigo Psychosis." In *Psychological Anthropology*, ed. Thomas R. Williams, 237–47. The Hague: Mouton, 1975.

Black Elk Speaks: Being the Life Story of a Holy Man of the Oglala Sioux as Told through John G. Neihardt (Flaming Rainbow). New York: William Morrow, 1932. Reprint, Lincoln: Univ. of Nebraska Press, 1988.

Blight, David. "W. E. B. Du Bois and the Struggle for American Historical Memory." In *History and Memory in African-American Culture*, ed. Geneviève Fabre and Robert O'Meally, 45–71. New York: Oxford Univ. Press, 1994.

Bodnar, John. *Remaking America: Public Memory, Commemoration, and Patriotism in the Twentieth Century*. Princeton: Princeton Univ. Press, 1992.

Boelhower, William. *Through a Glass Darkly: Ethnic Semiosis in American Literature*. New York: Oxford Univ. Press, 1987.

Boyle, T. Coraghessan. *World's End*. New York: Penguin, 1987.

Brandon, George. *Santeria from Africa to the New World: The Dead Sell Memories*. Bloomington: Indiana Univ. Press, 1993.

Brehm, Victoria. "The Metamorphoses of an Ojibwa *Manido*." *American Literature* 68, no. 4 (Dec. 1996): 677–706.

Budick, Emily. "Absence, Loss, and the Space of History in Toni Morrison's *Beloved*." *Arizona Quarterly* 48, no. 2 (summer 1992): 117–38.

Budick, Sanford, and Wolfgang Iser, eds. *The Translatability of Cultures: Figurations of the Space Between*. Stanford: Stanford Univ. Press, 1996.

Burunat, Silvia. "A Comparative Study of Contemporary Cuban American and Cuban Literature." *International Journal of the Sociology of Language* 84 (1990): 101–23.

Busia, Abena P. A. "What Is Your Nation? Reconnecting Africa and Her Diaspora through Paule Marshall's *Praisesong for the Widow*." In *Changing Our Own Words: Essays on Criticism, Theory, and Writing by Black Women*, ed. Cheryl A. Wall, 196–240. New Brunswick: Rutgers Univ. Press, 1989.

———. "Words Whispered over Voids: A Context for Black Women's Rebellious Voices in the Novel of the African Diaspora." In *Studies in Black American Literature*, vol. 3, *Black Feminist Criticism and Critical Theory*, ed. Joe Weixlmann and Houston A. Baker Jr. 1–41. Greenwood FL: Penkevill, 1988.

Butler, Judith. *Gender Trouble: Feminism and the Subversion of Identity*. New York: Routledge, 1990.

Butler, Thomas, ed. *Memory: History, Culture and the Mind*. Oxford: Basil Blackwell, 1989.

Cadava, Eduardo. "The Haunted Ethics of Paul Celan." In *Alphabet City Magazine* 4–5 (1995): 68–75.

Cahan, Abraham. *Yekl and the Imported Bridegroom and Other Stories of the New York Ghetto*. *Yekl*, D. Appleton, 1896. *The Imported Bridegroom and Other Stories of the New York Ghetto*, Houghton Mifflin, 1898. Reprint, New York: Dover, 1970.

Carpenter, Lynette, and Wendy K. Kolmar, eds. *Haunting the House of Fiction: Feminist Perspectives on Ghost Stories by American Women*. Knoxville: Univ. of Tennessee Press, 1991.

Caruth, Cathy. *Unclaimed Experience: Trauma, Narrative, and History*. Baltimore: Johns Hopkins Univ. Press, 1996.

———, ed. *Trauma: Explorations in Memory*. Baltimore: Johns Hopkins Univ. Press, 1995. An earlier version appeared in *American Imago* 48, no. 1 (spring 1991) and no. 4 (winter 1991).

Casey, Edward S. *Remembering: A Phenomenal Study*. Bloomington: Indiana Univ. Press, 1987.

Certeau, Michel de. *The Writing of History*. Trans. Tom Conley. New York: Columbia Univ. Press, 1988.

Chametzky, Jules. "Some Notes on Immigration, Ethnicity, Acculturation." *MELUS* 11, no. 1 (spring 1984): 45–51.

Cheyfitz, Eric. *The Poetics of Imperialism: Translation and Colonialization from The Tempest to Tarzan*. New York: Oxford Univ. Press, 1991.

Chopin, Kate. *The Awakening*. In *The Complete Works of Kate Chopin*, ed. Per Seyersted, 881-1000. Baton Rouge: Louisiana State Univ. Press, 1969.

Christian, Barbara T. "Ritualistic Process and the Structure of Paule Marshall's *Praisesong for the Widow*." *Callaloo* 6, no. 2 (spring/summer 1983): 74–84.

Churchill, Ward. *Fantasies of the Master Race: Literature, Cinema and the Coloni-zation of American Indians*. Ed. M. Annette Jaimes. Monroe ME: Common Courage Press, 1992.

Cisneros, Sandra. *Woman Hollering Creek and Other Stories*. New York: Random House, 1991.

Clarke, Deborah L. "'What There Was before Language': Preliteracy in Toni Morrison's *Song of Solomon*." In *Anxious Power: Reading, Writing, and Am-bivalence in Narrative by Women*, ed. Carol J. Singley and Susan Elizabeth Sweeney, 265–77. Albany: State Univ. of New York Press, 1993.

Clarke, Joni Adamson. "Why Bears Are Good to Think and Theory Doesn't Have to Be Murder: Transformation and Oral Tradition in Louise Erdrich's *Tracks*." *Studies in American Indian Literatures* 4, no. 1 (spring 1992): 28–48.

Clifford, James, and George E. Marcus, eds. *Writing Culture: The Poetics and Politics of Ethnography*. Berkeley: Univ. of California Press, 1986.

Cohen, Rabbi Harry A. *A Basic Jewish Encyclopedia: Jewish Teachings and Practices Listed and Interpreted in the Order of Their Importance Today*. Hartford: Hart-more House, 1965.

Cohen, Sarah Blacher. *Cynthia Ozick's Comic Art: From Levity to Liturgy*. Bloomington: Indiana Univ. Press, 1994.

Colombo, John Robert, ed. *Windigo: An Anthology of Fact and Fantastic Fiction*. Saskatoon, Saskatchewan: Western Producer Prairie Books, 1982.

Connerton, Paul. *How Societies Remember*. New York: Cambridge Univ. Press, 1989.

de Beauvoir, Simone. *The Second Sex*. Ed. and trans. H. M. Parshley. New York: Alfred A. Knopf, 1971.

DeLillo, Don. *Libra*. New York: Viking, 1988.

DeMallie, Raymond J., ed. *The Sixth Grandfather: Black Elk's Teachings Given to John G. Neihardt*. Lincoln: Univ. of Nebraska Press, 1984.

Dinesen, Isak. *Out of Africa and Shadows on the Grass*. New York: Random House, 1985.

Du Bois, W. E. B. *The Souls of Black Folk*. Ed. David W. Blight and Robert Gooding-Williams. Boston: Bedford Books, 1997.

Ducrot, Oswald, and Tzvetan Todorov. *Encyclopedic Dictionary of the Sciences of Language*. Trans. Catherine Porter. Baltimore: Johns Hopkins Univ. Press, 1979.

Duran, Eduardo, and Bonnie Duran. *Native American Postcolonial Psychology*. Al-bany: State Univ. of New York Press, 1995.

Ellison, Ralph. *Invisible Man*. New York: Random House, 1989.

Erdrich, Louise. *The Bingo Palace*. New York: HarperCollins, 1994.

———. "An Interview with Louise Erdrich." Interview by Nancy Feyl Chavkin and Allan Chavkin. In *Conversations with Louise Erdrich and Michael Dorris*, ed. Allan Chavkin and Nancy Feyl Chavkin, 220–53. Jackson: Univ. Press of Mississippi, 1994.

————. *Jacklight*. New York: Henry Holt, 1984.

————. *Love Medicine*. Rev. ed. New York: HarperCollins, 1993.

————. *Tracks*. New York: Harper & Row, 1989.

————. "Whatever Is Really Yours: An Interview with Louise Erdrich." Interview by Joseph Bruchac. In *Survival This Way: Interviews with American Indian Poets*, ed. Joseph Bruchac, 73–86. Tucson: Univ. of Arizona Press, 1987.

————. "Where I Ought to Be: A Writer's Sense of Place." *New York Times Book Review*, 28 July 1985, 1, 23–24.

Erdrich, Louise, and Michael Dorris. "Bangs and Whimpers: Novelists at Armageddon." *New York Times Book Review*, 13 March 1988, 1, 24–25.

————. "An Interview with Louise Erdrich and Michael Dorris." Interview by Kay Bonetti. *Missouri Review* 11, no. 2 (1988): 79–99.

————. "Louise Erdrich and Michael Dorris." Interview by Laura Coltelli. In *Winged Words: American Indian Writers Speak*, 41–52. Lincoln: Univ. of Nebraska Press, 1990.

————. "Louise Erdrich and Michael Dorris: Writers." Interview by Bill Moyers. In *A World of Ideas: Conversations with Thoughtful Men and Women about American Life Today and the Ideas Shaping Our Future*, ed. Betty Sue Flowers, 460–69. New York: Doubleday, 1989.

Eriksen, Thomas Hylland. *Ethnicity and Nationalism: Anthropological Perspectives*. London: Pluto Press, 1993.

Farley, Christopher John. "No Man's Land: Three New Novelists Take On Asian-American Life." *Time*, 5 May 1997, 101–2.

Faulkner, William. *Absalom, Absalom!* New York: Random House, 1986.

Fentress, James, and Chris Wickham. *Social Memory*. Oxford: Blackwell, 1992.

Ferguson, Rebecca. "History, Memory and Language in Toni Morrison's *Beloved*." In *Feminist Criticism: Theory and Practice*, ed. Susan Sellers, 109–27. Toronto: Univ. of Toronto Press, 1991.

Ferraro, Thomas J. *Ethnic Passages: Literary Immigrants in Twentieth-Century America*. Chicago: Univ. of Chicago Press, 1993.

Flavin, James. "The Novel as Performance: Communication in Louise Erdrich's *Tracks*." *Studies in American Indian Literatures* 3, no. 4 (winter 1991): 1–12.

Freud, Sigmund. *The Standard Edition of the Complete Psychological Works*. Ed. and trans. James Strachey. 24 vols. London: Hogarth Press, 1953–74.

Friedlander, Saul. "Trauma, Transference and 'Working Through' in Writing the History of the *Shoah*." *History and Memory* 4, no. 1 (spring 1992): 39–55.

Friedman, Susan Stanford. "Identity Politics, Syncretism, Catholicism, and Anishinabe Religion in Louise Erdrich's *Tracks*." *Religion and Literature* 26, no. 1 (spring 1994): 107–33.

Furlong, Monica. *Thérèse of Lisieux*. New York: Virago, Pantheon Books, 1987.

Gans, Herbert J. "Symbolic Ethnicity: The Future of Ethnic Groups." In *On the Making of Americans: Essays in Honor of David Riesman*, ed. Herbert J. Gans, Nathan Glazer, Joseph R. Gusfield, and Christopher Jencks. Philadelphia: Univ. of Pennsylvania Press, 1979.

García, Cristina. *The Agüero Sisters*. New York: Alfred A. Knopf, 1997.

———. "'. . . And There Is Only My Imagination Where Our History Should Be': An Interview with Cristina Garcia." Interview by Iraida H. López. *Michigan Quarterly Review* 33, no. 3 (summer 1994): 605–17.

———. *Dreaming in Cuban*. New York: Alfred A. Knopf, 1992.

———. "A Fish Swims in My Lung: An Interview with Cristina Garcia." Interview by Allan Vorda. In *Face to Face: Interviews with Contemporary Novelists*, 61–76. Houston: Rice Univ. Press, 1993.

García Lorca, Federico. *Obras Completas*. Ed. Arturo del Hoyo. Vol. 1. 22d ed. Madrid: Aguilar, 1954, 1986.

Gardaphé, Fred L. *Italian Signs, American Streets: The Evolution of Italian American Narrative*. Durham: Duke Univ. Press, 1996.

Gates, Henry Louis, Jr. "'Authenticity,' or the Lesson of Little Tree." *New York Times Book Review*, 24 Nov. 1991, 1, 26–30.

Geertz, Clifford. *Works and Lives: The Anthropologist as Author*. Stanford: Stanford Univ. Press, 1988.

George, Rosemary Marangoly. *The Politics of Home: Postcolonial Relocations and Twentieth-Century Fiction*. Cambridge: Cambridge Univ. Press, 1996.

Gibson, Ian. *Federico García Lorca: A Life*. New York: Pantheon Books, 1989.

Gillis, John R., ed. *Commemorations: The Politics of National Identity*. Princeton: Princeton Univ. Press, 1994.

Goldman, Anne E. "'I Made the Ink': (Literary) Production and Reproduction in *Dessa Rose* and *Beloved*." *Feminist Studies* 16, no. 2 (summer 1990): 313–30.

Goody, Jack. *Death, Property and the Ancestors: A Study of the Mortuary Customs of the Lodagaa of West Africa*. Stanford: Stanford Univ. Press, 1962.

Gordon, Avery F. *Ghostly Matters: Haunting and the Sociological Imagination*. Minneapolis: Univ. of Minnesota Press, 1997.

Greenberg, Mark S., and Bessel A. van der Kolk. "Retrieval and Integration of Traumatic Memories with the 'Painting Cure.'" In *Psychological Trauma*, ed. Bessel A. van der Kolk, 191–215. Washington DC: American Psychiatric Press, 1987.

Griffith, James L., and Melissa Elliott Griffith. *The Body Speaks: Therapeutic Dialogues for Mind-Body Problems*. New York: Basic Books, 1994.

Halbwachs, Maurice. *The Collective Memory*. Trans. Francis J. Ditter Jr. and Vida Yazdi Ditter. New York: Harper & Row, 1980.

———. *On Collective Memory*. Ed. and trans. Lewis A. Coser. Chicago: Univ. of Chicago Press, 1992.

Hall, Stuart. "Ethnicity: Identity and Difference." *Radical Identity* 23, no. 4 (Oct.–Dec. 1989): 9–20.

Hamacher, Werner. "Journals, Politics: Notes on Paul de Man's Wartime Journalism." In *Responses: On Paul de Man's Wartime Journalism*, ed. Werner Hamacher, Neil Hertz, and Thomas Keenan, 438–67. Lincoln: Univ. of Nebraska Press, 1989.

Handley, William R. "The House a Ghost Built: *Nommo*, Allegory, and the Ethics of Reading in Toni Morrison's *Beloved*." *Contemporary Literature* 36, no. 4 (winter 1995): 676–701.

Harris, Middleton A., comp., with the assistance of Morris Levitt, Roger Furman, and Ernest Smith. *The Black Book*. New York: Random House, 1974.

Harvey, Youngsook Kim. *Six Korean Women: The Socialization of Shamans*. St. Paul: West, 1979.

Hawthorne, Nathaniel. *The Scarlet Letter*. Vol. 1 of *The Centenary Edition of the Works of Nathaniel Hawthorne*, ed. William Charvat, Roy Harvey Pearce, et al. Columbus: Ohio State Univ. Press, 1962.

Helg, Aline. *Our Rightful Share: The Afro-Cuban Struggle for Equality, 1886–1912*. Chapel Hill: Univ. of North Carolina Press, 1995.

Henderson, Mae. "Toni Morrison's *Beloved*: Re-Membering the Body as Historical Text." In *Comparative American Identities: Race, Sex, and Nationality in the Modern Text*, ed. Hortense Spillers, 62–86. New York: Routledge, 1991.

Herman, Judith Lewis. *Trauma and Recovery*. New York: Basic Books, 1992.

Herskovitz, Melville J. *The Myth of the Negro Past*. Boston: Beacon Press, 1958.

Hertz, Robert. "A Contribution to the Study of the Collective Representation of Death." In *Death and the Right Hand*, trans. Rodney and Claudia Needham, 27–86. Aberdeen, Scotland: Cohen & West, 1960.

Hijuelos, Oscar. *Our House in the Last World*. New York: Persea Books, 1983.

Hobsbawm, Eric, and Terence Ranger, eds. *The Invention of Tradition*. Cambridge: Cambridge Univ. Press, 1993.

Hollinger, David A. *Postethnic America: Beyond Multiculturalism*. New York: Basic Books, 1995.

Holloway, Joseph E., ed. *Africanisms in American Culture*. Bloomington: Indiana Univ. Press, 1990.

Holloway, Karla F. C. "*Beloved*: A Spiritual." *Callaloo* 13 (1990): 516–25.

Horvitz, Deborah. "Nameless Ghosts: Possession and Dispossession in *Beloved*." *Studies in American Fiction* 17, no. 2 (autumn 1989): 157–67.

Hospital, Carolina. "Los Hijos del Exilio Cubano y Su Literatura." *Explicación de Textos Literarios* 15, no. 2 (1986–87): 103–14.

Huggins, Nathan Irving. *Black Odyssey: The Afro-American Ordeal in Slavery*. New York: Random House, 1979.

Hunt, Lynn. "History as Gesture; Or, The Scandal of History." In *Consequences of Theory*, ed. Jonathan Arac and Barbara Johnson, 91–107. Baltimore: Johns Hopkins Univ. Press, 1991.

Huntington, Richard, and Peter Metcalf. *Celebrations of Death: The Anthropology of Mortuary Rituals*. 2d ed. Cambridge: Cambridge Univ. Press, 1979.

Jahn, Janheinz. *Muntu: An Outline of the New African Culture*. Trans. Marjorie Grene. New York: Grove Press, 1961.

———. *Neo-African Literature: A History of Black Writing*. Trans. Oliver Coburn and Ursula Lehrburger. New York: Grove Press, 1968.

James, Henry. "The Jolly Corner." In *The Novels and Tales of Henry James*, 17: 433–85. New York: Charles Scribner's Sons, 1937.

———. *The Sense of the Past*. Vol. 26 of *The Novels and Tales of Henry James*. New York: Charles Scribner's Sons, 1945.

Janet, Pierre. *Psychological Healing: A Historical and Clinical Study*. Trans. Eden and Cedar Paul. 2 vols. New York: Macmillan, 1925. Reprint, New York: Arno Press, 1976.

Johnston, Basil. *The Manitous: The Spiritual World of Ojibway*. New York: HarperCollins, 1995.

Kammen, Michael G. *Mystic Chords of Memory: The Transformation of Tradition in American Culture*. New York: Alfred A. Knopf, 1991.

Kauvar, Elaine M. *Cynthia Ozick's Fiction: Tradition and Invention*. Bloomington: Indiana Univ. Press, 1993.

Keenan, Sally. "'Four Hundred Years of Silence': Myth, History, and Motherhood in Toni Morrison's *Beloved*." In *Recasting the World: Writing after Colonialism*, ed. Jonathan White, 45–81. Baltimore: Johns Hopkins Univ. Press, 1993.

Keller, Nora Okja. *Comfort Woman*. New York: Viking, 1997.

Kendall, Laurel. *The Life and Hard Times of a Korean Shaman: Of Tales and the Telling of Tales*. Honolulu: Univ. of Hawaii Press, 1988.

———. *Shamans, Housewives, and Other Restless Spirits: Women in Korean Ritual Life*. Honolulu: Univ. of Hawaii Press, 1985.

Kennedy, Liam. "Memory and Hearsay: Ethnic History and Identity in *Billy Phelan's Greatest Game* and *Ironweed*." *MELUS* 18, no. 1 (spring 1993): 71–82.

Kennedy, William. *Ironweed*. New York: Penguin Books, 1984.

Kingston, Maxine Hong. "Interview with Maxine Hong Kingston." Interview by Shelley Fisher Fishkin. *American Literary History* 3, no. 4 (winter 1991): 782–91.

———. "A *MELUS* Interview: Maxine Hong Kingston." Interview by Marilyn Chin. *MELUS* 16, no. 4 (winter 1989–90): 57–74.

———. *The Woman Warrior: Memoirs of a Girlhood among Ghosts*. New York: Random House, 1989.

Koolish, Lynda. "Fictive Strategies and Cinematic Representations in Toni

Morrison's *Beloved:* Postcolonial Theory/Postcolonial Text." *African American Review* 29, no. 3 (fall 1995): 421–38.

Kremer, S. Lillian. *Witness through the Imagination: Jewish American Holocaust Literature.* Detroit: Wayne State Univ. Press, 1989.

Krumholz, Linda. "The Ghosts of Slavery: Historical Recovery in Toni Morrison's *Beloved.*" *African American Review* 26, no. 3 (fall 1992): 395–408.

Krupat, Arnold. "Postcolonialism, Ideology, and Native American Literature." In *The Turn to the Native: Studies in Criticism and Culture,* 30–55. Lincoln: Univ. of Nebraska Press, 1996.

———. *The Voice in the Margin: Native American Literature and the Canon.* Berkeley: Univ. of California Press, 1989.

———, ed. *New Voices in Native American Literary Criticism.* Washington DC: Smithsonian Institution Press, 1993.

Kutzinski, Vera M. *Sugar's Secrets: Race and the Erotics of Cuban Nationalism.* Charlottesville: Univ. Press of Virginia, 1993.

La Barre, Weston. *The Ghost Dance: Origins of Religion.* New York: Doubleday, 1970.

LaCapra, Dominick. *Representing the Holocaust: History, Theory, Trauma.* Ithaca: Cornell Univ. Press, 1994.

Lamm, Maurice. *The Jewish Way in Death and Mourning.* New York: Jonathan David, 1969.

Langer, Lawrence L. *Admitting the Holocaust: Collected Essays.* New York: Oxford Univ. Press, 1995.

———. *Holocaust Testimonies: The Ruins of Memory.* New Haven: Yale Univ. Press, 1991.

Lawrence, David. "Fleshly Ghosts and Ghostly Flesh: The Word and the Body in *Beloved.*" *Studies in American Fiction* 19, no. 2 (autumn 1991): 189–201.

Lederer, Mary. "The Passage Back: Cultural Appropriation and Incorporation in Paule Marshall's *Praisesong for the Widow.*" *Ufahamu* 21, no. 3 (fall 1993): 66–79.

Lerner, Gerda, ed. *Black Women in White America: A Documentary History.* New York: Random House, 1992.

Levin, Ira. *Cantorial.* New York: Samuel French, 1990.

Lindberg-Seyersted, Brita. *Black and Female: Essays on Writings by Black Women in the Diaspora.* Oslo: Scandinavian Univ. Press, 1994.

Linenthal, Edward T. *Preserving Memory: The Struggle to Create America's Holocaust Museum.* New York: Viking, 1995.

Lipsitz, George. "Myth, History, and Counter-Memory." In *Politics and the Muse: Studies in the Politics of Recent American Literature,* ed. Adam J. Sorkin, 161–78. Bowling Green OH: Bowling Green State Univ. Press, 1989.

Lowenthal, David. *The Past Is a Foreign Country.* Cambridge: Cambridge Univ. Press, 1985.

Mageo, Jeannette Marie, and Alan Howard, eds. *Spirits in Culture, History, and Mind*. New York: Routledge, 1996.

Marano, Lou. "Windigo Psychosis: The Anatomy of an Emic-Etic Confusion." *Current Anthropology* 23, no. 4 (Aug. 1982): 385–412.

Marshall, Paule. *Praisesong for the Widow*. New York: Plume, 1983.

Maso, Carole. *Ghost Dance*. Hopewell NJ: Ecco Press, 1995.

McDonnell, Janet A. *The Dispossession of the American Indian, 1887–1934*. Bloomington: Indiana Univ. Press, 1991.

Melnyczuk, Askold. *What Is Told*. Boston: Faber & Faber, 1994.

Miller, Arthur. *Death of a Salesman*. In *Arthur Miller's Collected Plays: With an Introduction*, 130–222. New York: Viking Press, 1957.

Mobley, Marilyn. "A Different Remembering: Memory, History and Meaning in Toni Morrison's *Beloved*." In *Toni Morrison*, ed. Harold Bloom, 189–99. New York: Chelsea House, 1990.

Momaday, N. Scott. *House Made of Dawn*. New York: Harper & Row, 1968.

———. *The Names: A Memoir*. New York: Harper & Row, 1976.

Mooney, James. *The Ghost-Dance Religion and Wounded Knee*. New York: Dover, 1973. Originally issued as "The Ghost-Dance Religion and the Sioux Outbreak of 1890," part 2 of *Fourteenth Annual Report of the Bureau of Ethnology to the Secretary of the Smithsonian Institution, 1892–93, by J. W. Powell, Director*. Washington DC: Government Printing Office, 1896.

Morrison, Toni. *Beloved*. New York: Plume, 1987.

———. "A Bench by the Road." *World* 3, no. 4–5 (Jan.–Feb. 1989): 4, 37–41.

———. "A Conversation: Gloria Naylor and Toni Morrison." Interview by Gloria Naylor. *Southern Review* 21 (1985): 567-93.

———. "A Conversation with Toni Morrison." Interview by Judith Wilson. *Essence* 12, no. 3 (July 1981): 84–86, 128, 130, 133–34.

———. "In the Realm of Responsibility: A Conversation with Toni Morrison." Interview by Marsha Darling. *Women's Review of Books* 5, no. 6 (March 1988): 5–6.

———. "Interview with Toni Morrison." Interview by Christina Davis. *Présence Africaine* 145 (1988): 141–50.

———. "An Interview with Toni Morrison." Interview by Nellie McKay. *Contemporary Literature* 24, no. 4 (1983): 413–29.

———. *Jazz*. New York: Alfred A. Knopf, 1992.

———. "The Pain of Being Black." Interview by Bonnie Angelo. *Time*, 22 May 1989, 120–22.

———. *Playing in the Dark: Whiteness and the Literary Imagination*. New York: Random House, 1992.

———. "The Site of Memory." In *Inventing the Truth: The Art and Craft of Memoir*, ed. William Zinsser, 101–24. Boston: Houghton Mifflin, 1987.

———. *Song of Solomon*. New York: Plume, 1977. Reprint, 1987.

————. "Toni Morrison: New Novel Is More Than a Personal Triumph." Interview by Gail Caldwell. *Boston Globe*, 6 Oct. 1987, 67–68 (Living/Arts section).

————. "Toni Morrison: Novelist." Interview by Bill Moyers. In *A World of Ideas: Public Opinions from Private Citizens*, vol. 2, ed. Andie Tucher, 54–63. New York: Doubleday, 1990.

————. "Toni Morrison Now." Interview by Elsie B. Washington. *Essence*, Oct. 1987, 58, 136–37.

————. "Unspeakable Things Unspoken: The Afro-American Presence in American Literature." *Michigan Quarterly Review* 28, no. 1 (winter 1989): 1–34.

Mukherjee, Bharati. "The Management of Grief." In *The Middleman and Other Stories*, 173–94. New York: Fawcett Crest, 1988.

Murphy, Joseph M. *Santería: African Spirits in America*. Boston: Beacon Press, 1993.

Murray, David. *Forked Tongues: Speech, Writing and Representation in North American Indian Texts*. Bloomington: Indiana Univ. Press, 1991.

Naylor, Gloria. *Mama Day*. New York: Ticknor & Fields, 1988.

Nelson, Robert M. *Place and Vision: The Function of Landscape in Native American Fiction*. New York: Peter Lang, 1993.

Nora, Pierre. "Between Memory and History: Les Lieux de Mémoire." *Representations* 26 (spring 1989): 7–25.

Núñez, Luis Manuel. *Santeria: A Practical Guide to Afro-Caribbean Magic*. Woodstock CT: Spring, 1992.

Oliver, Lawrence J. "Deconstruction or Affirmative Action: The Literary-Political Debate over the 'Ethnic Question.'" *American Literary History* 3, no. 4 (winter 1991): 792–808.

Olson, James S., and Judith E. Olson. *Cuban Americans: From Trauma to Triumph*. New York: Twayne, 1995.

Ortiz, Fernando. *Cuban Counterpoint: Tobacco and Sugar*. Trans. Harriet De Onís. New York: Alfred A. Knopf, 1947.

Ottenberg, Eve. "The Rich Visions of Cynthia Ozick." *New York Times Magazine*, 10 April 1983, 47, 62–66.

Ozick, Cynthia. Preface to *Bloodshed and Three Novellas*, 3–12. New York: Alfred A. Knopf, 1976.

————. "A Contraband Life." *Commentary* 39, no. 3 (March 1965): 89–92.

————. "An Interview with Cynthia Ozick." Interview by Elaine M. Kauvar. *Contemporary Literature* 34, no. 3 (1993): 358–94.

————. "Roundtable Discussion." In *Writing the Holocaust*, ed. Berel Lang, 277–84. New York: Holmes & Meier, 1988.

————. *The Shawl*. New York: Random House, 1990.

———. "Toward a New Yiddish." In *Art and Ardor: Essays*, 151–77. New York: Alfred A. Knopf, 1983.

Page, Philip. "Circularity in Toni Morrison's *Beloved*." *African American Review* 26, no. 1 (1992): 31–39.

Patterson, Orlando. *Freedom in the Making of Western Culture*. New York: Basic Books, 1991.

———. *Slavery and Social Death: A Comparative Study*. Cambridge: Harvard Univ. Press, 1982.

Pérez, Louis A., Jr. "Politics, Peasants, and People of Color: The 1912 'Race War' in Cuba Reconsidered." *Hispanic American Historical Review* 66, no. 3 (1986): 512–39.

Pérez Firmat, Gustavo. *The Cuban Condition: Translation and Identity in Modern Cuban Literature*. Cambridge: Cambridge Univ. Press, 1989.

Pérez-Torres, Rafael. "Knitting and Knotting the Narrative Thread—*Beloved* as Postmodern Novel." *Modern Fiction Studies* 39, no. 3–4 (fall/winter 1993): 689–707.

Peterson, Nancy J. "History, Postmodernism, and Louise Erdrich's *Tracks*." *PMLA* 109, no. 5 (Oct. 1994): 982–94.

Pollard, Velma. "Cultural Connections in Paule Marshall's *Praisesong for the Widow*." *World Literature Written in English* 25, no. 2 (autumn 1985): 285–98.

Power, Susan. *The Grass Dancer*. New York: Berkley Books, 1995.

Powers, Peter Kerry. "Disruptive Memories: Cynthia Ozick, Assimilation, and the Invented Past." *MELUS* 20, no. 3 (fall 1995): 79–97.

Pratt, Mary Louise. *Imperial Eyes: Travel Writing and Transculturation*. London: Routledge, 1992.

Prucha, Francis Paul. *The Great Father: The United States Government and the American Indians*. 2 vols. Lincoln: Univ. of Nebraska Press, 1984.

Rainwater, Catherine. "Reading between Worlds: Narrativity in the Fiction of Louise Erdrich." *American Literature* 62, no. 3 (Sept. 1990): 405–22.

Remmler, Karen. "Sheltering Battered Bodies in Language: Imprisonment Once More?" In *Displacements: Cultural Identities in Question*, ed. Angelika Bammer, 216–32. Bloomington: Indiana Univ. Press, 1994.

Rivero, Eliana. "Cubanos y Cubanoamericanos: Perfil y presencia en los Estados Unidos." *Discurso Literario* 7, no. 1 (1989): 81–101.

Rodriguez, Richard. "An American Writer." In *The Invention of Ethnicity*, ed. Werner Sollors, 3–13. New York: Oxford Univ. Press, 1989.

———. *Days of Obligation: An Argument with My Mexican Father*. New York: Penguin, 1993.

Rody, Carolyn. "Toni Morrison's *Beloved*: History, 'Rememory,' and a 'Clamor for a Kiss.'" *American Literary History* 7, no. 1 (spring 1995): 92–119.

Rosaldo, Renato. "Others of Invention: Ethnicity and Its Discontents." *Voice Literary Supplement*, Feb. 1990, 27–29.

Rosenman, Stanley, and Irving Handelsman. "Rising from the Ashes: Modeling Resiliency in a Community Devastated by Man-Made Catastrophe." *American Imago* 49, no. 2 (summer 1992): 185–226.

Rosenwald, Lawrence. "Buber and Rosenzweig's Challenge to Translation Theory." Introduction to *Scripture and Translation,* by Martin Buber and Franz Rosenzweig, trans. Lawrence Rosenwald and Everett Fox, xxix–liv. Bloomington: Indiana Univ. Press, 1994.

———. "Lost in Translation." *Boston Review* 11, no. 6 (Dec. 1986): 20.

Roth, Philip. *The Ghost Writer.* New York: Farrar, Straus & Giroux, 1979.

Rothenberg, Jerome. "We Explain Nothing." In *On the Translation of Native American Literatures,* ed. Brian Swann. Washington DC: Smithsonian Institution Press, 1992.

Ruppert, James. "Meditation and Multiple Narrative in Contemporary Native American Fiction." *Texas Studies in Literature and Langauge* 28, no. 1 (spring 1986): 209–25.

Rushdie, Salman. *Imaginary Homelands: Essays and Criticism, 1981–1991.* London: Granta Books, 1992.

Saldívar, Ramón. *Chicano Narrative: The Dialectics of Difference.* Madison: Univ. of Wisconsin Press, 1990.

Samuel, Raphael, and Paul Thompson, eds. *The Myths We Live By.* London: Routledge, 1990.

Scarry, Elaine. *The Body in Pain: The Making and Unmaking of the World.* New York: Oxford Univ. Press, 1985.

Schopp, Andrew. "Narrative Control and Subjectivity: Dismantling Safety in Toni Morrison's *Beloved.*" *Centennial Review* 39, no. 2 (spring 1995): 355–79.

Schwartz, Barry. "The Social Context of Commemoration: A Study in Collective Memory." *Social Forces* 61, no. 2 (Dec. 1982): 374–402.

Sequoya-Magdaleno, Jana. "Telling the *différance*: Representations of Identity in the Discourse of Indianness." In *The Ethnic Canon: Histories, Institutions, and Interventions,* ed. David Palumbo-Liu, 88–116. Minneapolis: Univ. of Minnesota Press, 1995.

Siegel, Richard, Michael Strassfeld, and Sharon Strassfeld, eds. *The First Jewish Catalog: A Do-It-Yourself Kit.* Philadelphia: Jewish Publication Society of America, 1973.

Silko, Leslie Marmon. *Almanac of the Dead: A Novel.* New York: Penguin, 1992.

———. *Ceremony.* New York: Penguin, 1986.

Singer, Isaac Bashevis. *The Magician of Lublin.* New York: Noonday Press, 1960.

Singh, Amritjit, Joseph T. Skerrett Jr., and Robert E. Hogan, eds. *Memory and Cultural Politics: New Approaches to American Ethnic Literatures.* Boston: Northeastern Univ. Press, 1996.

———, eds. *Memory, Narrative, and Identity: New Essays in Ethnic American Literatures.* Boston: Northeastern Univ. Press, 1994.

Smith, Barbara Herrnstein. "Narrative Versions, Narrative Theories." In *American Criticism in the Poststructuralist Age*, ed. Ira Konigsberg, 162–86. Ann Arbor: Univ. of Michigan Press, 1981.

Smith, Curtis C. "Werner Sollors' *Beyond Ethnicity* and Afro-American Literature." *MELUS* 14, no. 2 (summer 1987): 65–71.

Smith, M. G. *Kinship and Community in Carriacou*. New Haven: Yale Univ. Press, 1962.

Smith, Theresa S. *The Island of the Anishnaabeg: Thunderers and Water Monsters in the Traditional Ojibwe Life-World*. Moscow: Univ. of Idaho Press, 1995.

Smith, Valerie. "'Circling the Subject': History and Narrative in *Beloved*." In *Toni Morrison: Critical Perspectives Past and Present*, ed. Henry Louis Gates Jr. and K. A. Appiah, 344–55. New York: Amistad, 1993.

Sollors, Werner. *Beyond Ethnicity: Consent and Descent in American Culture*. New York: Oxford Univ. Press, 1986.

Stead, Deborah. "Unlocking the Tale," review of *Tracks*, by Louise Erdrich. *New York Times Book Review*, 2 Oct. 1988, 41.

Steinberg, Stephen. *The Ethnic Myth: Race, Ethnicity, and Class in America*. Rev. ed. Boston: Beacon Press, 1989.

Steiner, George. *After Babel: Aspects of Language and Translation*. 2d ed. Oxford: Oxford Univ. Press, 1992.

Stewart, Susan. *Nonsense: Aspects of Intertextuality in Folklore and Literature*. Baltimore: Johns Hopkins Univ. Press, 1979.

Stripes, James D. "The Problem(s) of (Anishinaabe) History in the Fiction of Louise Erdrich: Voices and Contexts." *Wicazo SA Review* 7, no. 1 (fall 1991): 26–33.

Stuckey, Sterling. *Slave Culture: Nationalist Theory and the Foundation of Black America*. New York: Oxford Univ. Press, 1987.

Styron, William. *Sophie's Choice*. New York, Random House, 1979.

Swann, Brian, ed. *On the Translation of Native American Literatures*. Washington DC: Smithsonian Institution Press, 1992.

Tan, Amy. *The Hundred Secret Senses*. New York: G. P. Putnam's Sons, 1995.

Teicher, Morton I. *Windigo Psychosis: A Study of a Relationship between Belief and Behavior among the Indians of Northeastern Canada*. Proceedings of the 1960 Annual Spring Meeting of the American Ethnological Society. Ed. Verne F. Ray. Seattle: American Ethnological Society, 1960.

Thelen, David, ed. *Memory and American History*. Bloomington: Indiana Univ. Press, 1989.

Thomas, Nicholas. "The Inversion of Tradition." *American Ethnologist* 19, no. 2 (May 1992): 213–32.

Thornton, Russell. *American Indian Holocaust and Survival: A Population History since 1492*. Norman: Univ. of Oklahoma Press, 1987.

———. *We Shall Live Again: The 1870 and 1890 Ghost Dance Movements as Demographic Revitalization*. Cambridge: Cambridge Univ. Press, 1986.

Todorov, Tzvetan. *The Conquest of America: The Question of the Other*. Trans. Richard Howard. New York: Harper & Row, 1984.

Travis, Molly Abel. "Speaking from the Silence of the Slave Narrative: Beloved and African-American Women's History." *Texas Review* 13, no. 1–2 (1992): 69–81.

Turner, Victor. "Death and the Dead in the Pilgrimage Process." In *Religious Encounters with Death: Insights from the History and Anthropology of Religions*, ed. Frank E. Reynolds and Earle H. Waugh, 24–39. University Park: Pennsylvania State Univ. Press, 1977.

Tuwim, Julian. *My, Żydzi Polscy . . . / We, Polish Jews . . . .* Ed. Ch. Shmeruk. Jerusalem: Magnes Press, Hebrew University, 1984.

van der Kolk, Bessel A. *Psychological Trauma*. Washington DC: American Psychiatric Press, 1987.

Van der Zee, James, Owen Dodson, and Camille Billops. *The Harlem Book of the Dead*. Dobbs Ferry NY: Morgan & Morgan, 1978.

van Gennep, Arnold. *The Rites of Passage*. Trans. Monika B. Vizedom and Gabrielle L. Caffee. Chicago: Univ. of Chicago Press, 1960.

Vecsey, Christopher T. *Traditional Ojibwa Religion and Its Historical Changes*. Philadelphia: American Philosophical Society, 1983.

Vizenor, Gerald. *Manifest Manners: Postindian Warriors of Survivance*. Hanover NH: Wesleyan Univ. Press, 1994.

———. *The People Named the Chippewa: Narrative Histories*. Minneapolis: Univ. of Minnesota Press, 1984.

———, ed. *Narrative Chance: Postmodern Discourse on Native American Indian Literatures*. Albuquerque: Univ. of New Mexico Press, 1989.

Wald, Alan. "Theorizing Cultural Difference: A Critique of the 'Ethnicity School.'" *MELUS* 14, no. 2 (summer 1987): 21–33.

Walpole, Horace. *The Castle of Otranto: A Gothic Story*. Ed. W. S. Lewis. Oxford: Oxford Univ. Press, 1982.

Waters, Mary C. *Ethnic Options: Choosing Identities in America*. Berkeley: Univ. of California Press, 1990.

Waxman, Barbara Frey. "Changing History through a Gendered Perspective: A Postmodern Feminist Reading of Toni Morrison's *Beloved*." In *Multicultural Literatures through Feminist/Poststructuralist Lenses*, ed. Barbara Frey Waxman, 57–83. Knoxville: Univ. of Tennessee Press, 1993.

Weber, Donald. "Reconsidering the Hansen Thesis: Generational Metaphors and American Ethnic Studies." *American Quarterly* 43, no. 2 (June 1991): 320–32.

Welch, James. *Winter in the Blood*. New York: Penguin, 1986.

Wharton, Edith. *A Backward Glance*. New York: D. Appleton-Century, 1934.

———. "The Eyes." In *The Collected Short Stories of Edith Wharton*, vol. 2, ed. R. W. B. Lewis, 115–30. New York: Charles Scribner's Sons, 1968.

———. *The House of Mirth*. New York: Penguin, 1985.

White, Michael, and David Epston. *Narrative Means to Therapeutic Ends*. New York: Norton, 1990.

Wiget, Andrew. "His Life in His Tail: The Native American Trickster and the Literature of Possibility." In *Redefining American Literary History*, ed. A. LaVonne Brown Ruoff and Jerry W. Ward, 83–96. New York: Modern Language Association of America, 1990.

Wilentz, Gay. "Towards a Spiritual Middle Passage Back: Paule Marshall's Diasporic Vision in *Praisesong for the Widow*." *Obsidian II* 5, no. 3 (winter 1990): 1–21.

Wilson, August. *The Piano Lesson*. New York: Plume, 1990.

———. "Round Five for a Theatrical Heavyweight." Interview by Mervyn Rothstein. *New York Times*, 15 April 1990, section 2, 1, 8.

Winsbro, Bonnie. *Supernatural Forces: Belief, Difference, and Power in Contemporary Works by Ethnic Women*. Amherst: Univ. of Massachusetts Press, 1993.

Winter, Jay. *Sites of Memory, Sites of Mourning: The Great War in European Cultural History*. Cambridge: Cambridge Univ. Press, 1995.

Wolff, Cynthia Griffin. "'Margaret Garner': A Cincinnati Story." *Massachusetts Review* 32, no. 3 (fall 1991): 417–40.

Wolfman Jack, with Byron Laursen. *Have Mercy! Confessions of the Original Rock 'n' Roll Animal*. New York: Warner Books, 1995.

Wong, Hertha D. "Adoptive Mothers and Thrown-Away Children in the Novels of Louise Erdrich." In *Narrating Mothers: Theorizing Maternal Subjectivities*, ed. Brenda O. Daly and Maureen T. Reddy, 174–92. Knoxville: Univ. of Tennessee Press, 1991.

Wong, Sau-ling Cynthia. *Reading Asian American Literature: From Necessity to Extravagance*. Princeton: Princeton Univ. Press, 1993.

Wyatt, Jean. "Giving Body to the Word: The Maternal Symbolic in Toni Morrison's *Beloved*." *PMLA* 108, no. 3 (May 1993): 474–88.

Yerushalmi, Yosef Hayim. *Zakhor: Jewish History and Jewish Memory*. Seattle: Univ. of Washington Press, 1982.

Yezierska, Anzia. *Bread Givers: A Struggle between a Father of the Old World and a Daughter of the New*. New York: Persea Books, 1975.

Young, James E. *Writing and Rewriting the Holocaust: Narrative and the Consequences of Interpretation*. Bloomington: Indiana Univ. Press, 1988.

———, ed. *The Art of Memory: Holocaust Memorials in History*. Munich: Prestel-Verlag, New York: Jewish Museum, 1994.

Index

Abraham, Nicholas, 19
acculturation: reciprocal, 11, 12, 175n.23; trauma and, 43–44, 54
Adorno, Theodor, 162
Africa, as mythic, 144, 151
African diaspora, 149–51
Afro-Cubanism, 111–14, 118
Agüero Sisters, The (García), 3, 94, 99, 115, 127–32, 194n.7
Allen, Paula Gunn, 180n.22
Almanac of the Dead (Silko), 3
Always Coming Home (Le Guin), 57
America: ghostliness within, 30–31, 89–90; racism in, 12–14, 89–90; Santería in, 111
Anaya, Rudolfo, *Bless Me, Ultima*, 3, 16
ancestor spirits, 2, 20–21, 31, 136, 137–38, 141, 185n.9, 201n.22; in *Beloved*, 64, 66, 67, 186n.15; in *Comfort Woman*, 158–59, 202n.38; in *Dreaming in Cuban*, 105–6; in *Praisesong for the Widow*, 147, 149–52
Anderson, Andrew A., 124–25
anthropology, 23–24
Asikinack, William, 181n.33
assimilation, 12, 21, 44–45, 144–46, 167, 175n.23
authenticity, 12–13

"'Authenticity,' or the Lesson of Little Tree" (Gates), 176n.29
Awakening, The (Chopin), 198n.51

Barth, Fredrik, 11
Belliard-Acosta, Marianella, 195n.25
Beloved (Morrison), 1, 5, 16, 21, 26, 96, 115, 170, 174n.8; ancestor spirits in, 64, 66, 67, 186n.15; cannibalism in, 10, 71–72, 77, 82; coda, 69–70, 89; commemoration in, 65–67, 91–92, 132–34; exorcism scene, 67, 84–88; haunted language in, 78–79, 189n.32; historical consciousness in, 88–92, 185n.6; memory in, 7–8, 27–28, 74–75, 81–82, 88; narrative style, 72, 75, 77–78, 91, 189n.32; rejection of history in, 70–71, 90; rememory in, 7, 74–75, 81; repetition in, 72–73, 74; romantic love in, 70, 88–89, 91; secondary burial imagery in, 64–70; temporality in, 73–77; women's role in exorcism, 85–86; writing in, 62, 65, 67–68, 87, 185n.4
Benjamin, Jules Robert, 196n.30
Benjamin, Walter, 180n.20
Binder, Wolfgang, 193n.2
Bingo Palace, The (Erdrich), 3, 32, 184n.61
Black Book, 184–85n.3

Black Elk, 183 n.44
Bless Me, Ultima (Anaya), 3, 16
Blight, David, 187 n.17, 192 n.52
Blixen, Karen. *See* Dinesen, Isak
Body Speaks (Griffith and Griffith), 177 n.42
Boelhower, William, 29, 38, 126, 173 n.7, 198 n.53
Borland, Isabel Alvarez, 193 n.2
Boyle, T. Coraghessan, *World's End*, 3
Brandon, George, 105, 111, 192 n.1, 194 n.11
Bread Givers, The (Yezierska), 178 n.51
Budick, Emily, 189 n.34, 191 n.47
Burunat, Silvia, 193 n.2
Butler, Judith, *Gender Trouble*, 177 n.47

Cahan, Abraham, *Yekl*, 4–5
cannibal ghosts, 9–10, 71–72, 82, 152, 153. *See also* windigo
Cantorial (Levin), 3
Carpentier, Alejo, 111
Caruth, Cathy, 71, 188 n.24
"Casida de las palomas oscuras" (García Lorca), 103–4
Castle of Otranto, The (Walpole), 2
Cather, Willa, 33
Celan, Paul, 192 n.55
Ceremony (Silko), 33
Certeau, Michel de, 17, 38
Chametzky, Jules, 175 n.23
Changó, 104, 109–10, 195 n.18, 197 n.36
Chippewa, 31–35, 38–39, 178 n.1, 181 n.32, 182–83 n.42; Ghost Dance and, 53, 56, 57, 59, 183 n.46; tuberculosis and, 39–40, 42, 43. See also *manitous;* Native Americans; windigo
Chopin, Kate, *The Awakening*, 198 n.51
Christian, Barbara, 145
Christianity, imagery of, 49–52, 58, 85, 92, 97, 155, 168, 170, 182 n.42, 191 n.48, 201 n.25
Churchill, Ward, *Fantasies of the Master Race*, 176 n.27
Circle dances, 8, 148–51
Cisneros, Sandra, *Woman Hollering Creek*, 3, 16
Clarke, Deborah L., 191 n.46
colonialism, 13, 36–37
Comfort Woman (Keller), 3, 9, 18, 28–29, 131, 132, 143, 152–60, 163, 202 nn.34,

35, 38; ancestor spirits in, 158–59, 202 n.38; gender issues in, 25–26; ghost-liness in, 154–55; Korean shamanism in, 156–58, 202 n.38; possession in, 152, 155–60; secondary burial in, 152, 154, 155–56, 159
commemoration, 22, 65–67, 91–92, 132–34, 138–44, 147–48, 151, 170–71, 199 n.2
Connerton, Paul, 138–39, 147, 198–99 n.1
consumption metaphors, 9–10, 42–45, 51–53, 82, 100–102, 167, 181 n.32. *See also* incorporation
continuity, cultural, 27, 111, 134, 140, 160–61, 170–71
Cuba: as myth, 3, 95; racism in, 113–14, 192–93 n.1
Cuban-American exile community, 93–95, 192–93 n.1
Cuban-American National Foundation, 94
cultural constructedness, 13–14
cultural haunting, 4, 16–19; commemoration and, 132–34, 138–40, 147, 148, 170–71, 199 n.2; vs. ghost stories, 5–6; group histories and, 5–6, 8–9, 17, 38, 130–31; involuntary nature of, 19; pervasiveness of, 28; women and, 24–25
cultural mourning, 22–23, 53–54, 66–67, 132–44, 170–71. *See also* commemoration; mourning; secondary burial

Days of Obligation (Rodriguez), 3
de Beauvoir, Simone, 14
Debussy, Claude, *La Soirée dans Grenade,* 124
DeLillo, Don, *Libra,* 6
Di Cicco, Pier Giorgio, 29
Dickinson, Emily, 5
Dinesen, Isak, *Out of Africa,* 33–34
Dorris, Michael, 32, 200 n.14
Dreaming in Cuban (García), 3, 26, 28, 143, 170, 193 n.2, 193–94 n.4, 194 n.5; aesthetic imagery in, 118–19; ancestor spirits in, 105–6; biculturalism and, 94–95, 109–10, 115, 120; bridge imagery in, 126–27; consumption metaphors in, 100–102; genetic imagery in, 118–20; ghostliness in, 95–96, 107; imagery of exile in, 114–17; imagination in, 99, 102–3, 121–22, 194–95 n.17; language

in, 94, 98–99, 102–3, 106–10; ocean imagery in, 124–25, 198nn.51, 52; organization of, 96–98; relationships in, 197n.37; Santería in, 105–15, 117–18, 196nn.31, 35, 198n.52; secondary burial imagery in, 96–98, 100, 127; translation in, 94–96, 102–4, 106–10; tree imagery in, 144–47

Du Bois, W. E. B., 15

Ellison, Ralph, 15, 174n.8; *Invisible Man*, 6
embodiment, 10, 64, 74, 77, 80–82, 85, 86, 130–31, 136–37, 140, 143, 146, 167–68
Erdrich, Louise, 31–36, 43, 179nn.16, 17, 194n.4; *The Bingo Palace*, 54; Ghost Dance and, 54, 183nn.44, 46; land and, 32–35; *Love Medicine*, 32, 43; on tradition, 32, 141; "Whatever Is Really Yours," 178n.1; "Windigo," 181n.34. See also *Tracks*
Eriksen, Thomas Hylland, 176n.31
Espiritismo, 111
ethnic anxiety, 19, 131
ethnicity, 174n.10; anti-essentialist view, 11–12, 14; cost-free, 13; form vs. content, 11, 14; as ghostly, 151–52, 159–60; invented, 13–14, 38, 99, 118–20, 161, 175–76n.25; memory and, 130; as performance, 22, 138–39; as process, 11–12, 14, 22; self-ascription and, 12–13, 176n.31; subrational level and, 19. *See also* identity, ethnic
Ethnic Options (Waters), 176n.28
Ethnic Passages (Ferraro), 173n.7
ethnogenesis, mourning and, 21–23, 134–40, 142, 143–44
ethnographer, writer as, 23–24, 110–11, 134, 135, 138, 143–44, 171
exorcism, 6, 8, 165, 171; group history and, 8–9, 88–89, 91; possession and, 19–20, 41, 46, 66–67; reenactment and, 79–80, 83–85; revisionism and, 19; silence and, 11, 65, 71, 81–82, 91, 134; storytelling and, 79–80, 83–84, 92
"Eyes, The" (Wharton), 5

Fantasies of the Master Race (Churchill), 176n.27
Faulkner, William, 4, 33, 34, 174n.8
Ferguson, Rebecca, 189n.32

Ferraro, Thomas J., 139–40, 173n.7
Firmat, Gustavo Pérez, 196n.33
Fischer, Michael, 19
Forked Tongues (Murray), 36
Freud, Sigmund, 19–20, 67, 74, 138, 186n.14
Friedman, Susan Stanford, 182n.42

"Gacela de la huida" (García Lorca), 124
Galapagos (Vonnegut), 57
Gans, Herbert, 13
García, Cristina, 3, 94, 109, 110, 174n.9, 193n.3, 194n.6; black culture and, 110, 113; Morrison and, 114, 116–17. See also *Agüero Sisters, The; Dreaming in Cuban*
García Lorca, Federico, 103–4, 116, 124–25, 194n.9, 195–96n.26, 196n.28; *Gypsy Ballads*, 112, 196n.31
García Márquez, Gabriel, 34, 174n.9
Garner, Margaret, 8, 62, 64, 68, 138, 185n.6, 187n.19
Gates, Henry Louis, Jr., "'Authenticity,' or the Lesson of Little Tree," 176n.29
Geertz, Clifford, 23–24
gender issues, 25–26
Gender Trouble (Butler), 177n.47
generational issues, 21, 166, 177n.46
Ghost Dance, 27, 37, 53–60, 183n.44, 184nn.57, 59
Ghost Dance (Maso), 3
ghosts: ambivalence and, 20–21, 25, 66; cannibal ghosts, 9–10, 42, 71–72, 82, 153; cultural continuity and, 19–20, 27, 31, 111, 134, 170–71; demons, 20–21; erased history and, 2, 71, 133–34, 185n.9, 187nn.19, 21; as intermediaries, 6, 16, 47, 177n.36; internalization of, 43–44, 154; kinship and, 12, 13, 171; memory and, 130–32; pan-ethnic traditions and, 2–4, 11–12, 174n.8; as reconstructive agents, 31–32, 53, 171; revisionism and, 4, 11, 13, 19; social crisis and, 2; transformation of, 19–20; vampiric, 9, 10, 70; windigo, 10, 37, 42–44, 49, 51, 52, 181nn.32, 33
ghost stories, 5–6, 18. *See also* cultural haunting
Ghost Writer, The (Roth), 6
Goldman, Anne E., 190n.36

Goody, Jack, 186 n.13, 187 n.20
Gothic elements, 1–2
Grass Dancer, The (Powers), 3
Grenada, 112
Griffith, James L., 177 n.42
Griffith, Melissa Elliott, 177 n.42
Guillén, Nicolás, 111
Guirao, Ramón, 111
Gypsy Ballads (García Lorca), 112, 196 n.31

Halbwachs, Maurice, 130, 142
Hall, Stuart, 23, 176 n.33, 177–78 n.48
Hamacher, Werner, 71, 90, 192 n.55
Hamlet (Shakespeare), 86
Handelsman, Irving, 92
Hansen, Marcus Lee, 177 n.46
Harris, Middleton A., 184 n.3
Harvey, Youngsook Kim, 158, 202 n.38
haunting. *See* cultural haunting
Hawthorne, Nathaniel, 4, 174 n.8
heir-ethnographers, writers as, 23–24,
    110–11, 134, 135, 138, 143–44, 171
Henderson, Mae, 83, 84, 85–86, 187 n.21,
    190 n.43
Herman, Judith Lewis, 188 n.24, 189–
    90 n.35
Hertz, Robert, 22, 66, 67, 89, 186 n.15
Hijuelos, Oscar, *Our House in the Last
    World*, 3
historical consciousness, 5–6, 8, 38–39,
    88–92, 140–41. *See also* past
historical fiction, 6, 72
history, 38; erased, 2, 18, 21, 29, 63, 71–
    72, 132–34, 185 n.9, 187 nn.19, 21; fic-
    tion and, 17
Hobsbawm, Eric, 175–76 n.25
Hollinger, David A., 13
Holloway, Karla, 189 n.32
Holocaust, 162
Holocaust narratives, 71, 76–77, 90, 92,
    192 n.54
home, concept of, 34, 179 n.16
Hospital, Carolina, 193 n.2
House of Mirth (Wharton), 24
Howard, Alan, 111
Howe, Irving, 160
Huggins, Nathan, 192 n.52
Hundred Secret Senses, The (Tan), 3
Hunt, Lynn, 17
Huntington, Richard, 186 n.13

Ibo Landing legend, 147–49, 201 nn.24, 25
identity, ethnic: memory and, 130–31, 145,
    147; oppositional, 14–15; redefinition
    of, 111, 134–35; as syncretic, 11–12,
    104–5
imagination, 99, 102–3, 121–22, 144, 151,
    162, 194–95 n.17
immigrants, 15–16; language and, 94, 98–
    99, 102–3, 161; three-generations model,
    21, 177 n.46
incorporation, 34–36, 37, 101; mourn-
    ing and, 41–44, 162–63, 165, 167; as
    revision, 34–35. *See also* consumption
    metaphors
inheritance, 160–61
Invention of Tradition (Hobsbawm and
    Ranger), 175–76 n.25
Investigation, The (Weiss), 192 n.54
invisibility, 10, 15, 25, 30–31, 113, 196 n.31
Invisible Man (Ellison), 6
Ironweed (Kennedy), 3, 15, 131, 135, 142,
    171, 204 n.63

James, Henry, "The Jolly Corner," 5;
    Sense of the Past, 61–62, 63, 64
Janet, Pierre, 7–8, 9, 73, 79–81, 83, 188 n.24
Jazz (Morrison), 190 n.44
"Jolly Corner, The" (James), 5

Kaddish, 170, 204 n.62
Kazin, Alfred, 33
Keenan, Sally, 185 n.6
Keller, Nora Okja, 152–53. *See also Com-
    fort Woman*
Kendall, Laurel, 157, 158, 202 n.38
Kennedy, Liam, 199 n.4
Kennedy, William, *Ironweed*, 3, 15, 131,
    135, 142, 171, 204 n.63
Kingston, Maxine Hong, 15, 21, 123, 200–
    201 n.16. *See also Woman Warrior, The*
kinship, ghostly, 12, 13, 171
Kroeber, Karl, 36–37
Krumholz, Linda, 185 n.6
Krupat, Arnold, 36, 179 n.16, 180 n.20
Krystal, Henry, 188 n.24
Kutzinski, Vera, 111–12, 113

La Barre, Weston, 58
La Llorona, 3
land, tradition and, 32–37

Langer, Lawrence L., 76–77, 188 n.24
language: haunted language, 78–79,
189 n.32; immigrants and, 94, 98–99,
102–3, 161; lost, 102–4; physicality and,
84–87, 89, 99, 156, 159, 190–91 n.45;
survival and, 45–50; translation and,
35–37, 58–59, 106–10, 122–23, 126–
27; of traumatic memory, 80–82, 90–
91, 189 n.32; voice/voicelessness, 10–
11, 45–46, 100, 102. *See also* translation;
writing
Lanzmann, Claude, 192 n.54
La Soirée dans Grenade (Debussy), 124
Lawrence, David, 83, 189 n.31
Legba, 148
Le Guin, Ursula K., *Always Coming
Home*, 57
Levin, Ira, *Cantorial*, 3
Libra (DeLillo), 6
lieux de mémoire, 140–41, 142, 151–52,
200 n.12
Lindberg-Seyersted, Brita, 201 nn.24, 25
literature, as form of burial, 65, 66–67,
91–92. *See also* secondary burial
Lovecraft, H. P., 5
Love Medicine (Erdrich), 3, 32, 43

Macbeth (Shakespeare), 2
Mageo, Jeanette, 111
Malinowski, Bronislaw, 175 n.23
Mama Day (Naylor), 1, 16, 18, 21, 131–32,
135–36, 141, 142; commemoration in,
141, 142, 143
"Management of Grief, The" (Mukherjee), 3, 15, 143
manitous, 32, 35, 40, 46, 57
Marano, Lou, 181 n.33
Mariel migration, 93, 192–93 n.1
Marshall, Paule. See *Praisesong for the
Widow*
Maso, Carole, *Ghost Dance*, 3
Melnyczuk, Askold, *What Is Told*, 3
memory: collective, 130–31, 140–41, 151–
52, 163, 198–99 n.1, 200 nn.14, 15; commemoration and, 132–34, 138–39, 142,
147, 148, 170–71, 199 n.2, 200 n.12;
ethnic identity and, 130–31, 145, 147;
ghosts and, 130–32; mourning and, 28–
29, 80–83, 145; rememory, 7, 74–75,
81, 84; sites of, 130, 133, 140, 142–43,

144, 149, 165; as suspect, 129–30. *See
also* embodiment; traumatic memory
Metcalf, Peter, 186 n.13
Middle Passage, 16, 68, 75, 143, 149,
189 n.32
Miller, Arthur, *Death of a Salesman*, 5
Mobley, Marilyn, 188–89 n.29
Momaday, N. Scott, 31, 33, 180 n.22
Mooney, James, 54, 184 n.57
Morrison, Toni, 12, 89, 115, 116–18,
132, 174 n.9, 191 n.49; *Jazz*, 190 n.44; on
memorialization, 133; on national master narrative, 191–92 n.52; on revision,
186–87 n.17; on slave narratives, 62–
63, 185 n.5; *Song of Solomon*, 116–17,
191 n.46; *Tar Baby*, 144; on writing, 64,
67–68
mourning: ambivalence and, 20–21, 154;
biblical imagery of, 97, 147, 148; circle
dances and, 150–51; cultural mourning,
22, 53–54, 66–67; cultural recovery and,
22–23, 66–67, 98; ethnogenesis and,
21–23, 134–40, 142, 143–44; incorporation and, 41–44, 162–63, 165, 167;
liminality and, 41, 66–67, 89; memory
and, 28–29, 80–83, 145; ritual, 22, 66–
67, 134–35, 138; stages of, 22, 41; translation and, 54. *See also* commemoration;
secondary burial
Mukherjee, Bharati, "Management of
Grief, The," 3, 15, 143
Murphy, Joseph, 105
Murray, David, *Forked Tongues*, 36

Nanabushu, 47, 182 n.36
Native Americans: incorporation and, 34–
37; as invisible, 30–31; writing and, 36–
37, 47. *See also* Chippewa; Ghost Dance
Naylor, Gloria, 65. See also *Mama Day*
Nora, Pierre, 140–41, 200 n.11
nostalgia, 21

Olson, James, 93, 192 n.1, 193 n.2
Olson, Judith, 93, 192 n.1, 193 n.2
Ortiz, Fernando, 111–12, 114, 175 n.23,
196 n.33
otherness, 14–15
Our House in the Last World (Hijuelos), 3
Out of Africa (Dinesen), 33–34
Owen, Wilfred, 190 n.35

Ozick, Cynthia, 160–63, 203 nn.44, 53, 203–4 n.57, 204 n.60; "Rosa," 162; "The Shawl," 162. See also *Shawl, The*

Page, Philip, 189 n.29
Pannwitz, Rudolph, 180 n.20
past: continuity with, 19–20, 22–23, 31; group identity and, 130–31; historical loss and, 18, 21, 23, 29, 54, 63, 71, 133–34, 187 n.19; historical perspective and, 38–39; reconstruction of, 61–66, 71; survival and, 38–41, 45–50, 53–60; traumatic memory and, 76–81, 83. *See also* historical consciousness
Patterson, Orlando, 89–90
Peterson, Nancy J., 182 n.36, 182–83 n.42
Piano Lesson, The (Wilson), 1, 8, 18, 136–37
"Poema de la siguiriya" (García Lorca), 124, 125
possession: consumption metaphors and, 9–10, 42–45, 181 n.32; exorcism and, 19–20, 41, 46, 66–67; Korean shamanism, 155–58, 202 n.38; Santería and, 106, 107; secondary burial and, 155, 156, 159; traumatic memory and, 6–10, 48–49, 63, 71–72, 99, 188 n.24; writing and, 67–68, 87
postcolonial theory, 92, 177 n.36, 179 n.16
posttraumatic disorders. *See* traumatic memory
Power, Susan, *The Grass Dancer*, 3
Powers, Peter Kerry, 161
Praisesong for the Widow (Marshall), 1, 16, 28, 144–52, 163, 195 n.20; African diaspora in, 149–51; ancestor spirits in, 147, 149–52; assimilation in, 144–46; Circle Dance in, 8, 148–51; darkness, imagery of, 145, 146–47, 149; generational issues in, 21; Ibo Landing legend, 147–49, 201 n.24; paleness, imagery of, 145, 146–47
Pratt, Mary Louise, 92
pregnancy, metaphors of, 9, 25, 49, 182 n.38
Puerto Rico, 111

Radin, Paul, 47
Rainwater, Catherine, 183 n.43
Ranger, Terrence, 175–76 n.25
reciprocal acculturation, 11, 12, 175 n.23

Remmler, Karen, 191 n.45
repetition: historical fiction and, 72–73; traumatic memory and, 6–10, 72–75, 78, 136
revisionism, 4, 11, 13, 24, 61–66, 71, 141–42, 186–87 n.17; exorcism and, 19; as incorporation, 34–35
Ring Shout dances, 8, 149–50, 151
Rivero, Eliana, 193 n.2
Rodriguez, Richard, 19, 30, 53; *Days of Obligation*, 3
Rody, Carolyn, 186 n.15
"Rosa" (Ozick), 162
Rosaldo, Renato, 13–14, 16
Rosenman, Stanley, 92
Rosenwald, Lawrence, 180 n.20
Roth, Philip, *The Ghost Writer*, 6
Rothenberg, Jerome, 58
Ruppert, James, 180 n.20
Rushdie, Salman, 120, 176 n.29

Santería, 105–15, 117–18, 194 n.16, 194–95 n.17, 196 nn.31, 35, 198 n.52; in America, 111
Savage, Kirk, 132–33, 199 n.2, 200 n.12
Scarlet Letter, The (Hawthorne), 174 n.8
Scarry, Elaine, 86, 190–91 n.45
secondary burial, 22, 27, 64–70, 87–88, 96–98, 100, 127, 152, 154, 155–56, 159, 169, 187 n.20
Sense of the Past, The (James), 61–62, 63, 64
Sequoya, Jana, 37, 179 n.16, 180 n.22
Shakespeare, William: *Hamlet*, 86; *Macbeth*, 2
shamanism, Korean, 156–58, 202 n.38
"Shawl, The" (Ozick), 162
Shawl, The (Ozick), 29, 143, 160–70; consumption metaphors in, 167; exorcism in, 165; generational issues in, 166; ghostliness in, 164–65; memory in, 165–66; Persephone myth in, 169, 204 n.60; secondary burial in, 169; writing in, 166–67; Yiddish and, 167, 169, 203 n.56, 204 n.58
Shell and the Kernel, The (Abraham and Torok), 19
Shoah, 192 n.54
Silberman, Robert, 36
silence, 11, 65, 71, 91, 110, 134

Silko, Leslie Marmon, 180n.22; *Almanac of the Dead*, 3; *Ceremony*, 33
Singer, Isaac Bashevis, 203n.56
slave narratives, 62–63, 71, 75, 91, 188–89n.29
slavery, as social death, 89
Smith, Barbara Herrnstein, 179–80n.18
Smith-Wright, Geraldine, 144, 145
Sollors, Werner, 11, 13, 14, 18, 29, 174n.10
Song of Solomon (Morrison), 116–17, 191n.46
Sophie's Choice (Styron), 6
Stead, Deborah, 200n.14
Steiner, George, 52
Stevens, Wallace, 121
Stewart, Susan, 47
storytelling, 134; exorcism and, 79–80, 83–84, 92; history as, 17; memory and, 79–80; vs. reenactment, 80–81, 83; stories of cultural haunting, 5–6, 18–19; transmission of stories, 18–19, 23
Stuckey, Sterling, 150
Styron, William, *Sophie's Choice*, 6
Supernatural Forces (Winsbro), 173–74n.7, 182n.39
Swann, Brian, 184n.61
syncretism, 11–12, 104–5, 114, 182–83n.42

Tan, Amy, *The Hundred Secret Senses*, 3
Tar Baby (Morrison), 144
Thérèse of Lisieux, 51
Thomas, Nicholas, 176n.25
Thornton, Russell, 183n.48
"Thoughts for the Times on War and Death" (Freud), 19–20
Through a Glass Darkly (Boelhower), 29, 173n.7
Todorov, Tzvetan, 174n.11, 180n.20
Torok, Maria, 19
Totem and Taboo (Freud), 20
Tracks (Erdrich), 3, 9–10, 26, 27, 95, 170; ambivalence of ghosts in, 20; biculturalism and, 37; Christianity in, 49–52, 58; consumption metaphors in, 44–45, 51–53; gender issues in, 25; generational issues in, 21; historical perspective in, 38–39; sites of memory in, 33–34, 142; storytelling in, 18, 35; survival in, 38–

41, 45–50, 53–60; translation in, 46–50, 52, 58–59; trauma in, 43–44, 54; tuberculosis imagery in, 39–40, 42, 43, 44. *See also* Ghost Dance; windigo
tradition, 31–32, 141; invented, 13–14; land and, 32–35; reinterpretation of, 11–13
transculturation, 114, 175n.23, 196n.33
translation, 11, 16, 27, 28, 46–50, 102–3, 196n.33; bicultural and bilingual, 94–95, 109–10, 115, 120; burial and, 102–4; ghostliness and, 95–96, 107; language and, 35–37, 58–59, 108, 122–23, 126–27, 180n.20; mourning and, 54; in Native American scholarship, 36–37, 184n.61; violence and, 58, 180n.20. *See also* language
traumatic memory: acculturation and, 43–44, 54; evasion of, 72–73, 98–99; faithfulness and, 80–81, 189–90n.35; language of, 80–82, 90–91, 189n.32; mourning and, 80–81; physicalization of, 81–82, 84–87, 101, 156, 159; possession and, 6–10, 48–49, 63, 64, 71–72, 99, 188n.24; reenactment of, 43, 80–81, 83; repetition and, 6–10, 72–75, 78, 136; storytelling and, 79–80; temporality and, 73–77; as unassimilable, 79–80, 82, 83, 87, 88, 90–91
trickster figures, 47, 148
tuberculosis, 4–45, 39–40, 42, 43
Turner, Victor, 41, 89
Turtle Mountain reservation, 33, 35, 178n.1, 182n.42
Tuwim, Julian, 203–4n.57

van Gennep, Arnold, 41, 43, 186n.13
Van Heemskerck, Jacoba, 108
Villanueva, Alma Luz, *Weeping Woman*, 3, 16
Vizenor, Gerald, 58, 59
voice/voicelessness, 10–11, 45–46
Vonnegut, Kurt, *Galapagos*, 57

Walpole, Horace, *The Castle of Otranto*, 2
water imagery, 16, 148, 149, 198n.51
Waters, Mary C., *Ethnic Options*, 176n.28
Weber, Donald, 177n.46
Weeping Woman (Villanueva), 3, 16
Weiss, Peter, *The Investigation*, 192n.54

Welch, James, *Winter in the Blood*, 31, 33
Welty, Eudora, 33
Wharton, Edith, "The Eyes," 5; *House of Mirth*, 24
"Whatever Is Really Yours" (Erdrich), 178n.1
What Is Told (Melnyczuk), 3
White Earth Reservation, 53
Wiesel, Eli, 92
Wilson, August, *The Piano Lesson*, 1, 8, 18, 136–37
windigo, 10, 37, 42–45, 49, 51, 52, 181nn.32, 33
"Windigo" (Erdrich), 181n.34
Winsbro, Bonnie, 173–74n.7, 182n.39
Winter in the Blood (Welch), 31, 33
Wodziwob, 183n.44
Wolfman Jack, 122, 197–98n.44
Woman Hollering Creek (Cisneros), 3, 16
Woman Warrior, The (Kingston), 3, 131, 152, 174n.8, 195n.20, 200–201n.16; ambivalence of ghosts in, 20; gender issues in, 25, 26; ghost stories in, 18; mourning and ethnogenesis in, 137–40, 142; possession and exorcism in, 8–9
women, cultural haunting and, 24–26
Wong, Hertha D., 182n.38
World's End (Boyle), 3
Wounded Knee, 53, 57, 183n.44
Wovoka, 183n.44
writing: vs. oral tradition, 141–42, 180n.22, 190n.36, 191n.46; possession and, 67–68, 87. *See also* language
Wyatt, Jean, 188n.24

Yekl (Cahan), 4–5
Yerushalmi, Yosef Hayim, 141, 142, 200n.15
Yezierska, Anzia, 24; *The Bread Givers*, 178n.51
Young, James, 90